STOMPING GROUNDS

STOMPING GROUNDS

*A Pilgrim's Progress Through
Eight American Subcultures*

W. Hampton Sides

WILLIAM MORROW AND COMPANY, INC.
NEW YORK

Library of Congress Cataloging-in-Publication Data

Sides, W. Hampton.
    Stomping grounds : a pilgrim's progress through eight American subcultures / W. Hampton Sides.
      p. cm.
    ISBN 0-688-09049-4
    1. Clubs—United States—Case studies. 2. Social movements—United States—Case studies. 3. Subculture—Case studies.
    I. Title.
HS2723.S53 1992
306'.1'0973—dc20   92-23616
                                                          CIP

Printed in the United States of America

First Edition

1 2 3 4 5 6 7 8 9 10

To my father, Toby Sides
An idealist, a poet, and an honest man
1931–1991

Acknowledgments

THIS BOOK REPRESENTS THE work of many people. First and foremost, I must express my appreciation to the eight groups in this book, whose dazzling energy and spirit attracted me in the first place, and who in almost every case welcomed me into their worlds with an encouraging smile.

I'm grateful to Jack Shafer at Washington's *City Paper*, whose honorable employ I forsook to venture on this odyssey; Ranger Rick Roese, a fine traveling companion, whose new car we quite nearly trashed in the high desert of Nevada; Darrow Montgomery, my photography consultant; Ann Lewis, who swam me through the strange undersea world of the black bass; Kerry Richardson, Webb Stone, William Domhoff, and Mary Moore, who acquainted me with the rites and rituals of the Bohemian Grove; Lawrie Pitcher Platt, Charles Fishman, and Amy Leviton, who helped me probe the mysteries of burping plastic.

My gratitude also to the following folks for their soft pillows and warm hospitality: Scott and Liza Stevens in Los Angeles; Jill and Scott Brewer in Union, Washington; Ben McCracken in Albuquerque; Morris Panner and Mark Crosby in Manhattan; and Ben and Sarah Fortna in Chicago. To a slew of kind hosts in the forty-ninth state, including Susan and David Anstine in Anchorage, Ray and Sally Collins in McGrath, KNOM radio in Nome, Fred and Naomi Klouda in Anchorage, and Dewey Halverson in Trapper Creek.

I'd especially like to thank Dr. Jon Cohen, who dared to plough through first drafts of my manuscript, and who always wielded a wise and steady scalpel. Also Jonathan Rauch, Marnie Goodwin, and Jim Higgason, who graciously read early chapters of the book and offered valuable criticism. Thanks also to those editors who got me through the book's birthing pains, including Bill Hogan, George Spencer, Charlie Trueheart, Bob Malesky, Bob Webb, and Rich Leiby.

To my agent, Joy Harris, of the Lantz-Harris Literary Agency, who helped me conceive this book, and who stuck with me through thick and thin. And to my editor at Morrow, Harvey Ginsberg, who rode out this project with studied patience, and whose squiggles were always on target.

I must also thank Tim Zimmermann, generous friend and landlord, and brother in procrastination; my magnificent folks and grandparents in Memphis, who supported me every step of the way; and Emma, whose daily comradeship on the trails of Rock Creek Park kept me sane.

But most of all, I thank my beautiful bride, Anne, who read every word, edited with skill, endured my love affairs with plastic bowls and aluminum RVs, weathered my occasional private hells, supported us through the lean times, and accompanied me on many of the wonderful journeys in this book.

—W.H.S.
Washington, D.C.

Contents

9

Preface

In the summer of 1977 I worked at a KOA campground in the Shenandoah Valley of Virginia, digging ditches and leveling sites for the big RV rigs that came in off Interstate 81. Late in the afternoon they'd start rolling in—the Winnebagos, the Holiday Ramblers, the big Avions and Corsairs, the jury-rigged pop-up campers molded into the sagging beds of Chevy trucks. By nightfall we'd have them all hooked up for water and sewage, and the woods would glow like a snug little village.

But over in a far section of the campground, there would usually be a cluster of identical silver trailers that looked like spacepods from Mars. They were the Airstreamers, owners of the Cadillacs of the RV industry. The Airstreamers were organized into a kind of national family called the Wally Byam Caravan Club, named for the inventor of their distinctive silver bubble.

Whether the other campers envied the Airstreamers, or were annoyed by them, they had to concede that the Wally Byam Club had an interesting gig going. The Airstreamers were the proud land yachtsmen of the Interstate Highway System. They all had numbers affixed to their trailers, an identifying hieroglyph that only other Airstreamers could decipher. They traveled the country in caravans and attended a huge national

11

rally on the Fourth of July. We noticed that the Airstreamers liked to camp together, so over time we got to where we automatically stuck them off by themselves in a suburban enclave.

It struck me as strange and marvelous that even in the unassuming world of RVing, there had developed a code of association. What had once been a pastime had evolved into something more elaborate—something that might be called a *society*.

A few years later I worked for a weekly newspaper in the little mill town of McCall, Idaho. By the lake just outside of town, there was a tribe of hippies who lived communally out of an abandoned school bus. The lumberjacks down at the Foresters Bar made fun of the hippies, called them potheads and Communists, but I always enjoyed their company. They were friendly, good-natured, trusting to a fault. They smelled of patchouli oil and marijuana resins. Their kids had names drawn from the flora and fauna of the American West, names like Sequoia, Buzzard, Joshua Tree. They grew their own vegetables, baked their own bread, and sold hand-woven shoulder bags for spare cash.

Yet unlike most counterculturalists who lived on thousands of isolated communes across America, they were connected to something larger; they were part of a loose-knit tribe that called itself the Rainbow Family of Living Light. The McCall Rainbows had their hearts fixed on the following July, when another gathering would begin in another forest somewhere in the land.

I will always remember the look of childlike expectation that shined in their faces when they talked about those gatherings. Thinking back on it, I suppose it was the look of belonging. For the Rainbows, the year was not a seamless procession of days, but a natural unfolding of the seasons, the ebb and flow of solstice and equinox. Their calendar was built around one magical date that could be counted on like the coming of the full moon. Their bus might break down, the law might haul them off to jail, they might go broke and have to move on. But come July there was going to be a Gathering. And as always, the old faces would greet them with a wide smile and a kiss, and for a week, they would move together in the larger rhythms of the Family.

I saw the same look of belonging on the face of a woman I befriended while traveling in the Natal Province of South

Africa. Heather was a housewife in a little town that was an hour's drive from Durban. On the first afternoon of my stay in her home, I reached into her kitchen cabinet for a drinking glass, only to be buried in a landslide of . . . *Tupperware.* As I stooped to pick up the plastic containers scattered about the floor, she proudly informed me that she was a Tupperware saleslady—made a prosperous living at it, in fact. It was not merely a job, she said; it was a "way of life." Tupperware made her a precise person. It taught her how to set goals and economize her time. It gave her self-esteem. And Tupperware was the best way to combat what the company brochures liked to call "kitchen chaos." Indeed, Heather's kitchen was a triumph of Teutonic orderliness. In her refrigerator, the sealed modules of Tupperware were stacked in their manifold sizes and shapes, ensuring that no juices or gravies would ever mingle by accident.

Heather was saving her money for a trip to America to attend the annual sales convention at the Tupperware headquarters in Kissimmee, Florida. "The Jubilee," it was called. She had been planning the trip for years. She spoke of her coming pilgrimage in soft, reverent tones. She made Florida sound like a mythic holy land. At the Jubilee, she would hug the company president on stage. She would win prizes and recognition. She would sing the Tupperware anthem with her sisters from around the globe. And all along, she would learn subtle business secrets sure to boost her sales back home in South Africa. It was going to be a once-in-a-lifetime experience, like making the hajj.

IT WAS HEATHER'S EXAMPLE that finally got me interested in writing a book on the theme of the modern American subculture. I realized that there were scores of groups like the Airstreamers, the Rainbows, and the Tupperware salesladies —unusual but enduring tribes of a distinctly American character that had carved out discrete universes for themselves on the social frontier.

It occurred to me that the native genius of the American people is for seeking out fellow travelers across the vastness of a continent, and for forming groups. Such groups may be founded on the most compelling or the most banal of excuses; they may be composed of people from the margins of society, or from the mainstream. But modern America is a country of subcultures, a place where people's identities are shaped to a peculiar extent by the private enthusiasms which they may pursue with kindred spirits within an identifiable microcosm.

Most of these groups have established an annual gathering to summon their far-flung members back home. I don't mean a convention, merely, but a seasonal pilgrimage to a place of origin, like the swallows that return each year to Capistrano. This is what I refer to as the "Stomping Ground." The term has an etymology in jazz slang, and it conveys the idea of rebirth through reunion, the return to the familiar, reaching back to the roots of our true selves. The Stomping Ground is the place where the members of a society act out their communal rituals. It may be a sanctuary, a hallowed piece of land, or just a clearing in the woods. People come to the Stomping Ground to lose themselves in the pageantry of the group. Mostly it is a place of celebration: the bonfire dance, the powwow, the rodeo, the tent revival, the barnyard stomp, people gathered in a circle, turned inward toward the same idea.

I thought that the Stomping Ground was the ideal place to see the tapestry of a subculture unfurled. It seemed to me that to follow these pilgrims to their shrines and temples was the best way to explore a peculiarly American phenomenon.

AMERICANS HAVE ALWAYS been adept at what Alexis de Tocqueville called "the art of association." When Tocqueville visited the United States in the 1830s, he was astounded at the extraordinary diversity of groups that seemed to spring up without any provocation or encouragement from the government—the innumerable fraternal orders, charity organizations, temperance societies, and civic clubs. As a people, he observed, we did not take well to monolithic organizations, preferring instead to create smaller fellowships of like-minded souls. "Secondary associations," he called them.

The most conspicuous example of the subculture in our history, of course, has been the religious sect. This republic was largely founded by a religious subculture—the Pilgrims of New England—and the First Amendment has smiled on an endless procession of believers who have cut against the social grain: the Amish, the Shakers, the Mormons, the Mennonites, the Hutterites, the Jehovah's Witnesses, the Hare Krishnas, the Rastafarians, and today's New Agers, to name a few.

In the last half-century, a different variety of "secondary association" has emerged. An economic boom unparalleled in our history has given Americans of all classes the leisure time and disposable income to live a new kind of life. Prosperity has liberated us from our farms and factories and allowed us to define ourselves by our play. Increasingly, we are cell-dividing into a thousand insular isms and odd little clans, many of them built around the once marginal concern of "life-style." Just as our professional worlds are forever partitioning into subdisciplines, so too is our taste for avocation and whimsy. Living in a land where the pursuit of happiness is practically a constitutional imperative, we have chased our happiness into the remotest thickets. We have become a people of esoteric leisure.

It has been said that Americans are the true existentialists— that we have no general national character other than each American's individual desire to create his own universe, letting his true personality unfold in a kind of sublime isolation. Our culture is steeped in clichés of rugged individualism—Thoreau on Walden Pond, Teddy Roosevelt riding the Dakota Badlands, Natty Bumppo alone in the deep wood.

Yet despite our jealously guarded myth of self-reliance, most Americans, like people everywhere, need to feel an allegiance to a community. If Americans are existentialists, then we are *social* existentialists. Ayn Randers are big on solitude, but they have a national club like everyone else. Harley-Davidson bikers claim to be heirs to the cowboy individualism of the Wild West, but they ride around in identically dressed gangs and attend huge rallies of fellow "Hog" owners. Boxcar hoboes, perhaps the ultimate loners of industrial-age America, have held an annual gathering in Britt, Iowa, for over one hundred years. They call it, without a trace of irony, the National Hobo Convention.

In the 1973 film *A Touch of Class*, George Segal delivers a spirited monologue on the American passion for affiliation after Glenda Jackson describes his obsession with male sexual prowess as "typically American."

"I can't stand that phrase," Segal's character says. "There's no such thing as typically American. It's a big place, America. Which typically American American do you mean—the cabdrivers in New York? The coal miners of Pennsylvania? The students at Berkeley? The Mormons in Utah? The Harlem

Globetrotters? How about the Daughters of the American Revolution—are those the ones you mean? The only thing typically American about the two hundred million Americans is that they never do anything typically alike."

Ours is a land of refined fanaticism. Anything you could dream of doing, you can probably find a society of Americans who are already doing it, and doing it so intensely that they've organized their lives around it. They attend the annual gatherings. They subscribe to the national magazine. They buy the tools and toys. They decorate their cars with bumper stickers and vanity plates. They build up a circle of friends in the group. They meet their spouse in the group. They rear their children in the group. They spend their vacations doing whatever the group does. They slip into the subcultural lagoon, and by degrees of emotional and financial investment, they get themselves submerged.

In the early stages of this book, when I was still bouncing ideas off my friends, I once made the facetious observation that if an American was into tiddlywinks, he could start a national association, and tiddlywinkers in their thousands would come crawling from the woodwork. Then I found out that there really *was* a North American Tiddlywinks Association, headquartered in Silver Spring, Maryland. "I wonder if there is a single American who does not belong to some association," wrote journalist Ted Morgan in his classic study of U.S. cultural life, *On Becoming an American*. "I once thought I had found one, a hermit who lived in an abandoned silver mine in the wilderness area of Idaho's Salmon River. But he told me he belonged to the National Association of Hermits."

The 1992 edition of the *Encyclopedia of Associations*, the bible of booking agents and talk show hosts, lists more than 22,000 organizations in the United States. While it's true that many of these are conventional business and trade associations, several thousand of the entries fall under the broad category of "lifestyle." There are 1,174 hobby organizations, 839 athletic organizations, and 580 fan clubs—including 25 Elvis societies and 5 devoted to the TV series *Star Trek*. There are 80 national gardening associations, 49 numismatic groups, and 201 societies devoted to stamp collecting.

The Conchologists of America, headquartered in the unlikely marine capital of Louisville, Kentucky, is for "individuals interested in mollusks." The U.S. Trivia Association is based in Lincoln, Nebraska. The Aladdin Knights of the Mystic Light in Simpsons, Illinois, is for "collectors, dealers, users, and admirers of Aladdin lamps." If you're from Australia, you might consider the Free Throwers Boomerang Society of Delaware, Ohio. If you're a majorette, you might look into the National Baton Twirling Association of Janesville, Wisconsin.

All over America there are societies of pack rats devoted to every imaginable form of kitsch art, such as the Smurf Collectors Club of Massapequa, New York, the Beer Can Collectors of America, based in Fenton, Missouri, and the National Toothpick Holder Collectors' Society of Eureka, Illinois.

With admirable candor, many of the entries in the *Encyclopedia* are indexed expressly as "humorous organizations." To wit: Couch Potatoes of Dixon, California, is for "individuals who practice the esoteric art of prolonged television viewing and who enjoy a state of lengthy vegetation." DENSA, of Rochester, New York, is for persons who have been rejected by MENSA. Kill Devil Hills, North Carolina, is home of the Man Will Never Fly Memorial Society. The International Association of Professional Bureaucrats in Washington, D.C., is dedicated to preserving and expanding "the bureaucratic arts" (its publication is called *Fuzzify*). Bobs International is for "individuals who are named Bob or would like to be named Bob united to help those with the same name feel that Bob is not a boring name."

Untold thousands of other groups choose to keep a lower profile. The Rainbow Family, for example, wouldn't think of listing themselves in a guidebook like the *Encyclopedia of Associations*, nor would the Los Angeles–based Hung Jury, a heterosexual dating club for men with large penises.

SOCIOLOGISTS HAVE HAD A FIELD DAY trying to explain the American obsession with "life-style" subcultures. Some say it is the superabundance of options in America that has made people throw up their hands and choose a single thing with countervailing conviction. Some say the hugeness of the land has driven people into the familiarity of smaller worlds. Some contend that Americans in the Information Age increasingly find themselves numbed by abstract and pointless jobs devoid of a sense of craft or professional pride, and are thus moved to find meaning and fulfillment in weekend fantasies. Others argue that the faithlessness and cynicism of the modern era have made people hungry for ritual and belief, and that this spiritual drift has led people to claim their own absolutes.

I've found an element of truth to all of these explanations. But more often, simple loneliness lies at the root of the subculture explosion. In many cases, I've found, these groups have become extended families, filling the void left by the erosion of the neighborhood, the church, and the fraternal order. They provide scaffolding for people's lives. It should not be too surprising that these subcultures are flourishing most intensely in places that lack rootedness and a sense of history—notably in the condo kingdoms of Florida and the tract-housing sprawls of southern California. People want to belong somewhere. People want to believe in something. And people want to be masters of at least one small corner of the cosmos.

There is, of course, a dark side to the American passion for joining groups. If ham radio operators can form a national organization, so can child pornographers. If the First Amendment protects a Shriners convention, then it protects a conclave of skinheads as well. The United States has always been fertile ground for the formation of hate groups, bizarre cults, and netherworld gangs. The Ku Klux Klan is only one of the more sordid examples of our "art of association." Today we have the Aryan Nation, the Posse Comitatus, the Hell's Angels, and the Bloods and Crips. And we have always produced our share of spiritual mountebanks who pull in lost souls and rob them blind.

MADISON AVENUE HAS RESPONDED to the segmenting of popular culture in increasingly subtle ways, giving rise to a new lexicon ("narrowcasting," "micromarketing," "cocooning," "niche marketing"). A few years ago a book entitled *The Clustering of America* used an elaborate formula derived from postal ZIP codes to suggest that marketing professionals could break down the country into precisely forty-nine neighborhood types, each with its own descriptive tag: "Blue Blood Estates," "Furs and Station Wagons," or "Shotguns and Pickups."

Nowhere is the fragmenting of American tastes and pastimes more apparent than at the local newsstand. I like to browse at a little place near Dupont Circle in Washington called the Newsroom, where the magazine racks bulge with unfamiliar titles from the fresh frontiers of the American subculture. I can spend hours in there, poring over the garish gallery of characters that leap from those magazine covers—the well-greased bodybuilders, the mud boggers, the bungee cord daredevils, the tag-team wrestlers, the crossbow hunters on the prowl, the wan-faced Nintendo jocks, the even wanner-faced heavy metal rockers, the paintball warriors crouching deep in their jungles, and the medieval jousters from the Society for Creative Anachronism. There are currently twelve thousand magazines published in the United States, and the greatest growth has been in the field of the special interest magazine—periodicals like *Trailer Life, The Survivalist, Action Pursuit Games, Mushing Magazine, The Civil War Times,* and *Nude and Natural.* Publishers have found they can establish smaller fraternities of diehard readers if they simply push a given "life-style" theme to its logical conclusion.

I marvel at the collective energy that all those magazines represent. I salute the laissez-faire economy that produces so much well-routed data. But every time I go to the Newsroom, I wonder anew: Is this what Americans are really doing with themselves?

The fishing world provides a good example of the phenomenon. It used to be that the average angler, if he (or she) read periodicals at all, would subscribe to a general-purpose outdoors magazine such as *Field & Stream* or *Outdoor Life.* He ventured into the wilderness with a vague and indiscriminate image of himself as an American Sportsman.

Nowadays he is more likely to concentrate on a single variety of fish, like the largemouth bass, and buy the full arsenal that technology has devised for its capture. He owns a $20,000 metal-flake bass boat with a sonar depthfinder, a pH meter, and a foot-operated trolling motor. He gets *Bassmaster* magazine and tunes in to the various bass shows on his satellite dish. He joins the local chapter of the BASS society, and pays his annual dues. He knows more about the behavior of the bass than he knows about his next-door neighbor.

He is no longer an American Sportsman. He is something more fully realized. He is a Bassmaster.

Ray Scott, the millionaire entrepreneur from Alabama who more or less invented the whole bass fishing subculture, grasped the phenomenon as far back as 1967. Scott called it the Verticalization of America. Our culture was balkanizing, splintering into deep subspecialties. Scott thought that if a businessman could identify one of these untapped "vertical" markets, he could make a fortune, first by awakening people to the existence of a "life-style," and then amplifying people's desire to practice it with proficiency and a sense of high fashion.

"One of the great things about this crazy country of ours is that you can specialize in anything," Scott told me. "Hell, you can specialize in salt and pepper shakers if you want. Or better yet, just salt shakers. In my case, I specialized in a single species of fish and built a whole world on it."

THE FLOURISHING OF SUBCULTURES like the Bassmasters has been fueled in part by technological advances in communications. Facsimile machines, toll-free numbers, cellular telephones, personal photocopiers, scanners, answering machines, computer modems, and electronic mail have made it infinitely easier for groups to cross-pollinate. Meanwhile, advances in the field of personal entertainment—the camcorder, cable television, the VCR, home video games, and the satellite dish—have made it possible for people to choose their own diet of cultural influences. Instead of a single "global village," we have thousands of them. No longer at the mercy of a few network programmers in New York, Americans can fasten on to increasingly narrow wavelengths of the social spectrum. People can live anywhere and be electronically plugged in to the latest stirrings of the tribe. A devotee can stay in instantaneous communication with his fellows across four time zones, while bathing himself in images constantly beamed down from the subcultural headquarters.

And the headquarters can be just about anywhere. Running a new subculture is a cinch. Gone are the PR obstacles that have foiled visionaries down through the ages. Martin Luther had to nail his Ninety-five Theses to the church door. Today he'd just send them FedEx.

Lee Baxandall, founder of the Naturist Society, one of America's principal nudist organizations, runs his subculture out of a small Main Street office in the town of Oshkosh, Wisconsin. With a few choice tools, he's managed to turn his shop into the mission control of nudism. He's installed a computer bulletin board and a 1-800 number. He produces a four-color nudist magazine on his own computer. He receives faxes from fellow nudists around the country. When he steps inside his office, he is no longer living in Oshkosh; he is living in Nudistland.

Physical geography is thus being supplanted by a kind of social geography. A Mary Kay saleslady in Missoula, Montana, probably has less in common with the lady down the street than she has with a fellow Mary Kay saleslady in Milford, Massachusetts. The world of a Grateful Dead fan from Eugene, Oregon, is not likely to differ dramatically from that of another Deadhead from Athens, Georgia. In the hierarchy of distinguishing traits, it's no longer so much a question of where you live; it's what you're "into."

People so often say that America is becoming all the same, that the golden arches have swallowed the soul of the country. I don't think this is the case at all. Certainly much of our landscape has been bulldozed into sameness. But if you are willing to sail a little offshore, you will find a vast archipelago that is unimaginably wild and lush. If you want to see the diversity of America, you have to go island hopping.

A WORD OF EXPLANATION about my M.O. Obviously there were hundreds of subcultural groups I could have chosen to write about. At one point I had a working list of more than fifty, which I gradually narrowed down to the present collection of eight. I never wanted this to be an encyclopedia of subcultures. I thought it would be much more interesting to dive deep into several groups than to skim along the surface of many. Browsing through the subcultural shows on cable TV, it is typical for us to delight in these arcane groups, to ogle and stare and scratch our heads in bewilderment for a time, but ultimately to dismiss them as odd pieces of marginalia. We quickly zap them with our remote control and move on to the next channel. My instinct in this book was to pause on a few channels and to take these groups seriously—to watch and listen, to learn the argot, to see what the allure was about.

Besides, I felt that a focused approach would get me closer to answering the questions that applied universally to all groups: How do they communicate? How do they govern themselves? How do they resolve their disputes? How do they view the wider society? How do they mythologize their own leaders and celebrities?

I suppose you could say I arrived at this collection arbitrarily—following my own tastes and prejudices—but I did try to pick my groups carefully. I wanted to touch on as many levels of society as possible. I wanted the collection of events to spread evenly over the continent and the calendar. My search for the right mix kept me occupied for two exhilarating years, and sent me to thirty-eight states. It was the longest, strangest trek of my life, and I had a ball.

From the start, there were certain subjects I determined to avoid. For example, I wouldn't study criminal gangs or hate groups for the age-old reason that, for them, virtually all publicity is good publicity. I wouldn't visit any of the many thousands of conventions held each year by trade and professional associations, since I was more interested in how Americans play than how they work. I would avoid gratuitously weird or paranormal groups like, say, Bigfoot hunters or body-piercing cults. And I would stay away from the regional festival circuit—the quilting bees and rattlesnake roundups, the chili cook-offs and leaping frog races—deferring to Willard Scott.

My first criterion was that the groups had to have been around long enough to establish a Stomping Ground—a reunion with a mythic status.

I was especially drawn to subcultures that were founded by charismatic personalities. Anyone can start a local club, but it takes a visionary to make an idea catch on across a continent and survive through time. In nearly every case, the groups in this book are the lengthened shadows of a single man or woman.

I found I was drawn to groups that are built around an enduring human pursuit (like fishing, caravanning, or sled-dog travel). I also found I was intrigued by groups that nursed a certain nostalgia for a simpler past (such as the myth of Eden or the Wild West). Many of the subcultural pilgrims in this book like to suggest, in one fashion or another, that their way of life most closely approximates the natural state of man. They tend to view modern society as unhealthy—even unnatural—and they seek to revisit a purer and more innocent age, even if it's just for the weekend.*

---

* *Among the groups that I explored but didn't end up writing about*: the William Faulkner aficionados who meet once a year at the University of Mississippi for the Yoknapatawpha Conference; the Wiccan priestesses ("witches") who meet in Wisconsin every June for the International Pagan Spirit Gathering; the American Indian tribes that meet each spring in Albuquerque, New Mexico, for the Gathering of Nations, the largest intertribal powwow in America; adherents of the so-called Wildman Movement; American Hare Krishnas who meet every year at Prabhupada's Palace in the town of New Vrindaban, West Virginia, to celebrate Krishna's birthday; the yarnspinners who compete each October at the National Storytelling Festival in Jonesborough, Tennessee; the video game champions who compete at the National Nintendo Powerfest; the Westminster Dog Show in Madison Square Garden; the airplane buffs who fly into Wisconsin every summer for the Oshkosh Experimental Airshow; the National Spelling Bee in Washington, D.C.; and the Scottish clans who gather in July on North Carolina's Grandfather Mountain for the annual Highland Games.

PART I

BACK TO THE GARDEN

Nature boy, nature man, take me along
Deep in the woods we're undiscovered
     —The Talking Heads,
       "Totally Nude"

In Darkest Bohemia

Monte Rio, California

IF YOU DRIVE NORTH from the Golden Gate Bridge on Highway 101 for an hour or so, and then make your way west toward the town of Freestone, you will eventually pick up a little two-lane road known as "The Bohemian Highway."

The Bohemian Highway is one of the loveliest stretches of road in America. It cuts through twelve miles of vineyards and olive groves. It climbs over arcadian hills of pastel pink and burrows into ancient stands of redwood. It's all fog and mist and motes of primal forest dust dancing in pale shafts of light. But when you come to the little resort of Monte Rio, on the silty banks of the Russian River, the scenery suddenly shifts from somewhere in the south of France to Cold War Berlin. The road narrows and hooks to the right, and concertina barbed wire is strung up along a fence. The traffic signs grow in severity: NO THRU TRAFFIC. SPEED LIMIT 15 MILES. NO TRESPASSING. NO PARKING. PRIVATE ROAD. SLOW. CLOSED GATE AHEAD. MEMBERS AND GUESTS ONLY. NO TURN AROUND. The road stops at a gatehouse installation that looks like Checkpoint Charlie. A series of guard stations reaches far into the compound. Back in the redwoods, you sense a beehive of activity. You can hear buzz-

29

saws, hammers, forklifts, generators. Utility trucks are hauling cords of firewood up a paved canyon road. Valets are scurrying around in red jackets, toting luggage and parking cars.

The place has the air of rusticity achieved at stupefying cost. You have the odd sense of being in the wilderness, and at the same time, in the midst of formidable luxury.

Eventually a burly man in a forest ranger's suit will emerge from the gatehouse and ask you whether you can read English. "You're on private property pal," he'll say. "You gotta turn around." The burly man will have a very stern look on his face as he shows you the way out. And if for some reason you still do not get the picture, he will call the police.

You won't be the first person who's been turned away from this curious compound in the Pacific forest. The Bohemian Grove is the most exclusive summer retreat in America, if not the world. For over a century, members of the prestigious all-male Bohemian Club, an artistic and literary society in San Francisco, have made a pilgrimage to this redwood stand in Sonoma County. The men come here to escape their wives and the vexations of statecraft and corporate stewardship. The Bohemians call it the Midsummer Encampment; Herbert Hoover called it, simply, "The Greatest Men's Party on Earth."

For three weeks in late July, the Grove turns into a self-sustaining city. More than 2,000 members and guests sleep in Crusoesque treehouses with names like Derelicts, Cave Man, and Whiskey Flat. Some 450 waiters, electricians, bootblacks, and barbers work at the encampment, some of them living year-round on the Grove property. At the northern end of the Grove's central canyon is a clubhouse built in 1904 and designed by the renowned San Francisco architect Bernard Maybeck. At the other end is a warehouse stocked with California and European wines, many of the bottles wrapped in the Bohemian Grove label.

The Bohemians do a lot of drinking and pissing on redwoods. They shoot skeet, play dominoes, and go on nature hikes. Stanford botanists lead safari excursions on the perimeter of the Grove—"Rim Rides," they're called—in specially constructed open-air Land Rovers. Some members have been known to slip across the river for illicit evenings with hookers from the Vegas–Reno–Kentucky Derby circuit.

In a solemn Druidic ceremony that kicks off the first week,

the Bohemian high priests dress in crimson robes and burn a hideous effigy, known as Dull Care, that symbolizes all the travails of the workaday world. They arrange themselves around a sumptuous dining circle and feast on Pacific prawns and pheasant under glass. They gather on the greensward by the trout-stocked artificial lake and hear long-winded speeches by fellow Bohemians on subjects like "Third World Debt Restructuring" or "The California Condor." They crowd around the camp circle for bonfire sing-alongs, called "Afterglows," where they close out the cool evenings smoking cigars and lounging on futon-covered benches carved out of giant redwood logs.

Art and live music are omnipresent. Oil portraits by Bohemian painters sit on easels beneath the redwoods, gathering dust. Bagpipers and a cappella troubadours ply the canyons. The club has a 135-member orchestra and a 60-member chorus (all Bohemian Club members), and there are informally organized mariachi bands, Dixieland jazz bands, and string quartets. Over 50 pianos are stored in a dehumidified warehouse and wheeled out to cabins on demand. The Grove's pipe organ is housed in a special air-conditioned building. At the center of the compound is a 2,500-seat amphitheater where, on the peak night of the encampment, the club stages the annual "Grove Play," an extravagant epic drama written and performed exclusively by Bohemian talent and usually starring an odd cast of sprites and wood nymphs played by men in drag. Though a Grove Play typically carries a price tag upwards of thirty thousand dollars, it is performed only once.

But the Midsummer Encampment is much more than booze and thespian antics in the redwoods. It is the conspiracy theorist's greatest nightmare, a daunting roster of leading conservative politicians, corporate CEOs, and military brass who gather privately every year in a Tolkien forest to reaffirm their faith in big business, small government, and the good life.

Forget about the Trilateral Commission. Forget the thousand closed-door cabals of Wall Street. If the American plutocracy has a secret clubhouse, it is the Bohemian Grove. If the military-industrial establishment—hell, the Establishment, period—has an annual convention, it is here.

Left-wing political groups in California first caught wind of this decades ago. By the early eighties, a few hundred environmentalists, peaceniks, feminists, and lesbian separatists had

banded together to form a militant protest group called the
Bohemian Grove Action Network (BGAN). The demonstrators
held vigils at the entrance of the compound every summer to
denounce what they called "ruling class bonding." As Bohemians drove into the Grove, the protesters would stage sit-ins and
hold up placards bearing messages like "Boho Boys Profit from
World Strife," "El Salvador Grieves While Bohemians Play,"
and "Hail to the Keepers of the Divine Bomb." The BGAN logo
pictured a tuxedoed patrician in a top hat, swilling a martini as
he straddled an MX missile.

BGAN has called the Grove, with good reason, the birthplace of the atomic age. In the 1930s Berkeley physicist (and
Bohemian) Ernest O. Lawrence forged crucial ties to govern-
ment and business leaders at the Grove, paving the way for
construction of the first cyclotron, which led, in turn, to the
discovery of plutonium. In the autumn of 1942, Manhattan
Project physicists, wary of Hitler's spies, secretly met inside the
Bohemian Grove clubhouse to discuss isotope separation and
to map out the initial development plans for the atomic bomb.
BC member Edward Teller, the "unrepentant father of the
H-bomb," later worked with Lawrence and fellow Bohemian
Luis Alvarez to establish the Lawrence Livermore Laboratories,
the preeminent weapons proving ground connected with the
University of California.

Despite Lawrence's precedent, it is considered supremely
bad form to strike deals of any kind inside the Grove. The club's
motto is "Weaving Spiders, Come Not Here"—a line from *A
Midsummer-Night's Dream* meaning no networking or shoptalk
allowed. But contacts made beneath the gas-fed lanterns on
Saturday evening can, without effort or prolonged introduc-
tions, be followed up by phone calls on Monday morning. And
you can be reasonably sure that when executives from Boeing,
Northrop, IBM, ITT, and Lockheed meet for cocktails with,
say, the secretary of defense or a retired admiral from the navy,
they're not just reciting passages from Shakespeare. "The Grove
isn't designed for business, or even statecraft," observed one
fairly prominent member of the military-industrial establishment, Bohemian Caspar Weinberger. "But it's a very pleasant
place, and, inevitably, talk sometimes turns to substantive matters."

The Midsummer Encampment has long been a favored

retreat for mandarins in the Republican party. Teddy Roosevelt was the first in a long line of Republican presidents who've hobnobbed at the Grove, including William Howard Taft, Herbert Hoover, Eisenhower, Nixon, Ford, Reagan, and Bush. And striding in after them, all the presidents' men: Weinberger, George Shultz, James Baker, Henry Kissinger, Nicholas Brady, Harold Brown, William Clark, Donald Rumsfeld, William French Smith, and Alexander Haig are all Bohemian Club members, no doubt the most *un*bohemian lot ever assembled in one place.

Herbert Hoover is still affectionately known among Bohemians as "The Chief." Hoover joined the club back in 1913 and became a member of Cave Man camp, where he took great pride in being the earliest riser each morning. He wrote in his memoirs that in 1927, within an hour after Calvin Coolidge's announcement not to run again for the White House, "a hundred men—editors, publishers, public officials, and others from all over the country who were at the Grove—came to my camp demanding that I announce my candidacy." The following summer Hoover learned of his GOP nomination while "in residence" at the Grove. And it was largely at the Grove that ex-President Hoover, disgraced after the Great Depression, transformed himself into the party's elder statesman. From 1935 to 1964, Hoover was given the honor of delivering the final Lakeside Talk, and Republican hopefuls like Robert Taft and General Dwight D. Eisenhower made pilgrimages to Cave Man camp to pay him homage.

Modern GOP presidential aspirants have continued the tradition, using the Grove as a private testing ground for their candidacies. Nelson Rockefeller dropped all notions of running for the White House in 1964 after his Grove speech bombed. Richard Nixon's first successful run for the presidency was given a crucial psychological boost after Bohemians warmed to his 1967 Grove address, in which he first unveiled what would be his administration's policy of U.S.-Soviet détente. The Lakeside Talk, Nixon later wrote, offered "an unparalleled opportunity to reach some of the most important and influential men, not just from California, but from across the country." That same year, Governor Ronald Reagan met Nixon for a private chat beneath the redwoods and agreed not to challenge Nixon's run for the Republican nomination.

Jimmy Carter once visited the Grove, as did Robert Kennedy while he was attorney general, but Democrats have generally shunned this conservative salon in the woods. Bohemian William F. Buckley, Jr., likes to tell of the time he invited Harvard economist John Kenneth Galbraith to the encampment. "I asked him what he was doing the last week of July. He took out his book, and said, 'I'm sorry, that week I'm lecturing at the University of Moscow.' 'Oh,' I replied, 'What do you have left to teach them?' "

Republican honchos represent, to be fair, only a small fraction of the Bohemian membership. The club ranks are primarily composed of San Francisco businessmen and professionals, with a healthy smattering of professors from Stanford and Berkeley, research scientists from private R&D labs, policy Brahmins from the Hoover Institute, and a few wine barons from Napa and Sonoma Valleys. There are also an astounding number of nationally known authors and media stars, Hollywood celebrities, multinational corporate heads, press lords, old-money scions, and a few astronauts thrown in for good measure. A partial list of Bohemian Club members, past and present:

Walter Cronkite
John Kluge
Ray Kroc
Herman Wouk
Thomas Watson
Thomas Watson, Jr.
Allen Drury
Joseph Coors
Stephen Bechtel
Najeeb Halaby
Les Brown
William Randolph Hearst
Laurance and David Rockefeller
Henry Ford II
Merv Griffin
Art Linkletter
Dan Rowan
Eddie Albert

Tennessee Ernie Ford
Dick Martin
Bing Crosby
Edmund G. "Pat" Brown
Leonard Firestone
Irving Stone
David Packard
Admiral Thomas Hayward
Lowell Thomas
Union Oil Chairman Fred Hartley
Justice Potter Stewart
Charlton Heston
Christopher Buckley
Bob Hope

The wealthier Bohemians fly in from all over the world, parking their Learjets and company turboprops on the crowded tarmac at tiny Sonoma County Airport, fifteen miles from the Grove, near Santa Rosa. The airport officials have to arrange for added parking space and stock up on aviation fuel to handle the expanded traffic. Other Bohos take helicopters and limousines. Some have been known to sail their yachts up the Pacific coast and drop anchor in Bodega Bay. The less fortunate members just drive their ordinary Saabs and BMWs up from San Francisco.

There's an old saying in the Bay Area that you can't get any *real* business done in late July: Everybody who's anybody is at the Grove. The Encampment officially lasts for seventeen days, but most members just drop in for one of the two big weekends, when the bacchanalian revelry cranks up to its highest level. Some Bohos bring their sons along as guests, while others try to impress campmates by inviting their personal friend Howard Baker, or the prime minister of Singapore. Usually about two thousand members and their guests attend on these weekends, but by midweek the Grove population dwindles to as low as three hundred, mostly retirees and club diehards who plan extended vacations in Bohemia. The others jet back to their boardrooms and trusteeships on Monday morning. "Some of us have to *earn* a living," working Bohemians are fond of saying.

* * *

MY FIRST PLAN OF ATTACK is to go in by canoe.

The Grove keeps a floating boathouse on the Russian River where the Bohos sunbathe and swim laps in the milky green water. The club couldn't purchase rights to the whole river channel, try as it might, so visitors are free to drift by the boathouse and get a long—and legal—glimpse of Bohemians at play. It is the closest outsiders can get to Bohemia without risking a trespassing rap. Every year the tourists pile into rubber rafts and fishing dinghies and linger by the bend in the river, hoping to get a snapshot of Henry Kissinger's bay window, or Dan Quayle doing the backstroke. Late at night, the townsfolk say, you can spot the Bohos skinny-dipping by the boathouse under the moon and stars. And on the final day of the encampment, the members are known to gather here at the swimming hole for a big "water carnival."

My plan is simple: I'll paddle by the boathouse under the cover of night and hide my canoe in the brambles. Then I'll slip by the guardhouse and turn down Bohemia's main drag, River Road, toward the heart of the Grove.

On the first day of the encampment I head over to the public beach, a half-mile downstream from the Grove boathouse, and rent a banged-up metal canoe for five bucks. I want to scout the riverbank by day to see if my scheme will work. I paddle upriver against a gentle current, gliding past some ramshackle river cabins and the Northwood Lodge and Golf Course, where AWOL Bohos are out hitting a few rounds. An osprey hovers over the river, hunting for fish. Suddenly the channel grows shallow, and I find myself paddling through rapids. Finally I have to drag the canoe across the rocks and silt for twenty yards, struggling against the current. It looks suspiciously as if, long ago, the Bohemians had hired the Army Corps of Engineers to dam the river to discourage upstream traffic.

Beyond the rapids, there is an abrupt kink in the river, forming a naturally protected enclave for the Bohemian swimming hole. Here the river looks artificial, like the viscous, green-dyed lagoons of Disneyland. Instead of flamingos, a flock of turkey vultures broods on a sandbar. The boathouse is a sprightly affair with green-and-white canvas awnings and Adirondack chairs where a few Bohemians sit shirtless playing backgammon. A big American flag flaps in the breeze. From the dock, a bow-legged, ruddy-cheeked man in his sixties performs a perfect swan dive and surfaces with a howl. Farther out in the water, a liver-spotted old-timer is floating on his back and squirting geysers of water through his teeth. On the left bank, three bronze Bohos are lounging in the sun, flicking their toes in the sand. As I drift by, snippets of their conversation ("... get out the spreadsheets," "... interest-free loans," "bad judgment call ...") float over the water. One of the men, wearing a star-spangled meatsuit à la Mark Spitz, turns from the conversation, removes his sunglasses, and flashes me a proprietary look—an odd mixture of suspicion and obvious regret that this is a *public* river. "Nice day?" I falter, letting my paddle trail in the water. He coolly replaces his shades and resumes the discussion of spreadsheets.

I can see right off that my chances of getting in by the boathouse are slim. The bank is nearly vertical and overgrown with briars and thistles. The boathouse is swarming with activity. And there is a permanently manned guardhouse perched high above everything, linked to the river by a single wooden staircase that zigzags down the hillside.

It's obvious the Bohos took precautions against a river invasion a long time ago.

THE 2,300-MEMBER BOHEMIAN CLUB is in many ways the West Coast equivalent of New York's Century Club, or Washington's Cosmos Club. The six-story ivied brownstone at the corner of Post and Taylor streets in downtown San Francisco has the same sort of fusty Victorian charm: the creaky floors, the crystal chandeliers, the redolence of pipe tobacco and malt, the dapper old men sitting in overstuffed chairs reading moldering hardbacks from the library. Women, if they're invited in at all, must enter by a side door and confine themselves to the banquet halls downstairs. Membership comes dear: Voting members pay $8,500 to join, with monthly dues of $110. Men's clubs are said to be a dying phenomenon around the country, but the Bohemian Club has never been more popular. It typically takes fifteen years for prospective members to inch their way to the top of the three-thousand-name waiting list.

The club was started in 1872 as an informal drinking society for nightowlish journalists and authentic bohemians in the

San Francisco area who were interested in matters of art, literature, and music. At the time, the European notion of the "bohemian" life-style—the wandering, carefree *artiste*—had come into vogue in America. The term derived from the common French myth that Gypsies had originated in the Czech province of Bohemia (the French word for gypsies, in fact, is *bohémiens*.) The bohemian life-style gained wide currency after the publication of a picaresque novel of Paris life by Henri Murger, and later, with the production of Puccini's opera *La Bohème*.

Jack London, Bret Harte, Ambrose Bierce, and Mark Twain were among the club's early members, as were Sierra Club founder John Muir and economist Henry George, a radical social reformer chiefly known for his influential 1879 treatise, *Progress and Poverty*, which advocated the abolishment of all private property. The club was conceived as a refuge from the furious Mammon-worship that had overtaken the Bay City in the flush times after the Gold Rush and the completion of the transcontinental railroad. The club rented a few Spartan rooms at the Astor House on Sacramento Street, and blackballed all wealthy men as a matter of course.

But the Bohemians—being bohemians—couldn't pay their bills. So before long they reluctantly invited businessmen with professed avant-garde yearnings into the ranks of the club. "It was decided," wrote charter member Edward Bosqui, "that we should invite an element to join the club which the majority of the members held in contempt, namely men who had money as well as brains, but who were not, strictly speaking, bohemians." The bills got paid, and within a few years "men of affairs" dominated the club roster. By 1880, a group of BC painters were protesting that "the salt has been washed out of the club by commercialism, the chairs are too easy and the food too dainty, and the true Bohemian spirit has departed." Oscar Wilde, visiting the club as part of a transcontinental tour of America, was moved to remark: "I have never seen so many well-dressed, well-fed, businesslike-looking bohemians in all my life."

The ironies implicit in the club's name had been artfully troweled over by 1907, when the San Francisco poet George Sterling wrote what is still considered the quintessential Grove Play, *The Triumph of Bohemia*. The spiritual father of the club, Sterling was a former real estate speculator who conceived many of the early rituals that now lie at the heart of the Bohemian liturgy. In 1926, he took his own life by drinking potassium cyanide in an upstairs room of the city clubhouse, where he had lived his later years.

The Triumph of Bohemia involves an epic battle of the heavens in which the noble forces of Bohemia prevail over the money-grubbing spirit of Mammon. Sterling's story line, of course, flew in the face of the social realities of the club. "Sterling hadn't noticed," one writer later commented, "that the happy sprites and bacchic fauns whom he so proudly commanded in his onslaught of Mammon were in reality fat businessmen of San Francisco out on a summer picnic, ready to be amused and flattered by Sterling's plays."

Yet the name stuck, and membership in the Bohemian Club steadily grew, building on a curious alliance between businessmen and artists that could have thrived only in a city as wide-open and socially pliable as San Francisco in its youth. The Bohemians' musicals, reviews, and art shows grew more elaborate each year, and over time the club developed a latter-day version of Europe's court patronage system. Artistically gifted men were invited to join at greatly reduced rates, but were obligated to share their talents for full-paying members drawn from the wealthy class. The Bohemian Club thus gave the starving garret musician or actor of Victorian San Francisco what he wanted most—an appreciative audience and the financial freedom to perform—while the railroad tycoon could soften his philistine edges in the fashionable presence of similarly well-dressed, well-fed "bohemians." It was a social arrangement reminiscent of the Medici, and it continues to this day. "You have joined not only a club, but a way of life," the Bohemian Club admonishes initiates. "Talented types," as gifted members are called, are expected to put out. The club takes its dramatic and musical productions seriously. Scores and scripts have to be written, sets painted, dances choreographed. All members, even the rich and untalented ones, are expected to contribute in some way. It is not uncommon to find a board member of Chase Manhattan Bank hauling platforms for a Bohemian Club play, or an astronaut delivering a cameo performance as a sentry or a hamadryad. "Everyone carries a spear in Bohemia" is one of the club watchwords.

The first summer encampment, held in Marin County in

1878, was little more than a colorful picnic in the country.
The original 160-acre parcel of the current Grove property
was purchased in 1898 from a wealthy Sonoma County timber
baron named Captain Melvin C. Meeker. By 1925, most of the
Grove's 2,800 acres had been purchased, all for the paltry sum
of $99,000. In the early days, Bohemians took a ferry to Sausa-
lito, then rode a narrow-gauge train that stopped at a little
depot directly inside the Grove property.

The train service stopped in 1936, but the pilgrimage continued, year after year, the elaborate rituals becoming overlaid
with a bizarre combination of Greek drama, Druidic legend,
Shakespeare, the Book of Common Prayer, and the American
Wild West. Somewhere along the way, the Midsummer Encampment began to take on a vaguely spiritual aura. Today,
Bohemians at the San Francisco clubhouse speak of "going up"
in the reverent tones in which Jews speak of making aliyah.
Some members consider the Grove sacred ground. The Bohemian literature is strewn with descriptions of the Grove as a
"cathedral," "sanctuary," "temple." It is said that some Bohemians, upon their deaths, have had their ashes sprinkled over
the forest floor. Other Bohos concentrate their affections on
specific trees. At the base of a three-hundred-foot redwood not
far from the dining circle, you will find a little plaque that reads:
"I love this tree as the most sound, upright, and stately redwood
in the Grove. Let my friends remember me by it when I am
gone."

The Bohemians come here "to be boys again." Each spring
the club president officially welcomes the Bohemians back to
the Grove with a flowery appeal to adolescence: "Bohemians
come! come out and play, come with all the buoyant impetuous
rush of youth!" Going to the Grove, it is said, is akin to revisiting
the primeval garden, a wild place without laws or girls, where
a lad can be Lord of the Flies, and run half-naked in the woods
and roast meat around bonfires and sing old songs of forgotten
warriors and build treehouse hideaways with secret trapdoors
and urinate whenever and wherever he feels the urge. Those
ancient trees inspire a juvenility in old men. "We are grown
men now," reads a Bohemian Grove announcement from 1922,
"but to most of us it seems as if we have done little more than
progress from one schoolroom to another. And we have found
to our dismay . . . that the big school of life isn't very different

from the little grammar school we knew when we were eight. But each year, in the hard procession of our days, there comes, thank God, to us Bohemians, a recess time—it is upon us. Come out Bohemians. Come out and play!"

THE TOWN OF MONTE RIO is an improbable site for an Establishment retreat. Thomas Pynchon's *Vineland* could have been set in this frowsy burg in the heart of the fogbelt. The town's population of nine hundred is an odd fellowship of gays, hippies, loggers, bikers, and eco-bandits. It's the kind of place where Earth First! warriors strap themselves to condemned redwood trees and "Appropriate Technology" is the ruling creed. In past years, the area's largest annual event, aside from the Grove encampment, has been a conclave of lesbian motorcyclists who call themselves "Dykes on Bikes." A Bible camp and a Buddhist temple cling to the hills near the Grove. The Korbel Champagne Company, founded by two Czech brothers who moved to Sonoma County from the *original* province of Bohemia, owns a few thousand acres of vineyards nearby. Snaking through it all is the Russian River, named for the Russian fur trappers who, in the early 1800s, seasonally migrated here from the czar's colony in Alaska. Most of the original redwoods in western Sonoma County were cut in the late 1800s (neighboring Guerneville is still known as "Stumptown"), and the precious wood was skidded south to mills in Sausalito and Mill Valley, much of the lumber ending up in the stately rowhouses of downtown San Francisco. Local legend has it that the term "skid row," named for the cursed job of working the redwood skids, was coined here.

The Village Inn, where I'm staying, is a gracefully sagging Victorian hotel on the banks of the Russian River. It is less than a hundred yards from the Grove fenceline. Standing on the hotel steps that first afternoon, I can hear the report of shotguns booming down the hollow from the Bohemian trap and skeet range. Next door to the Inn is a modest residence faithfully guarded by two Doberman pinschers. Each blast of the shotguns sets the Dobermans off on a fit of barking, and they pace the length of a chain-link fence, beneath a sign that warns, "Trespassers Will Be Eaten."

The downstairs bar at the Village Inn is a popular hangout for Bohemian Club employees who've punched out for the night. The bar surface is strewn with an odd collection of toys and puzzles—Rubik's Cubes, Hot Wheels, trick ropes, battery-operated gizmos. On a busy night, you can meet Secret Service men, call girls, personal valets, and other servants of Bohemia gathered around the bar, fidgeting with the toys. A facetious cloak-and-dagger atmosphere pervades the place, *Casablanca* meets *Pee Wee's Playhouse*. Everyone is eyeballing each other. The guy knocking back tequila shots next to me wants to know how I'm connected to the Grove. A heavily perfumed woman in a leopard skin cocktail dress sits crosslegged on a barstool, drinking daquiris in a gauze of cigarette smoke. Two beefy men in dark suits stand in the shadows, playing with one of those metal-ball-pendulum-clackers from the early seventies: *Rackata-rackata-rackata-rackata*.

The locals are eager to share their "inside" tips on the Grove, but getting in, they assure me, is out of the question. If I had time, I could try to infiltrate the waiters' union that works up there. This is how San Francisco journalist John Van der Zee researched his 1974 book about the Grove, *The Greatest Men's Party on Earth*. Or if I knew a Bohemian Club member, I could try to wangle an invitation for myself. Some local hippies who protest at the Grove every year supposedly know a secret overland route from the backside of Bohemia. But I'd have to hack through miles of thickets and poison ivy, and I'd likely meet some pretty tough characters back in the hill country that surrounds the Grove, river rats straight out of *Deliverance* who wouldn't think twice about shooting me for trespassing on their property. And then, they said, there were guard dogs.

Even if I *did* succeed in penetrating the boundary some-where, the odds are I'd get hopelessly lost. The Grove, everyone reminds me, is three thousand acres of wilderness and steep meandering trails. I could wander around in there for days and never see a soul. It's all switchbacks and ravines and cul-de-sacs, a tangle of pathways in the green gloom of redwoods, whose massive fluted stalks all begin to look alike after a while.

The trail system, someone tells me, is designed so that each path eventually doubles back to a guard station. Some trails in remote areas even have infrared sensors that can detect an intruder's movements. Roving TV cameras stationed along the perimeter feed into a central monitoring station where Bohe-mian sentinels keep constant vigil. At strategic places, the Grove police have built treehouses high in the redwood canopy, where guards scan the pathways with binoculars. During the busiest days of the encampment, Secret Service agents comb the hillsides. And when the real big guns come to Bohemia—people like Reagan and Shultz—surveillance helicopters circle overhead.

"You might as well try to break into Fort Knox," the Village Inn bartender tells me, pouring another Bass Ale. "Trust me, you're going to wind up in the Santa Rosa jail with the worst cast of poison ivy you've ever seen."

THE VEIL OF SECRECY that hangs over the Bohemian Grove isn't just a product of barbed wire and fortified gatehouses. Secrecy is simply the Bohemian way of doing things, its modus operandi. Like Skull and Bones, the Grove is a place where secrets are kept for the sheer adolescent joy of keeping secrets. It's not that the Bohos have something really worth hiding, some black and unspeakable ritual which their high priests carry out in the dead of night. They don't drink baby's blood or mutilate chickens. They don't even, as is often rumored, perform the sacrament of onanism in a dank coffin. Yet everything about the Bohemian Club gives off a sly wink and a whisper. It is as if the Bohemians were playing some sort of practical joke on society, in the way the medieval Freemasons used to carve expletives high up in a cathedral vault, where no one else could see.

It wasn't always that way. In the early days, the Bohemian orchestra gave free concerts to the public. The club's plays and musical performances were regularly reviewed in the Hearst newspapers. But by the 1930s, when conspicuous elitism went out of fashion, the club gradually turned in on itself.

It also lost its sense of humor. The club denied membership to Will Rogers after the humorist told a reporter in 1928 that the Midsummer Encampment, which he'd just visited as a guest, was "a form of weekend divertissement for tired businessmen from which it took them about two weeks to recover." The Bohemians feared the joke would hurt the presidential bid of Herbert Hoover, who was then campaigning on a temperance platform.

The club mascot is itself a symbol of secrecy: the owl. Everywhere in Bohemia one sees owls. Owls on stationery, cuff links, and bolo ties. Stuffed owls, papier-mâché owls, bronze owls.

The forty-foot Owl Shrine, a dark and brooding concrete beast overgrown with moss and lichens, looms over the pond where the Bohos hear their Lakeside Talks. Originally the owl was chosen to reflect the nocturnal habits of the journalists who founded the club, but in the last half-century it has come to symbolize, quite succinctly, the shadowy perch to which the Bohemians have removed themselves. Bohemians like to point out that the owl, as the bird of Athena, has always served as a symbol of wisdom in classical literature. But the club's detractors speak of the owl as the screeching prey-bird of the night, all-knowing, all-seeing, silent in flight, the bird of Halloween and the occult. In the Middle Ages, they say, the owl symbolized the nonbeliever who dwelt in darkness. "Only in our culture does the owl represent wisdom," says Mary Moore, a local political activist and student of Bohemian iconography who has converted her entire guest house into a permanent archive on the Grove. "In other cultures, it represents evil, darkness, and death."

The Bohemian Club's patron saint is also a symbol of secrecy. He is St. John of Nepomuk, a martyred cleric from medieval Prague, capital of the *real* province of Bohemia, in western Czechoslovakia. The true story of St. John's death is shrouded in mystery, but here's the legend the Bohemian Club prefers to tell: It seems that around 1393 the Bohemian monarch, King Wenceslas IV, suspected his wife, Queen Sophie, of adultery. One day the jealous king demanded that John of Nepomuk, as Sophie's "spiritual director," betray her confessions. Being an honorable man of the cloth, John refused to break his priestly vow of confidentiality, and for that, Wenceslas had him drowned in the Vltava River. Like a good Bohemian, John knew how to keep a secret. Today, a statue of St. John of Nepomuk stands in the Bohemian Grove. Cloaked in robes, the Czech martyr is pressing his index finger to his lips, still keeping the queen's confidences.

Despite its persnickety adherence to secrecy, the Bohemian Club seems intensely interested in maintaining the Grove's place in history as a kind of American Olympus. Over the decades, Club archivists have seen to it that the major libraries in California, not to mention the Library of Congress, are supplied with the reams of official literature which the club publishes under

The cast of the 1909 "grove play" at the Midsummer Encampment of the Bohemian Club.

The dining circle at the Bohemian Grove, 1909.

The Cremation of Care, 1949.

its own imprint. At Berkeley's Bancroft Library, you can read the yellowed scripts of every Grove play ever produced, dating back to 1902. You can read all five hardback volumes of the club's tediously documented history, *The Annals of Bohemia*. You can spend weeks sifting through maps, wine lists, cartoons, lyrics, scores, transcriptions of Lakeside Talks, and tinted daguerreotypes of bewhiskered old men dressed in togas. The club seems to welcome the public's curiosity, as long as it takes the form of historical scholarship pursued through acceptable channels of research. It's the same sort of obsessive history-consciousness that led the Nixon White House to work its mischief behind closed doors, but all the while, *to tape-record everything*! Every word that is spoken in Bohemia is supposed to be off the record, and yet, absurdly, everything is recorded, photographed, and neatly catalogued for . . . for whom? Not for the general public, but for the faithful scribes of some far distant posterity. "What's the point of being brilliant," Henry Kissinger lamented at the opening of a 1982 Lakeside Talk, "if you have to do it in obscurity?"

Journalists, burning with a peculiar lust and feeling of entitlement, have been breaking into the Bohemian Grove ever since the start of the Woodward-Bernstein era. *Mother Jones*, National Public Radio, *Time*, the *Los Angeles Times*, CBS News, and *Spy* magazine have all snuck reporters in over the years. Jack Anderson once did an exposé on the Grove, as have a host of underground rags.

Interest in the encampment has by no means been limited to the news media. Grove crashing has long been a popular summer pastime for high school kids in Sonoma County. Two nonfiction books and several novels have been written about the place. An article in *The Harvard Civil Rights and Civil Liberties Law Review* has examined the legal arguments behind the club's steadfast refusal to admit women, and a Vanderbilt anthropologist has compared the Bohemians' elaborate rituals to those of a misogynist tribe of Indians in Central Brazil, the Mehinaku.

But the most indefatigable researcher of Bohemia is a shy free-lance photojournalist named Kerry Richardson. Working alone out of his parents' house in nearby Santa Rosa, Richardson has spent the past several years compiling a computerized dossier on every Bohemian club member. When I caught up with him he had just completed the *L*'s. Richardson is a tall, fair-complexioned man in his late thirties with thick spectacles and long dun-colored hair pulled back in a ponytail.

The fruits of his research can be found in a small underground newsletter that he publishes from time to time entitled, simply, *Kerry Richardson's Journal.*

If universities had a formal department for the kind of research Richardson does, it would be called Establishment Studies. His bookshelves sag with titles like *Missile Envy, The Man Who Kept Secrets, Friends in High Places.* He scours the Fortune 500, *Who's Who in America,* Standard & Poor's Index, and Dun & Bradstreet, hunting for clues to questions like which Bohemians sit on the boards of which of their friends' companies, or which Bohemians have made financial contributions in excess of one thousand dollars to the political campaigns of fellow Bohemians. He can tell you the names of the executive vice presidents of Lockheed, Rockwell International, and Pratt & Whitney. He can tell you whom Stephen Bechtel invited last year as a guest to the Grove. "There's a lot of evil concentrated up there," Richardson tells me, as he fries up a lunch of tofu wedges. "Or rather, there are a lot of people concentrated there who are responsible for . . . evil processes."

Richardson's real love is photography. Each summer he drives out to the Sonoma County airport and takes snapshots of Bohemian bigwigs as they step off their Learjets. He's got photo albums filled with photos of Reagan, Shultz, and Kissinger lugging briefcases down the tarmac. Most of the men aren't so easily recognizable, however. Richardson spends a lot of his time trying to verify the identities of those he's photographed. Sometimes he looks up the annual reports of major corporations and studies the official photographs of board members until he finds a likeness. Other times he copies down the tail numbers on the planes and writes the FAA to learn the owners' name. "I think that's John Kluge, but I'm not sure," he says, holding up a negative to the light.

One year Richardson put on diving flippers and swam by the Bohemian boathouse, taking photos with an underwater camera. "Why don't you just leave us alone?" one of the Bohos told him. Richardson snapped off a few more shots and then disappeared in the green water.

Interlopers like Richardson have justified their trespasses on the Grove by appealing to lofty principles: to expose the pernicious ways that power cross-pollinates, to hold the nation's oligarchs accountable. But for others, myself included, one suspects a baser motive. It is the ancient boyhood impulse to Get In—to break the spell of secrecy. It's not a noble enterprise, and certainly not a legal one. But it can't be helped.

When I first set out to do research on the Bohemian Grove, I called Kevin Starr, an eminent California historian and club archivist. I hoped that Starr, as a friend of a Bohemian Club member I knew, and as an author himself, might at least be willing to give me a background interview about the club's history and traditions. Starr was politely but resolutely mum. "The club has nothing to gain by talking to the press," he said. "We get crucified every time. We've got a dozen lawsuits in the courts right now. I'm sorry, but the last thing we need is more media attention." End of conversation.

So that was it. If I couldn't be above-board about it, then I would have to be a spy. The historical ironies were striking to me. Here was a club, conceived by newspapermen, whose gatherings are now utterly closed to them. There aren't even any journalists in the ranks of the club, unless you count Walter Cronkite. It was natural for me to imagine that my invasion by stealth would simply be the quiet revenge of the founders' ink-stained ghosts. And besides, it seemed to me the Bohemian Club had long ago forfeited its right to hermetic secrecy by playing an active role in hatching the atom bomb. Once a private place enmeshes itself in public policy—indeed, in the very fate of the earth—it is no longer a private place.

RACKATA-RACKATA-RACKATA. It's midnight at the bar at the Village Inn, and the toys are getting a workout. The joint is jumping with Grove employees, journalists, and a few off-duty hookers. A TV crew from San Francisco is here to gather footage for the national show *PM Magazine*, and so far, they haven't had much luck. "They don't make it easy for you," one of the cameramen is grousing. "The security is too rigid—it's like a military installation in there." In the dining room, there are four actual Bohemians wearing owl bolo ties and cardigan sweaters, but no one is paying them much attention. "Who cares about them?" a local woman tells me. "They're all a bunch of yawners!"

Most of the Grove workers are hired from the rolls of

the San Francisco waiters union, and are sworn not to assist journalists or other snoops in their research. But some are willing to cut a deal. Throughout the night, a Grove waiter in a pleated, food-stained tux shirt has been trying to sell me a "permanent pass" to the encampment for $500. "I could do it in a second," he assures me.

Holding court tonight is a garrulous fireplug of a fellow named Emmett who says he's been in charge of the Bohemian bar and grill for seventeen years. Emmett's discourse on Grove life is all good-natured bluster, his anecdotes reeled off in a tone of mock condescension that seems to say, *You don't have a clue about how this country* really *works.*

"Say Emmett," one of the locals blurts as he fiddles with a Rubik's Cube. "You must have seen some pretty heavy stuff up there in seventeen years. You know, political deals, CEOs divvying up the continent . . ."

"Man, they don't talk about shit up there," Emmett answers. "They talk about stuff like who stole the last bottle of Kahlua. They go someplace else to talk about their business."

"Who *you?*" Emmett asks me, breathing whiskey in my face.

A writer from Washington, I tell him.

"Don't be bullshittin' Emmett now. I've been keeping my eye on you. Seen you up there shootin' skeet. All you Secret Service cowboys think you're pretty hot shit with a shotgun, don't you?"

Emmett's got me pegged for some redneck hoss from the Secret Service and there's no convincing him otherwise.

"Listen up, James Bond. I'm the best shot in the state of California. I could break your neck before you even *get* to your gun. Who you workin' for? Reagan? Kissinger? Don't be messin' with Emmett. I'm the mayor of the Russian River."

Finally Emmett stumbles out with a fellow Grove employee. Later, I meet a chain-smoking waiter with lugubrious, bloodshot eyes who informs me that he's the shop steward of the San Francisco restaurant workers union that serves the encampment. "The Grove's a magical place," he says. "I've personally had eye contact with Ronald Reagan three times! *Three times.* Eye contact! Another time I heard Burt Bacharach singing with Merv Griffin on the piano. Or was it the other way around? But I mean, *together!*"

Now the enterprising fellow with the $500 Grove pass is

butting in again. No thanks, I tell him, I'll find some other way in. "Suit yourself," he scoffs. "But don't come running to me when they're hauling your ass off to jail."

That night, I crawl upstairs to my room, and doze fitfully to the barking of Dobermans. As my mind wanders, it suddenly hits me: There's one road into Bohemia that I still haven't tried. . . .

MONTE RIO AVENUE tumbles from the high hills above the Bohemian entrance. The only marker is a sign that announces, "Not a Thru Road." For me, this is an invitation. The "avenue" turns out to be a single-lane residential road that winds through a warren of cabins, then cuts along a steep ridge. In places, it is little more than a wobbly platform on stilts, cantilevered over a canyon. Finally the road doglegs to the right and dead-ends at a blocked entrance.

A sign over a gate says, "Beware of Dog," and judging by the general appearance of the place, it looks like a sign that means business. The wooden gate is half a foot thick, wrapped in chains, and padlocked shut. The fence is draped in barbed wire. Another sign announces unequivocally, "Private Property: No Trespassing."

I hurl a stone over the gate to stir up the dogs. It tumbles down the hillside, and I can hear it smashing into tree trunks before landing in a clump of maidenhair ferns. I think I hear barking, but at 4:45 A.M., I could be imagining things.

Down in a valley, through the tree limbs, I can see a parking lot filled with Jags and Mercedes-Benzes gleaming in the moonlight, and I am reminded of a piece of doggerel I'd read somewhere in the Bohemian literature:

Can't find your BMW?
You shouldn't let it trouble you
Don't worry where your auto is
Forget about it—Drive home *his*.

The road continues beyond the gate for a hundred yards or so, then drops behind a hill. It appears to be an old service road of some kind, an access route for trucks and heavy machinery, though it clearly hasn't been used in a long time.

I'm calling their bluff on the dogs. I'm going in.

I'm wearing my best approximation of a Bohemian uniform: a blue blazer, a cotton dress shirt, crisply pressed Levi's jeans, and a lived-in pair of dirty bucks. I'll be posing as a Bohemian early riser heading for his morning dip in the river, so I fling a towel around my neck and carry a pair of swimming trunks for good measure. In my coat pockets, I've stashed a penlight, a Sony tape recorder, and a faded map of the Bohemian Grove that I'd copied out of the Bancroft Library. The map is dated "September, 1935."

I spread the beach towel on the ground to shield my blazer from the dirt and conifer needles. I lie on my back and squeeze into the narrow passage under the gate. I can feel cobwebs brushing my face.

Now that I'm inside, I expect air raid sirens to go off, halogen floodlights, the squawk of a hidden PA system: *Turn back, intruder! This is a final warning!* Instead . . . nothing. Only the frogs and owls and miscellaneous thicket sounds of the forest. And as I creep down the spongy path, the only animal I see is a doe quivering in the shadows, her frightened eyes shining back at me through the silver moonlight.

There is a feathery artificiality about the trees, all those giant asparagus stalks stretching skyward in perfect uniformity. It's like a George Lucas movie set, not a real forest but a plastic Hollywood imitation. A deciduous forest is an imperfect world of crooks and elbows and broken limbs of different species rotting together in democratic heaps, and the leafy ground is always crawling with bugs. But not in a redwood grove. Where are the bugs? Occasionally I see a perfect spider spinning a perfect web between two perfectly straight trees, but no bugs.

The air is cool and damp and still as a cellar. The clump of my footsteps is swallowed by a corrugated wall of timber. But at times when the wind stirs in the upper reaches of the trees, the branches rub together to create a frightful keening sound, high-pitched and insistent, like the cry of a trapped animal.

The Grove is the last remaining old-growth stand of any size in Sonoma County, and it's a priceless piece of real estate. Some of these trees are two thousand years old. To walk in here is to walk among superlatives—oldest, biggest, tallest, darkest, thickest—not to mention the superlatives commonly associated with Bohemians themselves: richest, smartest, mightiest, best connected. Any living thing that was around during the reign of Charlemagne has a way of mocking you. "Redwoods are the nearest thing to living eternity that the planet affords," author Herman Wouk once wrote in a paper for the Grove archives. "They smile down on poor truants with majestic tolerance, as we sprinkle their greatness with our waste water." The Kayasha Pomo Indians who once lived and hunted in Sonoma County believed the groves were haunted places, filled with evil spirits. Just crawling over these ancient roots, I feel like an intruder twice over. On some cosmic level that transcends the mere illegality of trespassing, I sense I do not belong here.

According to my map, I'm on Mt. Heller Trail, but I keep blundering onto subsidiary paths that evidently didn't exist in 1935. I'm getting farther and farther from the encampment circle. Little cairns are laid out by forks in the path, but these tell me nothing. I fumble with the map in the darkness, but it's no use: I'm seriously lost in the Bohemian Outback. Members speak of the Grove as though it were its own country, Liechtenstein or someplace, and walking these extensive trails you begin to see why. Stow Trail, Chicago Trail, Snob Hill Trail, Rogers Hill Road, Middle Ridge Road—they swarm the map like a nest of tapeworms.

Occasionally I stumble upon a concrete trail marker bearing the chiseled image of an impish owl on the wing. But it's not until dawn that I see any convincing sign of Bohemian civilization. Taking Middle Ridge Road, I come to a desolate clearing that turns out to be the trap and skeet shooting range. The grass is drenched in dew and littered with the green casings of shotgun shells. Farther out is a thick dusting of pulverized terra cotta clay.

I walk for twenty minutes on an access road that winds out of the woods and climbs over several miles of weedy hill country. I've wandered clear off the map now, to some no-man's-land on the outskirts of Bohemia. In the distance, I can hear the rumble of a heavy truck, and it's growing louder. The Grove police, I suspect, making their hourly surveillance rounds. Now that darkness has lifted, the guards will spot me a mile away; there are no redwoods to duck behind out here. And they'll assume I'm a spy right off: I'm miles from camp, and farther still from the Russian River, where, ostensibly, I'm heading for a swim. No *real* Bohemians would be hiking this treeless periphery, certainly not at this godforsaken hour.

Now I can hear the police truck chuffing up the hill behind me, just a hundred yards back and gaining by the second. I'm sweating bullets, hunting for a place to hide. The sound of gears grinding, tires shaking the earth, Rommel's tanks. They're coming after me. *Closer . . . closer.*

I crawl into a culvert just before the vehicle crests the hill: a monster truck from the Bohemian utility fleet, fire-engine red, all clanking and rattling with chains, winches, heavy tools.

I'm in luck. No security men on board. I think they missed me, but I stay low for a few minutes until the coast is clear.

Now there's another engine approaching in the distance, only this time it's a helicopter. I'm assuming the worst—Grove aerial police—so I dive into a bed of ferns. Soon the chopper drops out of the sky. I can see television cameras peeping from the copter's windows as it floats by. Then I realize: It's not the Grove police, it's those cameramen from *PM Magazine* gathering bird's-eye footage. Sky pirates, violating Bohemian airspace in a rented whirlybird.

Another hour into my hike, and I still haven't seen any Bohemians. But I do have the good fortune of stumbling upon a piece of Bohemian tribal art. High in the crotch of a Douglas fir, someone has carefully placed a sculpture of a six-foot-long, fully erect penis. The sculptor obviously went to great trouble to achieve realism in his work: You can see bulging veins and ridges lovingly carved into the wooden phallus. This Bohemian Rodin, whoever he was, must have spent days on his masterpiece. All you can really say is that it is a very big penis—the kind of proud and muscular organ that Robert Mapplethrope might have appreciated.

PENISES, PISSING, AND PENILE PLUMBING are, in fact, a constant leitmotif in Bohemian literature. The Grove comic shows, called Low Jinx, are rife with double entendres about "tricky dicks" and "swollen members." But the Bohemian phallic genre may have reached a new plateau in 1982 when Alfred W. Baxter, a retired professor and member of Silverado Squatters Camp, penned this lamentation from the Berkeley hospital, where he was suffering from a prostate condition instead of sprinkling his favorite trees at the Grove:

Prostate, prostate, burning right
Up there where the plumbing's tight
What in hell persuaded thee
To plug the pipe through which I pee?
In what ocean, on what land
Grew the tissues of this gland?
What dread ailment fed increase
That caused my fluid flows to cease?

Such talk of prostates and penises only serves to underscore the controversy that has kept the club lawyers busy for years: the Bohemians' refusal to admit women as members. A steady succession of discrimination suits over the years has exerted considerable pressure on the Bohemians, but the club has held fast. (In 1989, however, the club was forced to hire women as Grove employees for the first time, the result of an employment discrimination suit brought by the State of California.) Several members, including former California governor Edmund G. "Pat" Brown, have testified in court about the disastrous effect women would have on life inside the Grove. Brown praised the right of men "to sit around in a pair of shorts and listen to stories that I don't want to listen to when my wife is there. . . . When women are around, any man is more genteel and careful of his words." Ladies might want to spruce up the place, Brown later argued, and would interfere with the time-honored Bohemian custom of walking around in "various states of undress." It was a matter of some irony that Brown, as the state's liberal Democratic governor during the 1960s, had signed into law much of the civil rights legislation that was being used to chip away at the Bohemian Club's males-only status.

Some Bohemians have speculated that the presence of women would create unwelcome sexual tensions. "I wouldn't want to meet last night's date at lunch," one San Francisco businessman observed, "or end up in the bushes with some other guy's wife."

"I don't mean to be sexist, but the housing is not that comfortable," club president Harry Scott argued at the time. "We're not up there to throw rocks at women. Women are wonderful. But the whole thing would be a catastrophe."

The feminist groups that have protested at the mouth of

the Grove in past years say the Bohemians throw plenty of rocks at women. "We are here to protest the longest, cruelest terrorist regime in the history of the planet," fumed Sonia Johnson, a former Citizens Party candidate for president, in a 1984 speech delivered outside the Grove gates. "This regime is five thousand years old, and it's called patriarchy. Patriarchy is the idea that God and man are all in this old boys' club together with God as president. As women, we have known for thousands of years that if we want to propitiate God, we had better stay on pretty good terms with his cronies, the Men. God trusts them a lot and likes them a lot, because they were made in his image. He therefore wants them to be the rulers, the prime ministers and kings of the world, the popes and prophets and priests. He wants them to own all the businesses and corporations and universities and media, and to make all the money."

Bohemians, of course, balk at these frequently leveled charges of chauvinism. They insist that the club is strictly an "art and literary club," not a business association, and is thus legally impervious to cries of gender-based discrimination. If anything, they say, it is the all-male club, and by inference, the entire male gender, that has been bullied by modern society. "The Bohemian Club," wrote Kevin Starr in a 1977 Grove talk, "is a sort of sanctuary designed to preserve an endangered species—the American Male. Like the great auk, the carrier pigeon, the sabre-toothed tiger, and the dodo bird, the American Male, in its flourishing, unintimidated variety, is on the endangered list. Each day a certain pernicious reverse-chauvinism threatens to deprive him of his natural virtues—his good humor, his self-pride and self-reliance. The Bohemian Club allows men to feel good about themselves."

The Bohemians' other major source of public criticism is the "Cremation of Care" ceremony, a kind of passion play that is held by the lakeside on the first official evening of each Grove encampment. Originally written by poet George Sterling, the Cremation is a solemn rite performed in King James English that involves a cast of two hundred men, most of them dressed in hooded robes. The effigy of Dull Care is placed on a barge and poled out across the pond. Care then addresses the Bohemians assembled on the shore:

Fools, fools, fools, when will ye learn that me ye cannot slay? Year after year ye burn me in this Grove, lifting silly shouts of triumph to the pitying stars. But when ye turn your feet again to the marketplace, am I not waiting for you as of old. Fools, fools, to dream you conquer Care!

The Bohemian high priest answers:

Year after year, within this happy Grove, our fellowship has damned thee for a space, and thy malevolence that would pursue us has lost its power beneath these friendly trees. So shall we burn thee once again this night, and in the flames that eat thine effigy we'll read the sign that, once again, midsummer sets us free.

With that, Care is set aflame, and the Bohemian band strikes up "There'll Be a Hot Time in the Old Town Tonight." Another year's encampment can finally begin.

The club gets a lot of grief for the Cremation of Care ceremony. More than a few critics have suggested its resemblance to a Ku Klux Klan rally. Others say it's unseemly for men of such power to consign the "cares" of the world to the flames. At the very least, the ritual reinforces the suspicion that the Bohemians really do view themselves as the tired custodians of the republic, overworked servants wishing only to unshoulder their White Men's Burden for a time. But the Bohemians insist the Cremation ceremony is a harmless tradition, steeped in romantic literature and ancient lodge rites; that it merely symbolizes the club's injunction to its members to lay aside all shoptalk and marketplace concerns. "[The Cremation of Care] is the shedding from each of us of the snake's skin we grow in the workaday world," Kevin Starr has written. "[It is] dropping the mask of pride, of position, of self-importance and greed and power. It cannot last, it is only a spell, but it is a magic spell."

JUST WHEN THOUGHT I'd managed to elude all of the Grove's fabled security traps, I round a corner and see that I'll have to pass by a guard station after all. I pick up the pace and try to look natural, swinging my towel over my shoulder and whistling a tune. To my surprise, the uniformed man in the little kiosk just smiles and waves me on through. I feel strangely disappointed by my good fortune. I'm thinking: *It shouldn't be this easy.*

It's about nine A.M. when I finally work my way down to River Road. The Grove is waking up now. There is the smell of bacon and percolating coffee. Smoke is curling from the camps, and everywhere you can hear the clinking of porcelain and flatware. Tyndall beams of light are angling through the canopy. Inside the camps, old guys are sitting in their boxer shorts, yawning, stretching, belching, hacking. On a hillside above Band Camp, a lone musician still dressed in his pajamas and slippers is softly playing the clarinet. Higher up, two stout souls in lederhosen burst out of the woods, their whittled walking sticks smacking the ground as they return from a brisk morning constitutional.

In many respects, the Grove is a rustic place. No TVs, stereos, or radios are allowed. Many of the camps are without electric heat or running water. Most of the buildings are rough-hewn cabins, their rickety steps carpeted in moss and forest needles. The public clearings are strewn with wood chips. A salt lick stands in the middle of the Grove, to attract deer. Tacked to a redwood tree near the dining area is an admonition to campers: GENTLEMEN! PLEASE NO PEEPEE HERE!

Each of the Grove's 135 camps has its own personality. Some are bungalows spread on the forest floor; others are jumbled boxes that bounce like pueblos down the hills. The public spaces are furnished with faded sofas and morris chairs, and all manner of bric-a-brac is lying about: stuffed animals, road signs, naked mannequins, fur pelts. Walking down River Road feels a little like strolling through Fraternity Row on a university campus, gauging the levels of sin emanating from frathouse to frathouse. But instead of Greek letters, the camps have boyish-sounding names that conjure up half-forgotten tales from *Treasure Island* and the works of Kipling: River Lair, Shoestring, Woof, Moonshiners, Toyland.

Aviary is the camp for singers. Tunerville is where the orchestra members stay. Medicine Lodge, a cluster of tepees, is inhabited exclusively by doctors. Lost Angels is a large camp for Bohemians from the Los Angeles area. ThreeThrees is a camp for Navy admirals.

Denizens at Highlanders wear their kilts to dinner. At Poison Oak Camp, they serve Bull's Ball Lunch, a hearty entrée of testicles from the castrated herds of a central California cattle baron. You can ride the funicular up to Mandalay and sample a certain gin and lemon juice drink.

Republican party stalwarts have tended to gravitate toward one of three camps: Mandalay (Shultz, Kissinger, Gerald Ford, Nicholas Brady, William French Smith, Stephen Bechtel), Cave Man (Nixon, Herbert Hoover, Emil Mosbacher), and Hill Billies (A. W. Clausen, William F. Buckley, Jr., Christopher Buckley). In 1989 a sign hung outside Hill Billies announced itself to be a "KINDER, GENTLER CAMP," a boastful tribute to its most famous member, George Bush. The senior Buckley once described a "typical" morning inside Hill Billies: "I play the harpsichord, [Apollo astronaut Frank] Borman talks about walking on the moon, and Bush talks about what he'll do when he's president."

Now that he *is* president, Bush has been unable to attend the Grove. For logistical and security reasons, incumbent presidents have been forced to forego encampment appearances. Nixon set the precedent in 1971, canceling a speech planned for the Lakeside after the press insisted on covering it. Nixon sent the Bohemian Club president an apologetic telegram, which now hangs in the city clubhouse. "Anyone can aspire to be President of the United States," Nixon wrote, "but few have any hope of becoming President of the Bohemian Club." Nixon urged the club to "continue leading people into the woods" and promised, as leader of the free world, that he'd redouble his efforts to "lead people out of them."

In 1989, former president Ronald Reagan made his first appearance at the Grove in almost a decade. Though no Sierra Club sentimentalist himself (he once observed that "If you've seen one redwood, you've seen them all"), Reagan has been a loyal member of the Owl's Nest Camp since 1975. His Lakeside Talk in 1989 touched on the lighter side of old age. "Loss of memory is one of the three things that denote old age," Reagan quipped, perhaps preparing for his imminent Iran-*contra* testimony, "and I can't remember the other two."

There is a boastful competitiveness about these little lairs.

You can sense the organizational principles of capitalism at work. The trademark cocktails are a kind of a mercantile gimmick. The fancy hinged signs that swing outside the camp entrances seem like a form of advertising, as if to say, *Come try life in our condo village.* Looking at the ruddy campmates hunkered over their fires, you sense that these men are instinctive company men, the kind of people who draw a large part of their identity from institutions. Their sweatshirts say EXETER, SEMPER FIDELIS, YALE CREW. Their baseball caps say AIR FORCE, UNIVERSITY CLUB, STANFORD LAW. One is conscious of property here: The borders of each camp are clearly marked with gates and tidy fences, bright flags and escutcheons. In one of the camps, someone has propped up a stolen sign from suburbia— "Warning: Neighborhood Crime Watch"—as if burglary were a problem in the Grove.

I'm a little young-looking to be a Bohemian (the average age in the club is fifty-five), though I could pass for a son or a nephew, or perhaps some junior executive that the boss brought along. But no one gives me a second look. It is the height of bad taste for a Bohemian to openly question the legitimacy of another guest's presence. The rules of decorum are such that once you've made it inside, you almost have to work at getting yourself kicked out.

Still, I've decided to forestall any suspicions by going out of my way to be friendly, making myself look at home here. As I stroll toward the dining circle, I'm constantly waiving, smiling, making direct eye contact with everybody I meet. Outside Monkey Block Camp, I have an encounter that gives me a start: It's the surly guy who wore the little Mark Spitz number on the Russian River the other day. But he clearly doesn't recognize me; this time he's all smiles. "How ya doing?" I gingerly ask him. He gives me a chipper salute and says, "Boy what a day! Goooooooooooood Morning, Bohemia!"

I wander over to the campfire circle and take a seat on one of the enormous benches hewn from redwood logs. The cinders from last night's bonfire are still faintly smoldering. Placed about the circle are full-length portraits of the men responsible for producing the various entertainments during the week. "Sires," they're called. A Sireship is a title of special honor and responsibility in Bohemia, and these portraits reflect it. All the Sires are depicted as discerning men of unerring taste. They stare off into the middle distance, their spectacles pushed back over their furrowed brows. In the backgrounds of the portraits, you often get a glimpse of the Sire's studio. It is a place of vigorous artistic activity piled high with manuscripts and musical scores. There is a martial cast to these portraits: The forces of Bohemia are still trying to conquer Mammon, and the Sire is the commanding general.

A young guitar player—a "Talented Type"—comes over to say hello. "What camp you in?" he asks politely.

"Bromley," I answer. (Bromley Camp is the large residential limbo at the Grove where most new members stay until they're assigned a permanent camp.)

"Oh, that's funny," he says. "I'm in Bromley, too. Where you sleeping, exactly?"

"Uhhhhhh," I stammer, "I-I-I . . ."

He gives me a long bewildered look. But then, lucky for me, one of his buddies comes over to congratulate him on a guitar performance he had given last night. I take my cue and disappear through the bushes and down the nearest trail.

At the Civic Center, fresh copies of the *Los Angeles Times* are laid out, and this morning Bohemian George Bush is pictured on page one, standing tall with other Western leaders at an economic summit. Over at the telephone bank, an unidentified Bohemian wearing only a towel and flip-flop thongs is deep in conversation with his broker. *"Whaddayamean he said no? Hey, I've got a controlling share."* Another gentleman in bermudas and a UCLA T-shirt is sipping a Bloody Mary and talking, in a somewhat defensive manner, with his "Grove widow" (as abandoned wives are called during encampment season). *"Honey, honey . . . l-l-look, I promise I won't get too smashed. I'm flying United down tonight, okay?"* At a little amphitheater near the museum, a Berkeley professor is delivering a lecture on the hot new scientific realm of "chaos." At the Main Stage, a team of techies is setting up the proscenium for the Grove Play, which this year will be based on the theme of Pompeii. The men are hammering sets, unloading flats, and stringing up floodlights with gels.

AN ORDINARY PERSON cannot stay very long inside a grove of *Sequoia sempervirens.* I've even heard die-hard Bohemians talk about the need to take a break, to get out of the gloom for a while. As beautiful as it is in there, all that cloistered monochrome green becomes suffocating. All you want to do is break loose and run for a thousand miles in the prairie. There is a spooky quality about the timelessness, the noiselessness, the *bug*lessness of this utopia. I'm beginning to understand why the Pomos believed the redwoods were haunted.

I don't linger long at the Bohemian Grove. It is a curious thing: I'd spent the past week snooping around like a jackal for a way in. Now that I've succeeded, I'm itching to leave. I can easily stay all week, crashing camp parties, attending free concerts, hearing Lakeside Talks until I'm Groved out of my mind. But I have no interest in it. I don't feel like hunting down celebrities or eavesdropping on policy eggheads as they carve up the planet. I have no interest in eating pheasant under glass or going on a Rim Ride.

At its worst, maybe the Grove really is all those evil things that Kerry Richardson and the BGAN protesters said it was: the playpen of the plutocrats, the spawning ground of God only knows how many nuclear weapons. Like all men's clubs, the BC is by its nature elitist, and, in frightening ways, it perpetuates a closed system of cronyism by which political leaders are often selected in this country.

But at its best, Bohemia is more than a men's club. It is founded on an intriguing idea, an illusion that is uniquely American and essentially Californian: the illusion that a man can shuck his identity for a time and bend reality to suit himself. The Grove is a fantasy land where masters of the American Dream can "cremate" the world they've conquered; where powerful men can feel talented, and talented men can feel powerful; where undistinguished men can feel famous, and famous men can melt into the crowd; where gentlemen of leisure can enjoy the amenities of cultured society while "roughing it" in the forest.

The Bohemians couldn't be a friendlier tribe. Perhaps this is part of the problem. Maybe, on some level, I wanted a *confrontation*.

I had believed the local lore. I had blanched with fear each time I heard about some new layer in the Grove's onion skin of security. I had imagined the Grove to be an impenetrable preserve, like some inner sanctum of the Vatican. But I just crawled under a fence and walked in here. Now I have the same queer feeling of disenchantment that Dorothy must have felt when she discovered that the Wizard was just a scared old man spinning knobs behind a curtain.

That afternoon, with a feeling of great relief, I crawl under the Bohemian fence and drive back to the Village Inn. Next door, the two Doberman pinschers are curled up in their little lot. But this time, when I walk by, they are wagging their tails.

Welcome Home, Brother

The Jarbidge Wilderness, Nevada

One by one we came to the woods
By random wandering
In the thousand lost directions we found
the real country we'd pledged our hearts to
all those years
While we covered our hearts with our hands.
We groped to a true divinity, the temple
they cut down to build the churches
the light we meditated on
Sunday after Sunday through the colored glass.
We gather in the fold of the unchurched
We, tired of preaching
We gather up the unloved
as disciples gathered crumbs after the feast
so that none go wasted
We, natives of one Mother, natives of one an-
    other
We gather on the ground of our common birth
and put up the flowering tents of our belief:

64

Colors as many as the gazes
that turn toward a single sunset, each
an outpost of the daylight
Shining on a while, into the dark.
We gather under the vast flag of stars
to chant the pulse and breathing of one body
dancing on a hundred thousand feet
we feed our fires with sticks of incarnated light
grasp hands in one more circle around the sun.
>   from Stephen Wing,
>   "In the Summer of the Dragon"
>   *All Ways Free*, the Rainbow newspaper

"LET'S BASH MCDONALD'S!"
>   *Right on, brother!*
"Let's bash Burger King!"
>   *Right on!*
"Let's paint 'em all with rainbows!"
>   *Ho!*

Five thousand people are gathered around campfires in a Nevada gorge, a happy tangle of tie-dyed shirts and gypsy gabardines. Though it is July, the night is chilly in the high desert. There is snow on the serrated peaks to the south. The sky is powdered with stars. Some people are wrapped in Indian blankets, while others draw closer to the hissing sage of the bonfires.

"Let's shut down every fast food joint in the land!"
>   *Dig it, brother!*
". . . and spraypaint 'em with graffiti!"
>   *Right on.*
"But hey, make sure you use organic paint!"
>   *Ho!*

The McDonald's basher takes his seat in the circle at the Rocky Mountain Camp, and there is a long silence as the group awaits the next inspiration.

A mile downstream, a dozen voices shout in unison, "We love you!" The neighboring camp responds in kind—"We love *you*!" Then the next camp, and the next, and the next, and for ten minutes the valley is a chain of salutations, a domino effect of love. Finally the Rocky Mountain Camp's turn comes, and

the chain continues up the gorge, growing fainter as it nears
the plateau of the mesa, where the magic buses and VW vans
are parked.

The Rocky Mountain Camp is quiet again. Someone throws
a log of mountain mahogany on the fire, and it spits in the
flames. After a few minutes, a meek woman in a Mexican serape
rises to her feet. Her body is draped in bells and bangles, and
a smiley face sticker is pasted on her cheek. She holds the
eagle's feather, which passes for a speaker's scepter, and softly
addresses the crowd:

"I am Condor Rising over the River, and I-I . . . I just w-
w-want to thank all you beautiful people. In all the relationships
of my life, I thought I was . . . *different.* I-I didn't fit in. People
thought I was . . . *strange.* Strange because I loved all people as
my brothers and sisters. Strange because I wanted to s-s-solve
the Earth Crisis. But ever since I came to this gathering, I know
there are thousands of others just like me. T-t-t-together we
can spread peace and love to all the world . . ."

We can do it, sister!

"We are SPECIAL people."

Right on!

"We are GENIUSES."

Right on, sister!

"We are members of the great human family! Gorby and
George can hear us now! All the leaders of the world are listening in! There's a collective consciousness that's tuning in on
our wavelength! Can you feel it? Can you FEEL IT! Isn't it
wonderful! Isn't it just beautiful! The planet is healing itself!"

"WE LOVE YOU!!" The domino effect has worked its way
to the upper end of the encampment and returned. "We love
you!" the Rocky Mountain Camp cries, and the chain of love
heads back downriver.

IT'S BEEN A QUARTER-CENTURY since Ken Kesey's bus trip, twenty
years since Woodstock, and fifteen years since the head shops
in Haight-Ashbury turned into fern bars. And yet scattered
across the country, there are still enclaves of flower children
who never gave up the dream of the garden. Once a year, they
put their dream into practice. Every July a loose-knit tribe of
hippies known as the Rainbow Family of Living Light has been
gathering in a different state, in a different national forest,

to erect a cooperative encampment for a week. First held in Colorado in 1972, the Gathering of the Tribes, as it is called, is a commercial-free whole earth festival of love. As many as twenty thousand Rainbows have attended these mystical celebrations in the woods. Long a nemesis of the National Forest Service, the Rainbow Family insists on its right to assemble in "the cathedral of nature" without the need for supervision by the forces of "Babylon." The Rainbows like to think of themselves as citizens of a sovereign country that has been temporarily carved from the wilderness. They set up an experimental community with vegetarian kitchens and a loving police force that roams the hillsides hugging people.

The Rainbows call their camp, simply, "Home." Home is a place without fences, guns, banks, clocks, locks, or shopping malls. It is a place where grown men cry without shame and mothers breast-feed in the open air. At Home, work is purely voluntary, and the economy is based on individual contributions to the Magic Hat. All events are run on "Rainbow Time," which means you can show up whenever you feel like it—or not at all. There are no deadlines at Home, only "*live*" lines." Music plays throughout the camp, but unlike Woodstock, no rock stars are invited to perform, since their presence would introduce the element of money and ego—and, no doubt, T-shirt sales.

The gathering is an interesting study in anarchy. There are no leaders. The week follows no script. Information travels by word of mouth, and rumors spread like wildfire. Decisions are reached by consensus, in open meetings held every day at twelve o'clock noon (*Rainbow Time*, of course). Life in the encampment may be confusing and exasperatingly vague, but the Rainbows claim this is how most tribal societies were once organized. To come to a Rainbow gathering, they believe, is to return to the communitarian innocence of natural man. "The gatherings are closest to how nature intended humans to act toward one another," Rainbow literature proclaims. "It's like visiting any foreign place—strange customs, strange costumes—yet it's uncannily familiar. After wandering awhile the feeling seeps in that this is how we would all be living if we weren't so busy out there surviving. It's a place where the twisted logic of 'civilization' does not apply."

On the Fourth of July, which the Rainbows call "*Inter*dependence Day," a Technicolor version of the American flag is unfurled. Everyone joins hands in silence around a circle and prays for peace. Some Rainbows hum mantras or raise amulets to the sky. After a few hours of meditation, the camp breaks into song. Many Rainbows believe that the goodwill generated at this vigil creates a "peace vortex," a concentration of positive energy that spins outward from the site and sweeps over the land, "healing" the earth.

When the week is over, Rainbow volunteers spade the ground and reseed the worn paths with native grasses. They lay down water-bars to prevent erosion. They fill their latrines, scatter their campfires, and pick up every shred of trash. The camp shrinks in on itself, and then one day, like the last tendril of fog burning off a mountain, it dissolves without a trace.

Finding out about the Rainbow Family can be difficult, because officially the Rainbows don't have spokespersons. They don't have an office, for that matter, or a central P.O. box. Their headquarters is, as they like to say, "the third stone from the sun." The Family does have a newspaper, a psychedelic tabloid called *All Ways Free.* But the paper has no fixed address and it's impossible to get a subscription.

The Rainbow Family of Living Light is what political scientists call an "acephalous society," a group without hierarchy. Rainbows insist that it is not a legal entity at all. There are no annual dues, no cards to carry, no catechisms to memorize. Anybody can be a member, though that's beside the point, since there is no membership roster, indeed no real group to be a member of.

An article in *All Ways Free* once described the Family as "a diverse and decentralized social fabric woven from the threads of hippie culture, pacifist-anarchist traditions, Eastern mysticism, and the legacy of depression-era hobo street wisdom." There are a lot of aging Rainbows, but lately the Family has been attracting a following among a new generation of counterculturalists who are rediscovering sixties-style psychedelia. Well over half of the people at the gatherings are part-time Rainbows, people who work "straight" jobs most of the year and go by legal names instead of invented designations like One Who Talks to the Trees Who Dance in the Wind. Others are fulltimers who travel a circuit known as the Rainbow Trail, moving from gathering to gathering, commune to commune, practicing the vagrant arts of boxcar hopping and dumpster diving.

Rainbows are so free-ranging in their tastes and sensibilities that it's difficult to describe what the Family collectively believes in. Rainbow philosophy is a mélange of traditions that have yet to coalesce: Hindu, Taoist, Buddhist, Christian, Wiccan. At Rainbow gatherings, the goddess Gaia, the ancient Greek personification of Mother Earth, is sometimes called upon for spiritual guidance. Many Rainbow customs and beliefs are broadly derived from Native American culture—and in particular, from the Hopi tribe of the American Southwest. Rainbows commonly adopt Indian names, live in tepees, and worship Indian gods and spirits. Peyote and marijuana are considered "spiritual sacraments." Many Rainbows refuse to have their picture taken, subscribing to the Indian belief that a photograph steals a piece of the subject's soul. In fact, some Rainbows have been so presumptuous in adopting Indian ways that Native Americans in the Southwest have on more than one occasion dismissed them as "Wannabe Indians." During the Harmonic Convergence in 1987, the Hopis were forced to evict a group of Rainbows who had camped on an Arizona mesa and allegedly desecrated several religious shrines.

No one knows for sure how many Rainbows there are, though some estimates run in excess of two hundred thousand. Smaller, regional gatherings of Rainbows have been held in nearly every state and in many European countries, including Poland. Though the Family originally grew out of a small network of farms in the Pacific Northwest, Rainbow-affiliated communes or "scenes" now thrive in every region of the country. In recent years the Rainbows have talked of developing an international "peace village" in Belize.

But despite their wide dispersion in the world, the Rainbows remain an obscure fellowship, and they like it that way. They are still sometimes confused in the public eye with the "rainbow warriors" of Greenpeace, or with the Rainbow Coalition, Jesse Jackson's better known but completely unrelated political movement.

Part of the reason for their poor name recognition is that Rainbows are aggressively blasé about formal titles. They aren't even in full agreement about what to call themselves. Over the years, they have answered to such names as the Rainbow Nation, the Rainbow People, the Rainbow Tribe, the Rainbow Council, the Human Family, or simply We the People. Ask a Rainbow what Rainbow is, and he probably won't be able to tell you whether it is a religion, a philosophy, or just a beautiful party in the wilderness. He will likely describe it as something like "a consciousness," or "an idea."

All you have to do to be a part of the Rainbow is show up at the gatherings.

THE UNITED STATES FOREST SERVICE in Washington, D.C., has considerable trouble dealing with an "idea."

Over the past decade, the USFS has devised an elaborate disaster alert procedure, officially known as the Incident Command System, to respond to natural emergencies occurring anywhere on the 191 million acres of national forest lands. Ordinarily, the Incident Command System is invoked in the event of a major forest fire, tornado, or other act of God. (For example, the Service used the System after Hurricane Hugo smashed into the Carolina shores in 1989, and in the aftermath of the 1980 Mount St. Helens eruption.) The System amounts to a full-scale battle plan against the excesses of nature. An Incident Commander is dispatched to the scene. He, in turn, marshals firefighters, orders helicopters, alerts medical teams, establishes communications, and controls a sweeping interagency chain of command.

The Rainbow gathering enjoys the dubious distinction of being the only *human* event that regularly triggers the Incident Command System. Over the years the Rainbow gatherings have become one of the Forest Service's biggest headaches and something of an institutional joke. "The Rainbows are a special case for us," says one discreet Forest Service officer in Washington. "You could say they . . . *try our patience.*"

The Forest Service's worries are not just the niggling concerns of a jealous bureaucracy. When tens of thousands of people live together in the wilderness for a week, things can go seriously awry—forest fires, epidemics, landslides. A Rainbow gathering is tantamount to constructing a medium-sized town overnight, often on fragile soils not suited for crowds. And as in any city, thousands of logistical details—water, sewage, garbage, first aid—must be addressed.

The Forest Service contends that because the Rainbows welcome everyone, criminals can travel easily in their midst. In past years, the FBI has apprehended fugitives at the gatherings, and authorities have investigated several cases of kidnapping, child molestation, and runaway youths. Of equal concern are belligerent locals who have been known to crash the gatherings and assault innocent Rainbows. The Forest Service has to coordinate its efforts with the local and county police, state troopers, state health department representatives, Fish and Wildlife officials, and sometimes agents from the DEA, the FBI, and the Bureau of Alcohol, Tobacco and Firearms.

The Forest Service's already trying task is further compounded by the Rainbows' insistence on handling their own security matters. The Rainbow police force, the *Shanti Sena* (Sanskrit for Peace Center), is composed of volunteers trained in nonconfrontational persuasion techniques. Though the Shanti Sena tries to cooperate with the Forest Service, the two forces frequently fall into rancorous disputes over jurisdictional questions. The invisible border between Babylon and Home is hotly contested.

But the Forest Service's principal concern is with the land itself. Despite the Rainbows' diligent cleanup efforts, which forest rangers universally praise, the physical impact of the gatherings can be devastating. "The Rainbows are not terribly professional when it comes to locating sites that are environmentally conducive to encampments of large crowds," says Wayne Miller, a Forest Service officer in Atlanta who has worked with several Rainbow gatherings. "Whenever you put that many people together, there's gong to be a helluva impact: Resource destruction, compacted soils, erosion, displaced wildlife. It takes decades for some of these sites to recover."

The Rainbows refuse to consult the Forest Service in their site selection process. Instead, they follow an ethereal method known as the "Vision Council." The Vision Council essentially works like a Ouija board séance. Every year on the final day of the gathering, July 7, a group of Rainbows sit in a large circle and wait for an inspiration to tell them where the tribe will meet next. These inspirations are not infrequently coaxed along with magic mushrooms or buttons of peyote. Someone may be moved to blurt out a state's name, or his hand may fall on a certain region of a map. At the 1987 gathering in North Carolina, for example, someone claimed to have experienced a Hopi

Indian vision in which a white buffalo roamed a plain beneath a night sky lit by a single star. This "lone star" was interpreted to mean Texas. And so it was.

Once a state is chosen, a Scouting Council then sets up residence and scours the national forest lands in search of a suitable campsite. It can take up to ten months for the Scouting Council to find an ideal spot. As a result, Rainbows don't learn the precise location until a few months—sometimes only a few weeks—before the gathering. This gives the Forest Service little time to gird itself for each year's onslaught.

The Rainbows shrewdly capitalize on the Forest Service's loose command structure; the USFS is perhaps the most decentralized bureaucracy in the federal government. Information percolates slowly through the Service's nine largely autonomous regions. Law enforcement tips learned at one year's gathering aren't necessarily passed on to the next. Each year a new cast of rangers—and a new Incident Commander—must confront the Rainbow phenomenon, learning the arcane customs from scratch. The Forest Service has yet to appoint a national-level "Rainbow specialist." Thus, the Rainbows have kept one step ahead of the Service. As one Forest Service ranger from Washington State puts it: "They know us better than we know them."

The Rainbows enjoy an additional advantage: National forests are Uncle Sam's least regulated pieces of real estate. Forest lands fall under the management *not* of the Department of the Interior, but of the less conservation-minded Department of Agriculture. Codes governing the use of national forests, unlike national parks or wilderness preserves, are written to give campers the widest possible latitude. There's really not much the forest rangers *can* do but cross their fingers and watch the invasion happen.

The Forest Service has repeatedly tried to make the Rainbows sign a "special use" permit, a routine requirement for large gatherings, but the Rainbows have steadfastly refused on constitutional grounds. "The Forest Service is neither a landlord nor a host of public lands," one Rainbow pronouncement reads. "We do not need anyone's permission to gather. We sign away our right to peaceably assemble when we sign permits. The only permit required is the guarantee of this right provided in the 1st Amendment. If any power decides to try to prohibit or cancel our coming together, we will ignore that power. And if that entity wishes to stop us forcefully, the whole world will watch them fail."

Another reason Rainbows won't sign documents is that they have no accountable representatives who are authorized to do so. The Forest Service thus finds itself in much the same position as the Roman legion trying to get to the bottom of the slave rebellion: Which one is Spartacus? "There is a commendable logic to the Rainbow people," concedes Forest Service officer Mac Thomson, who works out of Ogden, Utah. "Since no one can take responsibility for anything, there is no individual accountability. The Rainbows are institutionally incapable of complying with regulations of any sort. They have the same identity as a mob."

The best the Rainbows can do is present the Service with a team of powerless emissaries known as "legal-liaisons." Well versed in Title 36 of the *Code of Federal Regulations* (the Forest Service's bylaws), legal-liaisons arrive early and establish a "seed camp" to begin laying out the gathering site. They listen to what the rangers have to say and then return to the camp to "council" on the question at hand. A conch shell is blown to signal the start of the meeting, and the person who holds the eagle's feather holds the floor. It's all admirably democratic but painstakingly slow. The Rainbows don't exactly follow parliamentary procedure. Participants may interrupt the discussion to recite poetry or hum a tune. The council process may take days or weeks. The Rainbow Family can make no decision until all persons present at the consensus circle are in complete agreement. Often unanimity is never reached, which is one of the reasons why the Family has promulgated only a handful of public statements in its two decades of existence. In 1988, a council came close to drafting a one-sentence pronouncement that said, "The only political position of the Rainbow Family is our right to gather on the land," but the statement was scrapped because somebody objected to the word "political."

To FIND OUT ABOUT THE 1989 GATHERING, I phone my local Rainbow "focalizer." Focalizers are the synapses of the Rainbow nervous system; their job is to verify the latest rumors and "focalize" the news. Their names and phone numbers are listed in the Rainbow Guide, a hard-to-find directory that is circulated at the gatherings. Focalizers are friendly and helpful, but (the

Rainbow sense of space being about as precise as the Rainbow sense of time) they are notorious for getting the directions wrong—miles, counties, sometimes whole states off course. This is somewhat understandable since the Rainbows choose to meet each year in the middle of literal and figurative Nowhere, in some uncharted bosk where the drums can pound far into the night.

The gathering, I learn, is in the Humboldt National Forest of northeastern Nevada, near a place called the Jarbidge Wilderness. The focalizer delights in telling me that the campsite is located "in the most geographically far-out place in the Lower Forty-eight." Humboldt Forest, he says, is in the no-man's-land where Nevada's border meets Idaho's, where Pacific Time meets Mountain. To get there, I'll have to cross the Great Basin and travel over hundreds of miles of rutted mountain roads that can break an axle. Then I'll have to hike for half a day into a deep gorge, past the ruins of an old Mormon homestead and an ancient burial ground of the Shoshone Indians. Altogether, it will be five miles before I get down to the center of the camp, at a spot called Robinson Hole on the east fork of the Jarbridge River.

"Good luck, brother," the focalizer commiserates. "But hey—it's worth the effort. The gathering will change your life forever. You won't be the same person after it's all through. It's like four years of college compressed into one week."

I fly to San Francisco and hook up with my old friend Rick, whom I'd once spent a summer with, during my college years, in the small town of McCall, Idaho. We lived on a mountain lake near a commune of the Rainbow People, and since then, we'd always been curious about their gatherings. Rick had ridden a ten-speed bike across America from his hometown in upstate New York and had stopped in McCall on a whim. At the lakeside cabin where we stayed, we read Kurt Vonnegut novels and listened to a lot of the Grateful Dead. Some nights we'd ride out to the town amphitheater and play reggae music with the Rainbows under the starry skies.

It's been ten years since that rustic summer in Idaho, and we've both got our feet firmly planted in Babylon now. We're paying taxes, car notes, insurance premiums . . . the whole catastrophe. Rick moved to San Francisco, where he's become a graphic artist and a successful merchant in the printing business. I, on the other hand, landed on the East Coast, where my fall from paradise was even more profound.

But now, for a week at least, we're going back to the garden.

We load Rick's car with camping gear and bags of gorp trail mix. In the late afternoon, as the sun drops over the Golden Gate, we leave the city smogs behind and head east toward Home. We climb the Sierra Nevada Range. We pass the Reno casinos. We hurtle across the alkali sinks of the Great Basin, past Imlay and Winnemucca, past the signs that warn "Prison Area—Hitchhiking Prohibited," past chalky wastelands inhabited only by a few Basque shepherds and their flocks.

Finally we pull off the interstate and stop in Elko, a town of nine thousand. Though we're still a hundred miles from the gathering site, the focalizer had told us that Elko would be our last chance for provisions before we dropped out of civilization altogether and headed north into the lunar desolation of the Jarbidge Mountains. And sure enough, the Elko supermarket is overrun with Rainbows, most of them in the bulk bin section, stuffing their sacks with lentils, dried apricots, and banana chips. The Elko locals, meanwhile, are stocking up for their *own* Fourth of July celebrations—piling their shopping carts with cases of Budweiser, T-bone steaks, Off insect repellant, lighter fluid, and bags of sour cream potato chips. The weekly newspaper on display at the checkout counter warns of "naked hordes" invading Elko County, but the locals don't seem to mind. "Those hippies just want to get nekkid and smoke a little maryjane, is all," one rancher says. "I say let 'em. They ain't causing no trouble." According to one estimate printed in the paper, fifty thousand Rainbows will be descending on Humboldt Forest. Elko County Sheriff Jim Miller is striking a martial pose: "We're gearing up for the worst, and hoping for the best."

Up to this point, the focalizer's directions have been impeccable. But from Elko on, the going gets dicey. We take a gravel road, which on the map is a suspiciously vague-looking series of dotted lines snaking through the mountains. We creep along for several hours, soaking up the rugged country, which grows stark and beautiful as we climb up from the Basin. The roadsides are choked with piñon and juniper. Umber rock formations hang over us. An aspen grove quivers like a pointillist painting.

Then, in a mountain pass, we round a corner to find ourselves staring at a wall of . . . *snow*. The road is impassable. There are ruts in the shoulders where disheartened pilgrims evidently turned back for Elko. Previous wayfayers have tacked handwritten notes to the snowdrift—

"We give up!—Ded Hed Fred."
"Good luck, Tipi Dave."
"Snow got us—take the low road. No kidding!
Really!"

The notes are written in a loose, childlike script that's sprinkled with hearts and peace symbols. Looking around, Rick and I can spot other Rainbow touches: On the ground, someone has arranged a collection of rocks in the form of a medicine wheel. Hanging in the trees are scraps of colored fabric, a wind sock, a corkscrew mobile. There is a fairy-tale mysticism about the way these little artifacts have been placed out here, as if they were personal gifts to the tree elves.

We take a nearby logging road that appears to head in the right direction but is studded with boulders and treacherous stumps. For two hours, we bounce down the mountain, fishtailing through bogs of mud, stopping along the way to clear brush from the road. Nightfall is fast approaching and still no sign of Home.

At dusk, we happen upon a forest ranger who is relieving himself behind his 4×4. "Excuse me, officer, can you tell us where the Rainbow gathering is?"

"Sure can," the ranger says with a robust laugh. He points east. "Thataway, fifty miles. You're about two hours off course, son. I s'pose the snow got you folks, too?"

We're in a bad humor when we limp into the town of Jarbidge (pop. 29), a mining outpost set on the floor of a dark ravine. Jarbidge, we learn, is only five miles from the Rainbow camp "as the crow flies," but an hour's journey by car. But spirits are high in Jarbidge, and the townspeople soon cheer us up. It's Saturday night, Fourth of July weekend, and the air is alive with expectancy. The town's only street buzzes with talk of the Rainbows. How long will they stay? Are they friendly? Are they all whacked-out on drugs? The gathering looms in the town's imagination. Dionysus is stomping at the edge of Thebes; the drums are pounding, the wine is flowing, and it's all happening *over the next hill!* A strange, quivering dance is going on in their midst, and it's hard for them to ignore it.

"This Rainbow life-style—it's fine and all, for a vacation," one of the local mossbacks tells me as I fill up Rick's car with gas. "But you couldn't *live* that way. Who's going to do the work? Who's going to pay the bills?"

Rainbows have been streaming in, buying oats and safflower oil, fixing flats, eating their last kitchen-cooked meals for the week. Right now a couple of Rainbows are at the Trading Post, Jarbidge's general store, buying rolling papers and tins of Bugler Brand tobacco. The store's guestbook is scrawled with the names of other Rainbows who've passed through town: Wonton Dave. Metallica Dude Lester. Spirit Godkin from Albuquerque. Sound and Light from San Bernardino. Gypsy Rose Marie from "the U.S.A."

Jarbidge is one of the most isolated towns in America, about as far from Babylon as you can get and still find a pay phone. The last recorded robbery of a U.S. stagecoach happened here in 1916. The town's name is an English bastardization of "Tsawhawbitts," an evil monster who, according to Shoshone Indian legend, roamed the surrounding mountains and valleys by day collecting humans in a basket, and then returned each night to a lair in the canyon to dine on his quarry. Indians and white men alike avoided the haunted gulch of Tsawhawbitts until 1909, when another kind of quarry was discovered: gold. Soon Jarbidge was a boisterous tent city, and by 1920, the town had the largest gold mine in Nevada. But the prospectors never struck the mother lode, and when extraction grew too expensive during the Great Depression, mining operations closed down for good. Today the mineworks glower over town, tangled ruins rusting alongside piles of crushed gravel that have lain undisturbed for sixty years.

The prospectors may be gone, but life in Jarbidge is still much like a scene from the pages of Mark Twain's *Roughing It.* A few of the old saloons remain open. School is held in a trailer. The nearest hospital is three hours away. And law enforcement rests in the hands of one stouthearted man: Justice o' the Peace John Williams. Most people around these parts just call him "The Judge."

The Judge is the town father, town celebrity, and town eccentric rolled into one. The *Los Angeles Times* once featured him in a story on the most remote JP's in America, and he was later asked to be on *The Tonight Show*. An ornery old billy goat with a glass eye, the Judge speaks in riddles and half-answers and generally likes to get a rise out of people who pass through town. Ask him where he fishes and he'll answer, "In the river." Ask him where in the river and he'll say, "Sometimes upstream, sometimes down." Once he made a public bet that he could bite his own eye. A skeptical visitor plunked down twenty dollars, whereupon the Judge popped out his glass eye, and "bit" it in front of the speechless man. The Judge then wagered the man another twenty dollars he could bite his *other* eye. Figuring this was a truly impossible feat, the man agreed to the bet. The Judge promptly removed his dentures and "bit" his real eye.

Tonight the entire town, including the Judge, is gathered at the Outdoor Inn ("Booze•Grub•Rooms"), an old sportsman's bar with grizzly heads lunging from the walls and a knife collection hung over the cash register. Slot machines natter in one corner; in another, a fiddler saws out a Highland jig. The townspeople have taken to calling each other Rainbowesque nicknames. "Here comes Butterfly Ears!" they shout. "Why if it isn't old Mooncalf out on the dance floor!"

A teenaged waitress named Stormy is serving up prime rib dinners, the house specialty every Saturday night. "The Rainbows are okay," Stormy allows, sizzling platters of beef stacked on her arm. "A couple of 'em *did* run out on my tab—the jerks. But really, I'm glad they're here. Kinda spices things up. Life can get pretty dull in Jarbidge."

The Judge has been on the floor dancing a furious flatfoot, and now he returns to his seat, puffing. "Those Rainbows are harmless," he concurs. "A little bit 'Out There,' maybe. But nice folks, most of 'em. Still, we got cops running all over the county like it's a war or something. I think it's a goddamn overkill. I'm planning to go over and pay 'em a visit myself. Not going to take my clothes off, though. Nossir. Don't want my caboose to get sunburned.

"Hey, I bet you a hunnerd dollars I can bite my own eye . . ."

"WELCOME TO THE YOUNG REPUBLICANS' CONVENTION!" greets the man the Rainbows call Parkinglot Patrick. "Park your car

AMY SNYDER

The Rainbow Gathering, July 4, 1989.
The Jarbidge Wilderness, Nevada.

Rainbow Family elder Garrick Beck.

Rainbow dancers at the
Nevada gathering, 1989.

on the right side of the field. Don't forget, brothers: Stay clean and stay legal!"

Bus Village is a maze of antediluvian VW's and International Harvester buses patched together with bungee cords and coat-hanger wire. The field serves as a kind of temporary weigh station for recent arrivals who haven't yet mustered the energy for the five-mile hike down into the gorge. The smell of curried vegetables hangs in the air. A folk guitarist strums a Dylan tune. Rainbow mechanics sip herbal tea and compare notes on magic bus maintenance. The bumper stickers say, BETTER MUSIC THROUGH CHEMISTRY, HUGS ARE BETTER ON DRUGS, U.S. OUT OF NORTH AMERICA. On one of the buses, the airbrushed image of John Lennon stretches across the side panel with the word I M A G I N E. Engine blocks lie out in the field, oozing oil. Dust devils dance in the gaps between the buses. A New Age wizard stands at the edge of the precipice, his arms outstretched like a scarecrow, chanting "Ommmmmm."

We pull alongside a Datsun pickup from Madison, Wisconsin, that's also just arrived. Two weary young lovers emerge from the camper and stretch in the morning sun. Nearby, a group of bandana'd Deadheads from Boulder juggle Hacky Sack as a bootleg tape of "Sugar Magnolia" plays on the tape deck of their vintage BMW. ". . . *We can have high times if you would like, We can discover the wonders of nature, growing in the brushes down by the riverside. . . .*"

Parkinglot Patrick is a veteran Rainbow from Oregon who for years has taken it upon himself to manage the parking scene at the front gate. He is a wiry, hyperactive man with a walkie-talkie in his hand and a bright Guatemala pouch slung over his shoulder. Standing on the edge of the mesa, we look back over the valley and see the Rainbow rigs approaching in steady succession, tiny dots growing on the horizon, kicking up contrails of dust. It's an impressive sight, especially considering the staggering logistics involved in the trip: Somehow through the thousand reefer-fogs of imprecision that hang over the Rainbow world, all of these people got the word, got the directions, scraped together the money for the long trip, and actually found this crazy marooned corner of the country. Now here they are, five thousand strong and still dropping in every two minutes like planes at O'Hare.

Patrick beams with pride at the incoming pilgrims. "Kesey was going to show us what some really with-it hippies could do if they put their heads together," he says. "Hey, the Merry Pranksters fizzled out. But look at us! Look how far we've come! We've been at this for eighteen years and we're still truckin'!"

Patrick says a lot of Rainbows have doubts about the campsite choice this year. To them, Nevada, with its toxic dumps and weapons proving grounds, seems an inauspicious place for a Hippie High Mass. Free love in a nuclear desert? A peace vortex in the bottom of a uranium mine? The joke is that in addition to bottled water and trail mix, the Rainbows were supposed to bring Geiger counters this year. Some Rainbows are upset by a report in the *Los Angeles Times* announcing that the Department of Defense will be detonating a new nuclear device somewhere in the Nevada desert during the week. Though the explosion will be a mile underground and clear across the state, the sad coincidence is casting a pall of negative energy over the gathering.

Other Rainbows question whether people will be able to survive out here. The landscape looks like Venus. The hillsides are home to scorpions, black widows, and rattlesnakes. The ground is strewn with tiny volcanic rocks that collect in shoes and sleeping bags. And the howling mountain winds can rip a tent in two, or stir up clouds of fine dust that sting people's eyes and grit up the food.

To make matters worse, law enforcement, the Rainbows' perennial worry, is notoriously tough in Nevada. As far back as the 1960s, conventional hippie wisdom has held that Nevada is one of the two states that you never wanted to get busted in (the other being Texas). Of course, "vice" is a relative concept in a state with legalized prostitution, drive-in liquor stores, and neon casinos winking at every exit. A Nevada trooper may give you a summons for driving ninety miles an hour with a hooker in your lap on your way to Bally's, but possession of a single seed of marijuana is a felony in the Sagebrush State, punishable by one to six years in prison and up to $5,000 in fines.

Patrick is griping about the police hassling. "They're using Rambo tactics!" he rants. "They're just looking for an excuse to stop people so they can search for grass. It's a big turkey shoot, man!"

"Thing is"—he grins—"for every ounce they get, a pound's going to slip through!"

Earlier in the day, Patrick says, the Nevada highway patrol stopped the Rainbow food supply truck en route from a supermarket in Twin Falls, Idaho. "They got it in their heads that our supply chain was running narcotics," Patrick says. "They'd slice open big bags of rice and just pour it out on the ground. Pricks didn't even have a warrant, man."

Now an Elko County Sheriff's officer is running a drug-sniffing dog through the middle of Bus Village, while two other officers work the wings on horseback. Someone sprinkles the ground with cayenne pepper to throw off the scent. Rainbow sentinels run ahead to forewarn their brothers and sisters. "Six up! Six up!" they shout, code language for "Pigs a'coming." Others cluster around the officer to "insulate" the gathering from the evil vibes they say emanate from the handgun holstered to his side. "Shield the violence! Shield the violence!"

Rick and I strap on our backpacks and begin our long descent into the gorge. At the head of the trail, someone gives me a free crystal mined from a Family commune in Arkansas. Farther along, someone hands me a sack of cornmeal to haul down to the free public kitchens. By now, hundreds are walking ahead of us, hundreds behind, in a long, tattered column. People are carrying two-by-fours, guitars, shovels, watermelons, PVC pipe, toilet paper, jugs of bottled water. Some are skipping arm-in-arm down the path. Occasionally some daredevil sails past us on a mountain bike. The sun beats hotter on our backs, and the drums grow louder with each switchback in the path.

Finally the steep grade levels off and we come to a clearing where the Rainbows have set up a kind of welcoming station. Here we are met by a friendly earth mother in harem pants, with *National Geographic* breasts, lobster-red from the sun. She flashes us a snaggle-toothed smile and says, "Welcome home brothers!" Then she gives us each a hug and shows us the way to the campsites. "Just keep on going until the energy is right! Feel the vibe, listen to the harmony around you, and add your unique note!"

An aspiring young Rastaman in blond dreadlocks hands us a copy of the so-called "Rap 107," a one-page sheet that lays down the rudiments of Rainbow living. "Read and heed!" he shouts.

Please protect this beautiful land. Walk softly. Allow plants & animals to be harmonized. Blend in. Everyone sharing makes a strong human tribe! Keep all soap out of streams and springs. Use the latrines, cover your paper & waste with ashes and lime. Camp together—establish neighborhoods. Separate garbage for recycling. Use your own bowl & spoon. You *are* the gathering. Respect your sisters' and brothers' energies. Notice the balance: Earth, sky, trees, water & people. We ♥ you!

On both sides of the path are tepees and flimsy tarpaulin structures. In the public clearings, the Rainbows have set up vegetarian kitchens with names like Joy of Soy, Taco Mike's, the Wild Rose Cafe. People sit on their haunches and eat from upturned Frisbees while shirtless cooks stir enormous vats of lentil stew. At one kitchen, a volunteer washes dishes with a foot-pedaled contraption that dispenses bleach. Nearby, a hairy-legged woman hikes up her granny dress and squats to pee, in plain view of the diners.

The main path is a crush of Third World textiles—batiks, madras, Andean woolens. The air is pungent with patchouli oil and incense, and everywhere is the constant polyrhythmic pounding of congas. A doleful Rainbow wearing an "Abbie Lives" T-shirt cruises the pathways looking for hugs. "Hug Patrol! Hug Patrol!" he cries. "Gimme your hugs! Gotta have 'em. Need 'em bad."

We pass Kid Village and the Love'n Oven Bakery. We pass the Judgment-Free Uplifting Space and the Olympian Nudist Temple. Finally we set up camp on a secluded hill overlooking the Main Circle. Our nearest neighbors are two belly dancers from California.

As the sun goes down over the Jarbidge Mountains, Rick and I sit on our hillside perch and survey the mayhem below. The primal pulsing of humanity is inescapable. People are fluttering around with languid smiles and dilated eyes. Shit and piss and sweat and water and earth are commingled, a single biology. The drums do not stop.

At dusk, the belly dancers emerge from their tent, all decked out for the night's performances. One by one, the bonfires light up the gorge.

*   *   *

"WHO'S IN CHARGE HERE?" It's a question the Rainbows hate to hear and refuse to answer. The Family may not have chiefs, but it does have "elders," silver-haired hippies who've been around since the tribe's early days and who have attained a measure of respect. The names keep cropping up in *All Ways Free*: Plunker. Rainbow Hawk. Swami Mommy. Thumper. Medicine Story. John Buffalo. Emmy Rainwalker. But of all the elders, one in particular seems to be universally recognized; anyone with half a clue about who the Family is and how it evolved will tell you to go see Garrick.

Garrick Beck is the author of *Basic Rainbow*, a seminal pamphlet that lays out the Family's ideals and early history, and serves as the Rainbows' answer to *The Federalist Papers*. Beck is also one of the founding members of the Rainbow Farm, the original commune near the logging community of Drain, Oregon (not far from Eugene), which for years was the nerve center of the burgeoning Rainbow movement. Beck lived at the Rainbow Farm for twelve years, where he raised a family, grew organic vegetables, and dabbled with the dulcimer and guitar.

Beck is known as the word man, the righteous Rainbow rapper. He can mesmerize audiences for hours with his soaring metaphors. Beck makes the Rainbow Gathering sound like the loftiest of social experiments, a creative upwelling of the human spirit that is connected to the flowerings of all mystic tribal cultures through the ages. He'll tell you about the time the Rainbow Family saw a Great White Buffalo appear in the snow on the face of a mountain. He'll tell you about the gathering in New Mexico, when the Rainbows floated fifteen thousand "organic grapefruits" two miles down the Gila River to get them into camp.

Some say Beck is the closest thing the Rainbows have to a patriarch, but he dismisses the notion out of hand. "That's in the department of Forget It!" he balks. Beck is loath to play the role of High Holy Hippie, the tie-dyed grandpaw who scoffs at the younger generation's efforts while saying, "It ain't like it used to be. . . ."

Beck still owns seventy-seven acres of rolling land at the Rainbow Farm, which today is a quiet, stable commune with few remaining ties to the Gatherings. In the early days, the Farm had been a legendary stopover point for Pacific Northwest hippies who were drawn to the music and marathon acidfests (the hand-painted sign over the door of the main cabin said NEVER A DULL MOMENT), but clearly the party has been over for years. I dropped by the Farm on a warm spring day and got only blank stares when I asked about the Rainbow Family's origins there. "Look, we're just human beings who happen to live at a place called the Rainbow Farm," one of the residents snapped, obviously put off by my intrusion.

Today Garrick Beck lives, of all places, in Manhattan. I visit him at his apartment in Alphabet City, where he sells jewelry and gemstones through a small mail-order outfit. Though he keeps a magic bus parked in New Jersey and still makes frequent trips to Rainbow Gatherings, Beck says the focus of his life is here.

Beck, who teaches gardening classes to public school kids, is a guru in the "urban greening" movement. All over Lower Manhattan, vacant city lots once filled with rubble have been transformed into vegetable plots. Beck walks me over to his own patch at the corner of Sixth Street and Avenue B. Outside the chain-link fence that surrounds the garden, sirens blare, tires screech, a drug casualty sits gibbering in a puddle of urine. But once the gate clicks shut, we are enveloped by calm. Tomato plants rustle in the breeze. The noise of the city is lost in the dappled drapings of vegetables. "The garden is a big part of my life now," Beck says, with a whispery reverence in his voice. "I see it as the Rainbow ideal in action."

It is much more beautiful than a garden in the country, this incongruous patch rising from the ruins. Beck could still be tending the vine back in Oregon, but instead he has chosen to be here, in the hives of Manhattan. Somehow it all seems right, this scaled-down version of the Rainbow, this circum-scribed idealism. And in the end, it is probably as close to the State of Nature as most Americans will ever get—a tiny strip of green surrounded by a tall, secure fence.

Garrick Beck is a thin-boned, fine-featured man in his early forties with a long, gray-flecked ponytail. His keen eyes are set deep inside a haggard face, and a large vein throbs in his temple. He wears faded blue jeans that smell vaguely of potting soil and *Cannabis sativa*. Beck is one of the few Rainbow "elders" I've met who actually goes by the name he was born with. "Garrick always sounded good to me," he reasons.

Ideas come to Beck like a summer storm gathering on the horizon, the distant flashes lighting up his eyes. Suddenly the bottom drops out of his imagination, and the words rain down in torrents.

"What is the Rainbow?" he asks. "You tell me. I don't know what Rainbow is. Is it a tribe? Is it a spiritual organism? Is it an organic evolution of the species? Is it a temporary cultural effect? I don't know. Time will spell it out more clearly."

The Rainbow Family was founded on what Beck calls "the true truth that humanity is not so fouled up." He argues that the ills of modern society are caused not by human nature, but by the problem of "authoritarian overlordism"—i.e., banks, corporations, governments. It is the leitmotiv that runs throughout Beck's *Basic Rainbow*, a theme that directly echoes Jean-Jacques Rousseau's most famous proposition: "Men are naturally good; it is only through their institutions that they have become bad."

"How many people tonight will go to bed ill fed, ill cared for, living in fear or living in prison?" Beck poses. "You add it all up and you say, 'My God, this is a mess here! It's all loused up!' Who are we going to blame? Well, the statesmen will blame the human spirit. They'll say, 'Human nature is foul. We need to defend against it with more police and more weapons programs. We need to defend ourselves against those bad people OUT THERE who have it in for us.' They see human nature as competitive, greedy. Survival of the fittest, and all that. But we think that's totally backwards. We say that the human spirit is magnificent and splendid. The 'fittest' is not necessarily a competitive kind of fittest. It may be that what the human race is really 'fittest' at is cooperating. And that cooperating is what put us ahead of the beasts."

Beck likes to think of the Rainbow gathering as a seasonal City on a Hill that is erected each summer to demonstrate how the cooperative process works. "To change the way things are done in the world is the vastest of all possible undertakings. To do it, society needs a vision of what it *could* be like. And so to present that vision, we make this little example. Here are ten thousand people who come together without anybody making a buck over it. We try to see what happens when food is given out to everyone for free and no one has to pay for parking. We relearn the art of community design, the thousand-and-one logistical tasks that need to be done in any village. We gather to show that peace among different people is possible. Christians, Muslims, capitalists, anarchists—all these people come together and make this beautiful village. It's a delicate experiment. It's a gentle little thing. But it's our hope that the world can learn something from it. At the very least, we have created a public space where an individual can come and make up his own mind whether society at large could be organized in this way."

The Rainbow gathering operates on an honor system of the grandest scale: Human nature is good, so we trust that you will be good, too. But what of the freeloaders who invariably will crash the party and abuse this public trust? Such malingerers are known as "Drainbows," since they "drain" the energy from the gatherings. "Every society is going to have its hangers-on and its spacecases," Beck concedes. "But the question is, What do you do with those people? Do you take an authoritarian point of view and *make* them work? Do you take a capitalistic point of view and *pay* them? Or do you take the Rainbow position and *inspire* them, assuming all along that eventually the work is going to get done and there's going to be enough for everyone? We are utopians. Ours is a very trusting scene. We are extremely tolerant of other people's trips. And believe me, we get a lot of people who subscribe to some very extreme ideas. We might get a group of holier-than-thou hippies who say that the only way to REALLY know the Mother Earth is to walk barefoot *at all times*, people who say that it's a sin to wear shoes. We are very tolerant of those people. We take the position that if it doesn't pick our pockets or break our legs, then let it be. Of course some people are going to take advantage of all this trust. Our system isn't perfect, for goodness sake. There are many situations where it doesn't work well. There are even some situations where it doesn't work at all."

"But," he says, as sirens wail outside his garden, "it works so much better than what's going on *out there* . . ."

THE PRECISE ORIGINS of the Rainbow Family of Living Light are shrouded in myth, and the Rainbows seem to prefer it that way. As one Rainbow elder puts it, "Legends are more interesting than facts. We encourage people to come up with their own creation myths."

According to most accounts, though, the idea for holding

the first gathering originated with Barry Adams, a.k.a. "Plunker." A self-described Jesus-Taoist who lately has kept an address in Missoula, Montana, Adams is a tall, lanky man with long braided hair. He wears a feathered cowboy hat and is often given to chanting. He is known for carrying around a homemade stringed instrument, carved from a coconut, which he likes to "plunk" on—hence his nickname. Rainbows describe Plunker as the Family's Jeremiah, a lone prophet wandering in the wilderness.

Plunker's story is spotty but it goes something like this: One day in 1969, he had an apocalyptic vision on Forty-fourth Street in Manhattan. It was Judgment Day. God was in heaven and all the souls of the universe were gathered around him. He had surveyed the mess that humans were making of the earth, and He was outraged. "You blew it, it's all over, you failed the test," God informed the souls. When Plunker awoke from his vision, he knew that time was running out for the planet, and that something *big* had to be done. It was then that he got the notion of holding a huge, free, countercultural get-together in the wilderness to pray for the earth's healing.

Plunker hooked up with a group of like-minded souls at the 1969 Renaissance Fair, an annual arts and crafts festival in Eugene, Oregon. Across the Pacific Northwest, an informal circuit of hippie communes and squatter camps was beginning to flourish, and the time was ripe for a gathering of the sort Plunker had envisioned. Two groups in particular were drawn to the idea: a family from northern Washington State called the Marble Mount Outlaws (chiefly known at the time for ferrying draft dodgers across the border into Canada), and the Temple Tribe, a group of arts and crafts people from Oregon. Among those involved with the Temple Tribe was young Garrick Beck, then a student at Reed College in Portland. "It was a rich and vibrant time," Beck recalls. "The Pacific Northwest was the Fertile Crescent of the back-to-the-land movement. All these new tribes and tribelets were being spawned. There were hipsters, tripsters, and dipsters. There was a constant flux of people cycling in and out of the scene. People were starting to live a totally different life behind what we called the Granola Curtain."

After the Renaissance Fair, the Temple Tribe joined the Marble Mount Outlaws at their camp in Washington to draw up definite plans for their "healing" event, which they were now calling the World Family Gathering. As they visualized it, the World Family Gathering would be a grander, greener, more spiritual version of the Human Be-In, the historic festival that had been held in San Francisco's Golden Gate Park a few years earlier. "Humans had been gathering as we envisioned since the dawn of our species," Beck writes in *Basic Rainbow*. "In historical terms, this practice has largely been in the domain of religious movements: the Buddha's meetings at Raj Gria, Jesus' assemblies at the Sea of Galilee, the Native American Ghost or Sun Dances. We saw ourselves as literally called upon to revive this form of human congregation. We had arrived at the conclusion that a spiritual understanding of ourselves as one human family was our best hope for avoiding certain destruction."

As a dress rehearsal for their own event, this (as yet) unnamed union of two tribes helped organize a free rock festival near Portland during the 1970 Labor Day weekend. The festival, called Vortex I, drew seventy-five thousand people. The planners of the festival set up a cluster of tepees at the center of the camp, and one of them was called the "Rainbow Tepee"— rainbow as in psychedelics. The Rainbow Tepee was set up as a kind of MASH unit to help bring unfortunate souls down from bad acid trips. At some point during the event, festival-goers started calling these tepee dwellers "the Rainbow People," and the name stuck. And so the two tribes became united under one name.

The Rainbow People set a date—July 1, 1972—and found a rendezvous site on Strawberry Lake, near the town of Granby, Colorado, at the headwaters of the Colorado River. For the next year, they roamed America circulating invitations. They visited food cooperatives, yoga ashrams, and college campuses. Every member of Congress and every delegation to the UN was invited. The Rainbows distributed five thousand copies of *The Rainbow Oracle*, a collection of countercultural drawings, articles, and poems that served as the group's manifesto. "Our politics were faith and elbow grease," Beck recalls in *Basic Rainbow*. "And the publicizing of the gathering was mostly word of mouth. We found as we talked with others that every so often someone's eyes would light up, as though they themselves had independently seen or desired this event to be. These people spread the word."

More than twenty thousand people showed up at the remote Colorado site, many of them hiking for days through the Rocky Mountains to evade police barricades. The Colorado governor put the National Guard on alert. The Forest Service closed down every campground within a radius of fifty miles. Undeterred, the Rainbows flooded the campsite. Before daybreak on July 4, several thousand people climbed Table Mountain, joined hands in a circle, and prayed for peace.

After Colorado, the Rainbow People went their separate ways; they had no intention of planning a second event. But the following spring, to everyone's surprise, a man who'd attended the Colorado meeting announced that he was holding his own "Rainbow Gathering" on the Wind River Indian Reservation in Wyoming. The problem was, he'd neglected to secure permission from the local Shoshone Indians, who were now threatening to arrest anyone who set foot on their land. But with thousands of invitations already in the mail, it was too late to call off the event. So, to avert an ugly confrontation with the Shoshone tribal council, some of the planners of the original Rainbow festival beat a path to Wyoming and, with the help of the Forest Service, hastily located a new site on nearby national forest lands. In the end, Wyoming turned out to be an even bigger success than Colorado. At the end of the week, somebody erected a sign that announced, "Next year in Utah." And so, quite by accident, the Rainbow Gathering became an annual event.

Since then, the Rainbows have met every summer in a different state. But over the years, the gatherings have consistently fared better in the West, where the wide-open expanses and more tolerant attitudes provide a more hospitable environment for pitching a Hippie Tabernacle. Nearly every summer that the Rainbows venture east of the Rockies, they run into trouble with the law, the weather, or the locals. In 1980, for example, the Rainbows met in the Monongahela National Forest of West Virginia, their first appearance east of the Mississippi. The West Virginia political establishment insulted them from the start. "You look like a bunch of Gypsies," blustered Secretary of State A. James Manchine in the local papers, managing to insult two groups at once. "There are already too many people out wandering around. Someone must stay home and take responsibility. What knowledge do you have to teach us—

how to eat berries?" The event ended in tragedy: Two Rainbow women were found murdered on a remote trail, shot evidently by irate locals.

At the 1987 gathering in North Carolina's Nantahala National Forest, the Family hit a new nadir. In part because attendance was so high—nearly thirteen thousand—a major epidemic of shigellosis dysentery broke out. More than six thousand cases were reported. Epidemiologists at the Centers for Disease Control in Atlanta later traced the spread of the dysentery to twenty-nine states. The North Carolina Department of Health, which closed down the area for a month, determined that the outbreak was caused by human feces coming in direct contact with the drinking water. But many Rainbows nursed conspiracy theories: They claimed that airplanes chartered by the Forest Service had dusted the campsite with strains of shigella. In fact, official planes *did* fly over the gathering, but the Forest Service maintained that they were simply performing routine reconnaissance missions.

While the Rainbows had no evidence to back up their "dousing" theory, the story became an accepted part of Rainbow folklore. "Given the CIA's history of dirty tricks in Chile and Cuba," Garrick Beck says, "I wouldn't be surprised if the government was sabotaging us by introducing microorganisms in our midst. Sounds perfectly reasonable to me."

But it wasn't only the dysentery outbreak that made the North Carolina event such a disappointment. A lot of Rainbows voiced concern that the old spirit was gone, that the tribe had begun to lose its idealism. "The Rainbow is in danger of falling apart!" one distressed Rainbow named Sanity Clause wrote in to *All Ways Free* after the North Carolina gathering. "This year there was no observable line of demarcation between those who came to work or play; between those whose hearts and minds prayed for peace or those whose loins lusted after fornication." Clause proposed that in future years, the site should be layed out in a yin-yang configuration, with one side of the camp for serious Rainbows ("OM"), and the other side for those who'd just come to party ("AH").

If North Carolina was a disappointment, the next year's rendezvous in the piney woods of East Texas was a disaster. Dysentery was about the only problem the Rainbows *didn't* experience in the encampment, which was pitched on the chiggery shores of Sam Rayburn Reservoir in the Angelina National Forest. A Rainbow woman named No Guns was critically injured in a hit-and-run incident involving drunk locals who had come to gawk at the nude dancing. Rainstorms, 100-degree heat, and last-minute legal wrangles conspired to make the Texas event the most miserable celebration in Rainbow history. "Too much sun, too little fun!" is how one Rainbow summed up the experience in *All Ways Free*.

In the months leading up to the Texas gathering, it had not been clear whether the Rainbows would even be permitted to cross the state line. Reactionary politicians in Austin raised the specter of twenty thousand dope-smoking hippies desecrating the pristine wilderness. The governor publicly vowed not to let the Rainbows within one thousand miles of the Lone Star State. U.S. Senator Phil Gramm threatened to call in the National Guard. "Like the Rainbows," Gramm snickered, "I too will be praying for world peace. But the Lord is more likely to answer the prayers of those not using drugs."

The authorities kept a tight rein on the gathering. All told, seventy-six Rainbows were arrested. To serve as Incident Commander, the Forest Service called in a law-and-order hoss and former DEA detective named Billy Ball, whose swaggering Texas-style policing methods (he had a habit of tackling his Rainbow suspects) won him the nickname "Ball Connor of the Rainbow Nation." Bull responded to public complaints about his alleged abuses this way: "Their brains are all baked, anyway."

But the Rainbows did enjoy one consolation—some called it a miracle—in the Lone Star State. At the close of their silent meditation for world peace, three thousand rain-soaked celebrants opened their eyes to behold a rainbow arching across the sky. Many interpreted it as a sign that the Family's tribulations were finally over. The Vision Council decided that the next summer the Rainbows would visit the only western state where they hadn't already met: Nevada. "We are now 18 summers old," one Rainbow wrote to *All Ways Free* before the Nevada gathering. "It's time for serious consideration of our passage into spiritual adulthood. Time to put aside childish ways and get back to the hard work needed to make our Visions real. No one said it was going to be easy to wage Peace."

* * *

IT'S EIGHT A.M., RAINBOW IME, and the encampment is beginning to stir. A rooster crows. Pots rattle. A Rainbow scout stands on the rimrock and blows a conch shell for no apparent reason. A Forest Service plane buzzes the length of the canyon. A few hug patrollers are already out getting their daily quotas of affection. Rick and I brew a pot of strong coffee and then head down to the information center, where the day's activities are posted on a message board:

9 A.M.	Sufi peace dancing.
9:30	Free metaphysicals.
10 A.M.	Midwifery techniques.
11 A.M.	Guided discussion group for white people who want to work on unlearning racism. The C.A.L.M. meadow.
TBA.	March to main gate to protest police harassing.
Noon.	Psychedelic workshop at the Mormon ruins.
3 P.M.	Regional focalizer meeting.
4 P.M.	Session on strengthening the human-animal bond.
5 P.M.	Stop Nuclear Testing mutual strategy session.
6 P.M.	Sunset vision quest.
8 P.M.	Silent vigil council after dinner in the Meditation Meadow.

Also displayed on the message board are open letters from the distraught relatives of missing Rainbows: "Dearest Wendy: No matter what, we will always love you. Love, Your Family." "Joel, 48, was living in Key West when he took off for the 1986 gathering in Pennsylvania. Not heard from since." "Ed is my brother. He is a loving good man who left his family and friends in 1971 and has not been in touch with us since."

A woman in a Flying Nun outfit is wandering around singing a ballad about how she smoked pot with Vice President Quayle—*fifteen times!*—back in Indianapolis. "I've got the dope on Dan Quayle!" she chants. No one pays her any attention.

A group of young New Agers dance in a circle, chanting, "Rama-Tow, Rama-Ta, Rama-Ho!" A Rainbow woman named

Geneva and her sixteen-year-old daughter Summer are frantically looking for their cat, which has been lost for days. Nearby, a bleary-eyed young woman, who's evidently been up all night tripping, has accidentally dropped her cigarette in a cattleguard. This has her terribly upset. She is trying to fish out the cigarette with a stick, but's all too much for her. She breaks down in tears.

At the Garbage Yoga Station, the camp's refuse has been diligently separated into seven categories: metal, aluminum, glass, paper, compost, plastic, lost and found, and "free." The Rainbow "garbage consciousness" system is based on the seven Hindu *shakras* and was devised by a yoga instructor from Hawaii named Swami Mommy. But during the night, the sierra winds sabotaged her valiant recycling scheme. Now the garbage is strewn over the hillside, and packs of dogs are running around scavenging for scraps.

Down by Robinson Hole, a dazed man named Tibor has just emerged from a long session in one of the Indian sweat lodges. "It's like returning to the womb," says Tibor, his face beet red and glistening. 'You get in there and you can see nothing but the glow of the igneous rocks. Sweats out the impurities." Tibor is a traditional buckskin tanner who lives on a commune near the town of Tonasket, Washington. He's been coming to the Rainbow Gatherings since 1976. This year's encampment, he says, is too spread out. "There's no center," Tibor complains. "Energy levels are low and unfocused. Too much walking."

The council circle, where the Rainbows' consensus decisions get made, is situated in an open field above the trail. For a few days there were actually two different "main" circles, each one rendering decisions without awareness of the other, but someone finally figured out the error. At noon someone blows the conch shell, and the council commences. About twenty-five Rainbows fall into a discussion about what the Family should do to protest "police hassling." A number of people want to bring a suit against the State of Nevada for "gross violations of our constitutional rights." After a few hours of debate, the group is ready to agree on a particular proposal, but one Rainbow vehemently disagrees. His filibuster drags on for over an hour, and the other Rainbows are annoyed. "What we usually do with motormouths like him," one Rainbow explains, "is fill them up with tea. Then, when they go to take a leak, we quickly vote. They come back and say, 'What's going on here?' and we say, 'Hey, brother, it was *unanimous*!'"

Rick and I hike over to the Center for Alternative Living Medicine, or CALM, the Rainbow first aid clinic. CALM specializes in homeopathy and chiropractic care. A patient is stretched out on a long massage table with acupuncture needles in her groin. One of the herbalists is on a walkie-talkie placing orders for more medical supplies. "We're getting low on pennyroyal and comfrey! And we're gonna need two more bottles of calamine."

Next in line is a hugely pregnant women who wants a spinal adjustment. The doctor is happy to oblige her, but he's worried about her lying directly on her swollen belly. He then produces a shovel and digs what he calls a "preggy pool" so her abdomen can hang freely in the ground while he manipulates her spine. "This is the third preggy pool I've dug this week," the doctor says.

Later, a bongo-player comes in with a complaint of psoriasis on his finger. "Can't bend it at all, man. See?" He offers the doctor his scaly finger.

"You been eating a lot of peanut butter lately?" the doctor inquires.

"Well . . . now that you mention it, yeah! . . . I have."

"There's your problem. Lay off the goobers."

"Thanks, doc!"

"*Ahhgggggrrrrrr!*" A blood-curdling shriek comes from behind the CALM tent. Several holistic nurses are holding a woman on the ground. She is pale and shivery, and breaking out in cold sweats.

"What's going on back there?" I ask.

"Rebirthing session," the doctor explains. "Semihypnotic regression all the way back to the womb. We've found it works better on women than men, because women's emotions are more easily tampered with."

"*Ahhgggggrrrr!!!*"

A man named Soaring Eagle is hiking up the main trail with a crate of crystals under his arm. He is trying to persuade a young Flower Maiden to adopt an Indian-style name like his own. The girl looks a little frightened about the prospect of changing her name. "Don't worry," Soaring Eagle reassures her, slipping his arm around her waist. "A name will come to you over time. You must have patience." He strokes her cornsilk hair. "Sometimes your initials will provide a clue."

A tall, sinewy man in his mid-thirties, Soaring Eagle is a self-described "spiritual wanderer." He has a shock of sun-scorched hair and the blazing eyes of a prophet. He says he's done three thousand hits of acid in his lifetime, and listening to him talk, I can believe him. "I am an eternally existing being," he proclaims, "currently utilizing this human form to manifest a positive reality for the Earth Mother and all of her inhabitants."

Soaring Eagle's spiritual odyssey began in 1974, when he "died" at the age of nineteen from an overdose of angel dust. He claims to have had an out-of-body experience in which his spirit floated through a tunnel of white light. When he awoke a few hours later in a Cincinnati hospital, he was a changed man. He studied Christian doctrine, Buddhist doctrine, Krishna doctrine, and every other doctrine he could get his hands on. He worked for a while in a tool and die factory in Ohio, then landed at a "spiritual sanctuary" in Tennessee. In 1987 he caravanned to his first national Rainbow Gathering. He later moved to Atlanta, where he participated in the Harmonic Convergence celebration, learned rod dowsing techniques, and studied the teachings of various New Age shamans. Now he lives in Santa Fe with a former disciple of the Bhagwan Shree Rajneesh and wanders around America seeking enlightenment.

Soaring Eagle says he is wanted on half a dozen counts of tax evasion. "I don't pay taxes because I don't agree with any-thing the government is doing—like building weapons of mass destruction. I don't want to participate in the annihilation of the planet. You know it really fucks up the consciousness of a planet when you splatter it all over the galaxy. I just don't want to be karmatically involved."

RICK AND I CAMPED at Home for a week, but Babylon finally called: Alas, we had to return to work. Besides, we were sun-burned, filthy, and exhausted by all the raging togetherness. And truth be told, seven days of eating lentil stew had given us horrible gas.

We realized that we weren't cut out to be full-time Rain-bows. But as we emerged from the gorge and gazed back over the throngs for the last time, we were moved by the guileless hopes and longings, the potent spiritualism, the sheer tribal wattage that suffused the encampment. It was comforting to go an entire week without spotting ® or ™, without hearing sirens or horns, without seeing money changing hands.

We found Rick's car on the mesa and pulled out at dusk. We rode in silence through the cool black night. We knew we'd finally crossed into Babylon when we saw the coruscating signs of Jackpot, Nevada. The casino lights seemed especially garish after our week among the Rainbows. We parked in the neon glow and walked into the loud casino restaurant, where the jukebox was playing Frank Sinatra tunes.

We ordered hamburger platters and Coca-Colas. The red meat tasted decadent. The French fries dripped with fat. The Coke cans said ®. A melancholy woman dropped a roll of quarters into a slot machine. And at the gaming tables, the gamblers threw the bones with lustful eyes.

The 1989 gathering in Nevada ended uneventfully. Only eleven people were arrested, most of them for minor drug offenses, and there were no deaths or serious injuries. According to Tom Beddow, the U.S. Forest Service officer who presided over the gathering as Incident Commander, the Rainbows left the camp in better shape than they found it in. The Rainbows did file a suit against the State of Nevada for unnecessary harassment and unlawful searches, but as of this writing, the legal proceedings have gone nowhere. The last two Rainbows to leave Robinson Hole were Geneva and Summer, the mother and daughter who had lost their cat. They camped out all summer and well into the fall before a forest ranger forced them to leave, fearing they'd freeze to death in the coming snows. Geneva and Summer never did find their pet, though they said they had "smelled" it several times. Most locals assumed the cat had been taken by a coyote or a mountain lion, though some speculated that Tsawhawbitts, the Shoshone monster, was on the prowl again.

PART II

ON THE ROAD

Allons! the road is before us!
It is safe—I have tried it—my own feet have tried it well—be not
  detain'd!
Let the paper remain on the desk unwritten, and the book on the
  shelf unopen'd!
Let the tools remain in the workshop! let the money remain unearn'd!
              —Walt Whitman, "Song of the Open Road"

The Silver City

South Bend, Indiana

"WE ALWAYS LIKE A GOOD PARADE!" Esther snorts. She salutes the Grand Marshal as he sails by in a Cadillac convertible, his blue beret pulled down at a rakish angle. "We like to get gussied up and look at ourselves."

"Oh, there's no beating a parade," agrees Esther's friend Pauline, holding a parasol to block the sun. "Especially on the Fourth of July!"

It's 96 degrees in South Bend and muggy as a swamp. The golden dome of Notre Dame towers over the Indiana flatlands. Outside the football stadium where Knute Rockne coached his last season, the marching band is playing John Philip Sousa—

Bum-Bummmmmmmmmmmnnnnn
bum-bum-bum
bum-bum-bummmmmnnnnnnnnnn—

—cymbals smashing, trombones punching the sky. Along the parade route, five thousand spectators are squeezed into lawn chairs or sprawled on picnic quilts, Velma and Clarence and Gertrude and Dale, zinc oxide slathered on their noses, hearing

103

aids squeaking in their ears. A drum-and-bugle corps shambles by, then a kazoo band, then a Dixieland jazz ensemble doing a Bourbon Street dirge. A group of ladies in floral print dresses and straw hats sip lemonade under a broad oak tree. "Oh what fun!" Esther chuckles. "This *is* a doozy! The best parade EVER!"

"My goodness, what a wingding!" Pauline agrees. "Have you ever seen such a thing?"

They're all hooting and horselaughing like kids at a pep rally, Orval and Mildred and Chester and Blanche, just watching the stream of humanity drift by: Pilgrims and Indians, kings and queens, Yanks and Rebs . . . a troika of Boy Scouts bearing flags, flapper girls dancing the Charleston, dignitaries doffing tassled hats . . . cowpokes, hoboes, baton twirlers . . . a motorcade of chrome and whitewalls and Simonized wax, Studebakers, Model T's . . . papier-mâché rockets, prairie schooners, a vintage fire engine with sirens screeching . . . an outhouse on wheels with a sign tacked to the door that says BACK OFF OR I'LL FLUSH! . . . a dozen lacquered beauty queens with their white-gloved hands tightly cupped and swiveling over the cheering crowds.

And finally, at the end of the procession, comes one of the familiar silver bubbles—the silver bubble that brought them all here in the first place—Horace and Twila and Ray and Pearl. Teardrop from the age of Sputnik, spaceship from the pages of H.G. Wells. The bubble noses down Juniper Road and coasts toward the famed "Touchdown Jesus," the fourteen-story mosaic on the facade of the Hesburgh Library that is directly aligned with the stadium goalposts and seems to depict Christ raising His arms to signal yet another touchdown for the Fighting Irish. On the side of the bubble, spanning the full length of its fuselage, a sign proclaims:

AIRSTREAMING IS A
WAY OF LIFE.

BEYOND THE PROCESSION, on the athletic fields where the Gipper once played, 3,350 Airstream travel trailers are parked in meticulous rows, a vast grid of metallic silver lozenges baking in the sun. The owners of these distinctive rigs have come to Indiana from nearly every state and Canadian province to celebrate the vision of their club patriarch, the late Wally Byam, dean of the American RV industry. Tinkerer, author, businessman, and tireless impresario, Byam was the inventor of the Airstream—arguably the best travel trailer in the world. Every July for three decades the Wally Byam Caravan Club International (WBCCI), the social club of Airstream owners, has picked a different site in which to hold its International Rally. In past years it's been in Duluth, Minnesota; Bozeman, Montana; and Ames, Iowa. The International is both a family reunion and a birthday celebration: As it happens, Wally Byam was born on the Fourth of July.

The Airstreamers come to toss horseshoes and go on metal-detecting excursions. They sit in on RV maintenance seminars to learn about the latest in tow hookups and septic tank chemicals. They perform skits and attend morning devotionals. A subgroup of single Airstreamers calling themselves "The Freewheelers" meets for happy hours and bridge socials. A Teen Queen (usually a granddaughter of one of the members) is crowned in an elaborate pageant at the end of the week. And, of course, there is the Independence Day parade.

As the powwow draws to a close, the Airstreamers form dozens of well-organized caravans and fan out across the nation, "rally hopping" their way home.

If they have a home. For more than six thousand WBCCI members, the trailer *is* the home, and Airstreaming is a permanent state of existence. These proud practitioners of the caravan ethic, called "full-timers," are treated with a certain deference within the club. Some full-timers park their rigs in exclusive Airstream villages—with names like Land Yacht Harbor or Port-O-Call. Others, called "snowbirds," migrate with the seasons. "We're not supposed to use the word 'gypsy,' but I guess I'm a gypsy at heart," says Edna Covar of Melbourne, Florida, who has lived in an Airstream for nineteen years with her husband Les, a retired police officer. "At first, I didn't think it was humanly possible to go full-time. I just figured you'd get claustrophobia in there. But I adjusted real quick. Now I don't even like to stay anywhere else *but* my Airstream."

"We don't get tired of traveling because we go home every night," explains Mary Tinga, from Castle Hayne, North Carolina, who lives in a 31-foot Airstream with her husband, Eelco, seven months of the year. "We sleep in our own beds. We eat

our own food at our own table. We look at our own TV set.
When we shut the door, we're home. And this is why we can
stay on the road six, seven months of the year. There's a little
saying in Airstream that goes, 'We have a cottage in the mountains, and a cottage at the shore, and a cottage in many places
we've never seen before.' That's our cottage out there, and we
just put it wherever we want it."

This is the twenty-first international rally the Tingas have
attended. "Coming to the rallies is like coming to a big family
reunion," Mary asserts. "We have very good friends from all
parts of the country who we see once a year—here. We leave
this rally counting the days until the next one starts."

Mary's husband Eelco is a serene man with a Carolinian
drawl as smooth as custard pie. "The Airstream's appeal is not
only a matter of aesthetics," he claims, noting that the Airstream's aerodynamic contour and lightweight aluminum construction diminish wind drag. "You've got to punch a hole to
drive through. With the Airstream, you make a nice round hole
in the air. You get great towability. That thing just pulls along
smooth, and you forget it's back there. It's all the legacy of Wally
Byam."

It was Byam who first conceived the name "Airstream" in
1936, when he introduced a new line of travel trailers with
riveted aluminum shells. Drawing from technological advances
in the airline industry, Byam's monocoque bubble was designed
to ride "like a stream of air." During the postwar boom, Airstream became wildly successful, etching itself into the popular
culture both as a product and as a way of life. The Shah of Iran
once had an Airstream, as did former Mexican President Lázaro
Cárdenas. NASA has used customized Airstreams as temporary
holding chambers for astronauts returning from space. And
today, the silver bubble is the official personnel vehicle for space
shuttle landings at California's Edwards Air Force Base.

Byam wasn't only a designer and businessman—he was a
traveler himself, a latter-day Bedouin who believed in the high
romance of group touring. He wore a blue beret, his sartorial
trademark and now the club's official headgear. Byam caravanned around the globe in a special gold-plated Airstream
(bearing the number "1") with an observation hole punched
through the roof, where he liked to perch himself and shout
instructions to his fellow campers through a bullhorn.

Byam was something of a pied piper figure; such was his charm that wherever he went, people followed him. And like the children of Hamelin in the Robert Browning poem, they often joined his caravans without much concern for the destination or the possible perils of the trip ahead. "We shall go where angels fear to tread," he used to exhort his friends and followers before embarking on his far-flung trips. "We shall lead our caravan down roads that are still but a gleam in a cartographer's eye."

Byam's caravans were logistical feats, mythologized in the pages of *National Geographic*. In 1959 he and his wife Stella led a team of Airstreams through Africa—from Cape Town to Cairo. In Addis Ababa, he gave an Airstream to Ethiopian Emperor Haile Selassie as a personal gift. Another caravan took him and a large group of friends to Central America along the Pan-American Highway. Other trips went through Europe, Asia, and pre-Castro Cuba. In addition to offering free publicity for the Airstream Company, these caravans served as field trials for the early models. Byam would wire telegrams back to the company engineers, demanding additions or structural changes in future models based on the torture-tests of these road trips. In his two books, *Fifth Avenue on Wheels* and *Trailer Travel Here and Abroad*, Byam's enthusiasm for caravanning bordered on the evangelical. "Trailering is practically a religion with me," he wrote in *Here and Abroad*. A life on the road, he believed, could cure ulcers, depression, marital problems, spiritual malaise, and the infirmities of old age. "Civilization seems to have solved the problem of keeping people alive longer. But it has done precious little about making these extra years happier and more fruitful. Many people have to work so hard all their lives that they never learn how to have fun."

So Byam taught them. His advice was always the same: Buy a trailer and hit the road. He said that he often felt like a minister because trailering enriched the lives of his older followers so much. "They come to me with a vague, lustreless look in their eyes, but after two years of trailering, they're suntanned, interested in life, a spring in their step."

Byam had a notion of traveling in what he called "the vehicular village," a moving town with its own constitutional bylaws and democratic institutions. "I wanted to show how much fun trailering could be en masse if we ran the whole shebang like a New England town meeting and let democracy have its head," he wrote. In the vehicular village, everybody had a job, each person contributing according to his ability, taking according to his need. There was a postmaster, a doctor, an official greeter, a keeper of the kitty, and a special rearguard officer called the "caboose." Byam himself wore several hats: He was, in the words of one fellow caravanner, "mayor, secretary of state, protocol officer, and toastmaster on ceremonial occasions."

The Wally Byam Caravan Club was organized by a group of Byam's friends who were taken with his idea of self-sufficient travel and thought caravanning might especially appeal to the newly emerging generation of postwar retirees, who had the leisure time and disposable income to travel year-round. The first International Rally was held in 1958 in Bull Shoals, Arkansas, deep in the Ozarks. The Airstreamers parked in a giant wagon wheel formation from the Wild West days, concentric circles of space capsules radiating from a central bonfire. Pat Boone's grandfather provided entertainment, and a fireworks display on the Fourth lit up the stormy sky with the words, "H-A-P-P-Y B-I-R-T-H-D-A-Y W-A-L-L-Y."

Byam drafted a kind of traveler's prayer, called "The Wally Byam Creed," that captured the original spirit of the club. Many Airstreamers recite it to this day: "To place the great wide world at your doorstep for you who yearn to travel with all the comforts of home . . . To keep alive an enduring promise of high adventure and faraway lands . . . To lead caravans wherever the four winds blow, over the twinkling boulevards, across trackless deserts . . . to the traveled and untraveled corners of the earth . . . To strive endlessly to stir the venturesome spirit that moves you to follow the rainbow to its end."

THE AIRSTREAMERS HAVE BUILT a self-contained city on the Notre Dame campus. They've set up their own post office, with a special ZIP code—46556. They have their own news program known as "Wally Byam Control." They've laid five miles of water hose and four miles of electrical wire. Everybody draws from the same water supply: a universal five-eighths-of-an-inch hose that courses through the Silver City and enters each trailer through a special Y-junction. A fleet of red Honda mopeds serves as the Wally Byam Scooter Patrol, delivering messages in the Silver City. There is a committee to oversee every facet of life: A lost and found committee, a macramé committee, even a pancake committee. But the most prestigious of these is, by all accounts, the sanitation committee, charged with the mal-odorous task of pumping the "black water" out of every Air-stream trailer. A quirky kind of esprit de corps has developed among the sanitation workers, who wear overalls and red roses and like to call themselves "the Effluent Society."

In the Silver City, everything is done in an orderly fashion, as if disorder were a disease. Every rally has a theme. Every trailer has a number. Every meeting follows parliamentary pro-cedure, and no decision is made unless the ayes have it. The Airstreamers pride themselves on what they call "precision parking." A team of traffic experts in orange vests and safari helmets docks the incoming rigs according to blueprints drawn up months in advance. Every row has an identifying code, and every section is marked off by color: Red-6, Gold-8, Blue-7. The exact location of every trailer is posted on a "Locator Board," so no one at the rally can remain incognito.

It's a neighborhood built on conformity and a shared com-mitment to serious leisure. To enter into the society you must buy a piece of property that looks exactly like everyone else's. The individual aesthetic merges with that of the community. Airstreamers take pride in private ownership and will talk to you at length about the nifty personal features of their rig. But at the same time, you can see on their faces the warm flush of fellow-feeling that comes from knowing that the couple parked next door has a nearly identical home. If the electrical system breaks down, or the water pump is on the fritz, an Airstreamer can always commiserate with neighbors who have had the same problem.

The club is open to people of all races and creeds, though the membership is overwhelmingly white and Christian. Every Airstream family belongs to one of the club's 175 local units that are organized into 12 geographical provinces. Members pay $35 in annual dues and must pledge to obey the WBCCI Code of Ethics, which essentially demands that they be nice people at all times. "[Members agree] to say or print nothing that may reflect unfavorably on others," states the Code. "Mem-bership in this organization is an assurance of our courtesy on the road and good will to all peoples and countries."

Though the median age of the club is sixty-six, it's difficult to think of the Wally Byam Caravan Club as a society of old folks. Everywhere you look, you see vigorous, ruddy-skinned people marching around the college campus, fighting age. Constant motion is the antidote to infirmity. There are square dances, shuffleboard tournaments, Jazzercise classes, talent shows. "The club extends the life of a good number of our members," avers WBCCI President Ed Minty, who theoretically lives in Phoenix but has been full-timing three years now with his wife, Pat. "We have a lot of people who are up in their eighties pulling trailers around. It keeps them interested in getting out and doing things. I know that's true in our case. This club's the best thing that ever happened to us."

Airstreamers are not the sort of people Albert Brooks had in mind when he filmed his RV comedy, *Lost in America*. Airstreamers know exactly where they are at any given time— longitude, latitude, county, precinct, and mile marker. They pride themselves on their navigational prowess. The interiors of their Suburbans and GMC trucks are rigged with compasses, altimeters, barometers, temp gauges, Triptik charts. Their consoles are neatly layered with atlases and contour maps. Crisp efficiency is the operative ideal—road science. Their seat cushions are orthopedically correct. Their soft drinks are securely anchored. Safety is put at a high premium. They keep a close eye on weather patterns two time zones away, and their hands are firmly wrapped around the wheel, ten and two. "Truck drivers always toot their horns at us," one club member tells me. "It's a form of salute. They say Airstreamers are the best drivers on the road."

Walking down the long rows of docked trailers with model names like Excella and Land Yacht, you can see the blue flicker of television sets inside; occasionally the sweet smell of cakes or brownies wafts from the kitchen ovens. Filmy gray water from the drains of bathtubs and kitchen sinks trickles out of hoses and seeps into the soft ground. Old guys in floppy fishing hats and lime green golf slacks whir through the alleyways on their Rascal electronic carts. The air crackles with CB radios, as the announcer from Wally Byam Control breaks in: *"All parties who wish to participate in the cribbage tournament should meet in Room two-fifty-eight at nine o'clock for further instructions."*

In Blue-19, an Oregon woman sits under her Zip-Dee

ratchet awning doing needlepoint and listening to Paul Harvey on an AM transistor radio, while her husband rummages through his rock collection piled in the back of their Silverado.

Next door, a couple from Nebraska is setting out a garden of wooden tulips and artificial grass. Two rows over, a foursome from Arizona drinks cans of Schlitz beer wrapped in plastic foam huggies while one of the wives brings out an hors d'oeuvre tray piled high with pimento cheese and deviled egg sandwiches.

At the RV market, they're selling antisway bars, telescoping drains, skunk deodorant, and potty toddy tabs. In a side lot by the stadium, an Airstream dealer from St. Louis is showing off the 1991 Model 350 Motorhome, a sparkling 35-footer with touch-sensitive door locks and a rear video camera for backing up (List Price: $130,000). *"Drivability,"* the salesman intones, *"is further enhanced by the composite multiaxle torsion bar suspension system. . . ."*

In Gold-6, a couple from Delaware is practicing dance steps to a Glenn Miller tape (the music periodically interrupted by a sizzling sound coming from their electric bug zapper). The sticker on the back of their trailer says

NO PHONE

NO CLOCK

NO WORRIES

NO MONEY

Actually, bumper stickers like this one are a rarity among Airstreamers, who pride themselves on their discretion. They like the handsome look of all that unsmirched aluminum, and have trouble understanding why an RV owner would want to junk up his rig with detritus from his travels—tacky souvenirs in the I DID YELLOWSTONE vein. It's understood within the club that you're not allowed to tinker with the exterior of your Airstream. You can gut the insides if you like and customize everything yourself, but the silver shell has to remain intact. Sometimes an Airstreamer will affix a small map of America to his trailer, with the states he's visited highlighted in blue, but it's all very tasteful and unobtrusive.

Discretion is an important part of the role Byamites have assigned themselves as ambassadors of the much-maligned RV world; they hope to show by their example that trailering can be a classy pursuit. Section C of the Wally Byam Code of Ethics requires members "to conduct ourselves in a manner to inspire others engaged in trailering . . ." Boorish or conspicuously tacky behavior is forbidden. Things you won't find at an Airstream rally: shirts hanging on clotheslines, litter of any kind, whiskey bottles, tattoos, tank tops, barefootedness, shirtlessness, loud dogs, loud stereos, loud kids, or loud mufflers. The club's members, who have a median income of $43,000, are acutely offended when the media portrays them in any way that might be construed as proletarian. When NBC's documentary show *Real Life with Jane Pauley* opened a segment on Airstreaming with a quick glimpse of a woman in haircurlers, the club hit the roof. "Why would they want to go and show a thing like that?" one club member griped to me. "That's *not* the image we want the public to see. We're not like those other tin-can trailer owners you see on the road."

At the same time, members are just as concerned about the club's reputation for snobbery. At parks and RV camps like Kampgrounds of America, Airstreamers tend to stay together. Over the years this cliquishness has led more than a few owners of less distinguished rigs—Winnebagos, say—to resent Airstreamers as the self-appointed Brahmin class of the RV world. The charge of elitism is only reinforced by the lexical habits of Airstreamers, who sometimes refer to other RV makes as "cheeseboxes" or "SOB's" (some other brand). At times this perceived elitism leads to a kind of facetious reverse-discrimination. A sign at the entrance to a trailer park in Melbourne, Florida, says: "Welcome All Campers—Left to Registration; Airstreamers—Turnaround."

"Oh sure, there are a lot of people who think Airstreamers are just plain stuck up," concedes Carl Bateman, a retired Caterpillar equipment dealer from Nashville. "But we're not stuck up—most of us, at least. It's not that we think that Airstream is so much swankier than all the others. Personally, I think Holiday Rambler [one of Airstream's major competitors] has got the prettiest rigs on the market. It's just that you're naturally friendlier with someone who's got something in common with you. It's human nature."

Carl shifts in his Zip-Dee lawn chair and squints at the spacepods glinting in the afternoon sun. "The other thing that makes people think we're snobs is that when we caravan around the country, and go to these rallies, we don't need a whole lot of contact with the outside. We don't mean to sound snooty about it, but anything that we need, we got it right here. You want music? We've got our own orchestra. Feeling sick? We've got retired doctors in the club. You see, we're a city unto ourselves."

OVER THE YEARS, SOUTH BEND has become a favorite rendezvous for the WBCCI; the club has held numerous regional gatherings and four International Rallies at Notre Dame, more here than in any other place. This university town of 110,000 is steeped in its own legacy of trailer travel. Throughout the 1800s, South Bend was nationally known for the manufacture of covered wagons and horse-drawn carriages. The most prominent of the local industrialists was the Studebaker family, who made the switch to automobiles around the turn of the century.

South Bend has welcomed the Airstream invasion with typical Hoosier hospitality. Cafeterias are doing a particularly brisk business. The Chamber of Commerce estimates that Byamites will contribute $3 million to the local economy—a nice infusion of cash, the local paper notes, but somewhat less than the impact of the average Notre Dame football game.

The week began inauspiciously in the Silver City. Sweltering temperatures sent more than sixty Airstreamers to the hospital with heat exhaustion. There have been ten emergency ambulance calls, and at least one participant died—evidently of a heart attack. It got so hot one day that hundreds of Byamites left the rally and spent the entire afternoon in an air-conditioned mall. Later in the week, an elderly woman was hit by a car and broke her hip. Another man was struck by lightning. Rainstorms have turned the parking fields into mud (someone erected a sign in a water puddle that says "Warning: Alligator Crossing"), and there have been two tornado watches in the area. Worst of all, hailstorms are in the forecast. Airstreamers are particularly leery of hailstones, which can leave tiny pockmarks on the soft aluminum skins of their trailers—an unsightly and difficult-to-treat condition known as "Airstream Acne."

Luckily, much of the action has been indoors at the Notre Dame auditorium. On Sunday night, Rhonda Knight ("Miss Ontario") was crowned Teen Queen before a howling crowd of seven thousand. On Tuesday night, the 1990–91 officers, attired in white tuxedos and blue berets, were installed in a formal pageant that featured the national anthems of Canada, Mexico, and the United States. And, later in the week, Vegas crooner Roger Miller gave a concert, singing his old classic "King of the Road" for an encore—*Two hours of pushing brooms buys an eight-by-twelve four-bit room, I'm a man of means by no means . . . King of the Road.*

"IT'S A LIFE-STYLE THAT GETS INTO YOUR BLOOD," says Gene "Stubby" Stubbs of Vienna, Virginia. He and his wife Shirley have been members of the Wally Byam club for fourteen years. Stubby is president of Region 2 of the WBCCI, a large dominion that extends from Ontario to Maryland. "We're the kind of people who, when we get into something, we give it a hundred and ten."

The Stubbses are more than happy to give me the grand tour of their new rig, a 1990 34-foot Limited (#277), Airstream's top-of-the-line. The Stubbses' trailer is parked near the stadium, its big wheels leveled and chocked, its liquid propane tank glimmering in the sun. It has all the options: Corian galley tops, oak cabinets, a cedar-lined closet, overhead tambour storage bins, wooden venetian blinds, mixer, convection microwave, blender, solar panels, shag carpeting, ceiling fans. There is a Panasonic color TV with cable hookup, a fifty-gallon freshwater tank, and a dinette that converts to a single bed. It's a cheerfully decorated world appointed in soft burgundy hues, with an AstroTurf welcome mat and a needlework greeting by the door that says, "Home Sweet Home." A macramé Kleenex cozy sits on a doily-covered credenza. The mailbox welcomes in cheerful letters, "The Stubbs." The magazine rack is stashed with copies of *Trailer Life* and *Blue Beret*, the club's monthly journal. Everything folds out, slides in, tucks under, and snaps down. "A marvel of space utilization." Stubbs beams, leaning back in the swiveling captain's chair and sipping an ice-cold Coke fresh from the fridge. "Now you take a trip in one of these, and you won't ever want to stay in a motel again. That living out of a suitcase business is for the birds, let me tell you. You get a trailer, and it's personalized to fit you. It's such a simple life. You know where everything is. You just kick off your shoes and you're all set."

Aerial view of the International Rally of the Wally Byam Caravan Club.

Airstream founder Wally Byam greeting Ugandan tribe in 1959.

Airstreamers gather at the base of the Egyptian pyramids in 1959.

Gene and Shirley Stubbs of Vienna, Virginia, in their Airstream, 1992.

Stubby is an avuncular man of six-foot-five who wears a gemstone bolo tie and hefty turquoise rings. A model Airstream bulges from his belt buckle. A semiretired accountant for a division of the Department of Defense that researches what he calls "way-out Buck Rogers stuff," Stubby was born in northern Alabama and grew up on a Navajo reservation in New Mexico, on the eastern slope of the Great Divide. An ace at running committee meetings, he is a natural politician and something of a ham. Stubby speaks glibly, informally, with a slight south-by-southwest drawl, though occasionally little phrases from *Robert's Rules of Order* crop up in his speech. "I got an Airstream trailer because it was the only RV I could stand up in," Stubby jokes, noting that he's installed a customized seven-foot bed in the back so he can get a decent night's rest. "From the very beginning, we liked the *idea* of an Airstream. It was aerodynamic. It was all aluminum. There was nothing to break or bend. It was just the ultimate."

Stubby's wife Shirley is an attractive woman in her early sixties with twinkling eyes and a warm smile. "You know, to tell you the truth," she confesses in a conspiratorial whisper, "when we first joined the Wally Byam Club, Stubby and I thought it was all a little too much togetherness. Everything was so regimented. We weren't used to being so structured all the time." She chuckles. "Now look at us!"

"With Airstream, you have instant friendships," Shirley says. "People come up to you from out of nowhere and say, 'I'm an Airstreamer too.' It's a big silver magnet that draws people together." She points out that if she or Stubby were to spot another Airstream driving down the road, they could look up the number in a membership directory and immediately find out who's driving and where they're from. For example, if they were to pass Airstream number 21383, a quick glance in the directory would tell them that Howard and Mildred Dixon of Chattanooga, Tennessee, were behind the wheel. The Stubbses could then pick up their CB radio and talk directly to the Dixons on 14, the channel that all WBCCI members use, and perhaps they would agree to meet for lunch somewhere down the road.

Another amenity to be found in the club directory, the Stubbses point out, is "Courtesy Parking." Nearly one thousand members across the country offer free parking space for any Airstreamer who happens to be passing through town. These generous hosts have the designation "CP" at the end of their personal listing in the directory. If an Airstreamer finds himself in, say, Kenai, Alaska, he can park his rig on the property of Jack and Willie Mae Bowen (#5708) (CP). If he's in Oldtown, Idaho, he can drop anchor in the driveway of Hilmer and Dot Malm (#7541) (CP). Courtesy parking amounts to a national motel chain for Byamites, enabling them to hopscotch across the country and never pay a cent for camping or lodging fees.

More than 50 percent of all Airstream owners decline to join the Wally Byam Club. Such killjoys are called "baldies." Their rigs have no affixed ID numbers and thus are "bald." Byamites view baldies with a mixture of pity and disappointment, laced with a healthy dose of club evangelism: It is hoped that today's baldie will be tomorrow's convert. Stubby concedes that he might be less likely to stop for a broken-down baldie than for a properly numbered Byamite trailer. "Oh, I might stop just because I'm a Good Samaritan. But once I've stopped, you can be sure I'll be working on him, trying to get him to join our club. I want him to know what he's missing."

> *The Airstream is a symbol of motion . . . both nostalgic and somehow futuristic, suggesting the optimism of an earlier time when space travel was only imaginary.*
> Airstream, a company history
> by Robert Landau and James Phillippi

AT ITS ESSENCE, the WBCCI is a club built around a shape.

The Airstream plant in Jackson Center, Ohio, manufacturers a host of lesser-known box-shaped trailers and vans with the "Airstream" name attached to them; but only owners of the classic bubble-shaped trailers and motor homes are eligible for membership in the WBCCI. "You see, it's the *styling* that we like," says club President Ed Minty, who defines Airstream's distinctive shape and sheen as, simply, The Look. "The Winnebagos and all these others, they're good trailers. But they don't have that classic look about them. There's a lot of nice trailers on the road, but this one . . . well, there's a reason why it costs more. It just looks different. It's round. It's that aluminum—it gives. It's flexible. Boy, that thing's alive!"

The debate currently raging within the club is whether it should open the ranks to the owners of a new box-shaped trailer manufactured by Thor Industries, Airstream's parent company. WBCCI purists dismiss the controversial newcomer as a "Squarestream" and have so far succeeded in blocking its admission. "We've got a good thing going here—let's not tinker with it by trying to square the circle," one of the club diehards protests at a special hearing on the Squarestream issue.

"We don't mean to be arrogant about it," argues Bill Taylor of Nashville, Indiana, a longtime owner of a classic Land Yacht Airstream. "But once you open the door to one model, all the standards go out the window. You have to draw the line somewhere, or else everybody will want to start calling himself an Airstreamer."

Eelco Tinga likes to explain the club's obsession with uniform roundness this way: "If you go by a pasture where there's Holstein cows, they're all black and white, and it looks good. If you go by another pasture where they're mixed in with Jerseys and Guernseys and beef cattle, they look—*pfffff*. Right? See, this is what we like about what we've got here. Uniformity. Everything looks the same."

The Airstream "Look" has long held a peculiar fascination for students of American iconography. It is a kind of national pop symbol in the same vein as the Warholean soup can. Jazz guitarist Pat Metheny pictured Airstreams on the cover of his *American Garage* album. In television ads, Madison Avenue has snuck in a glimpse of an Airstream to help sell blue jeans, cars, and beer (much to the chagrin of the Airstream trademark attorneys). In Paris, not far from the Eiffel Tower, an American-style diner has been carved from the shell of an old Airstream trailer—the seamless fusion of two Yankee icons.

A film crew from Ithaca, New York, has come to Notre Dame to shoot a documentary on *Aging in America*. At Notre Dame's divinity school, a class on "Ritual Studies" has spent the week exploring the Airstream rituals taking place outside the classroom windows.

Club members are often bemused by the public's interest in the Airstream subculture. For example, no one in the Silver City can figure out why a certain young couple from Edmonton, Alberta, has come all the way to South Bend to spend their honeymoon documenting the ID numbers on all the 3,350 Airstream trailers parked at the rally. Mike Orchard, the groom, says that Airstream-gazing has been his hobby ever since he was six years old; for some reason, he's taken it upon himself to memorize the sequences on hundreds of Airstreams. Though he doesn't own an Airstream himself, he and his new bride, Terri, hope to get one someday.

Stories of other Airstream fetishists abound. Gene Stubbs like to tell of the time a photography editor for *The Washingtonian* magazine insisted on using his Airstream as a backdrop for a fashion shoot. "Boy, this guy had a thing for Airstreams. He wanted to have models in evening wear and high heels slinking around on the roof of my trailer. I said, 'Now w-w-w-wait a minute. That trailer costs fifty thousand dollars.' He wouldn't take no for an answer."

SELF-CONTAINMENT. That was the lifelong ideal of Wallace Merle Byam. He spoke the phrase like a mantra. From his earliest days in the business, Byam wanted to construct a trailer that could keep its septic fluids and foul odors to itself. With the careful arrangement of battery packs, propane tanks, and storage cells, he sought to build a traveling vessel that could go for weeks without having to drop umbilical cords to the outside world. For Byam, self-containment amounted to a declaration of independence from the messy uncertainties of the road. One of the names of his early models neatly captured the spirit of self-containment. He called it "The Sovereign."

Byam was a distinguished-looking man with piercing eyes and downy silver hair. He had a chiseled face and an aquiline nose popping with capillaries. When he was deep in thought, he had a habit of nibbling at the ends of his thick, black-rimmed reading glasses. In the company photographs, he was often pictured leaning against a globe in a black flannel suit, looking like an august patron of the Explorers Club.

Details about Byam's life are spotty in places, and the club has done a fair amount of embellishing over the years. "There are so many myths," warns Byam's cousin Helen Schwamborn, a longtime employee of the Airstream Company who is now a widow living in Bakersfield, California. "Many of the myths were Wally's doing, of course. His imagination was a lot better than his memory, and he had a way of exaggerating things. You see, Wallace was a showman. We used to say, 'Wally, if you had been born a little earlier, the circus would have been called Barnum, Bailey and Byam.' "

He was born in Baker, Oregon, on July 4, 1896. His parents died when he was young, so Wally, an only child, went to live with his grandparents in the dry foothills of eastern Oregon's Blue Mountains, where he spent his summers working as a shepherd. His interest in self-contained vehicles is said to have dated back to these summers, when he would live for weeks at a time out of a donkey-drawn cart that was equipped with a sleeping mat and a kerosene stove.

He went to sea as a cabin boy before attending Stanford, where he graduated in 1921 with a B.A. in history. In the early twenties he worked as an advertising copywriter for the *Los Angeles Times* and then published how-to carpentry magazines. One of his magazines ran an item showing how to build a trailer on the chassis of a Model T. The item brought complaints from readers, who said the instructions were faulty. Byam tested the plans himself and agreed, so he set out to design his own. In the next issue of his magazine he wrote an article about his new trailer, claiming it could be built for less than one hundred dollars, including materials. He sold instruction booklets by mail and began working as an "after-five mechanic" in his backyard—building weird-looking contraptions straight out of Jules Verne, with bat wings and portholes and webbed fins of chrome. With each new model he made subtle improvements: He dropped the floor between the axles so people could stand upright; he put in water pumps and chemical toilets; he installed gas stoves, iceboxes, heaters. The first trailers were built out of plywood, Masonite, and furring strips, much of the raw material pulled from the junkyard.

By then other moonlighters were building travel trailers, too. In the late twenties, trailer construction had become a thriving cottage industry in the U.S., and in Europe the trailer business was even better established. Most of the new trailers were improbable-looking vessels with names like "the Auto-Kamp" and "the Prairie Schooner." It became fashionable among wealthy adventure-seekers to tour Europe in customized rigs, dubbed "house cars." Harvey Firestone, Thomas Edison, Henry Ford, and John Burroughs traveled around together in one such house car, with Edison's bulbs lighting up their camps at night.

During the Great Depression trailer travel began to acquire an unsavory reputation. Increasing numbers of itinerant laborers and Dust Bowl refugees were living out of trailers, migrating around the country to find work. The newspapers were filled with screeds about "Okie trailer squatters and motor gypsies." J. Edgar Hoover warned that trailer parks were becoming "dens of vice and corruption, haunted by nomadic prostitutes, hardened criminals, white slavers, and promiscuous college students." Health department officials feared that unhygienic trailerites were spreading contagion. State governments fretted over how to tax the new class of "tin can tourists," and progressive-minded municipalities blackballed trailers as an eyesore. By the mid-thirties, legislation was passed banning the construction of homemade trailers, which were often so poorly built that the highways of some states had been turned into eerie elephant graveyards; the chief of the Texas Rangers reported at the time that the plains of the Lone Star State were "littered with the bones of trailers that didn't make it."

But Byam saw a brighter future for the travel trailer. In 1930, he closed down his magazine publishing operation and entered the business full-time. During the initial years, he worked from his hip pocket, borrowing three-hundred dollars from his fellow workers to finish the first few models. In 1933, he built his first teardrop-shaped trailer, the "Torpedo Car Cruiser," and sold the design plans by mail for five dollars. Three years later, working under the new company name of "Airstream," Byam unveiled "The Clipper," an aluminum-shelled trailer with a cedar closet and an experimental air-conditioning system that worked on dry ice. Cost: $1,200.

Impetuous, flamboyant, prone to manic spurts of inspiration, Byam built his trailers in much the same way that Preston Tucker built his futurist cars. He was a maverick, brilliant with his hands, expert in the theatrics of promotion—but the sort of man who sometimes forgot to dot his *i*'s. From a practical standpoint, he was a terrible businessman. But he was smart enough to surround himself with competent people, and charming enough to retain their loyalty. "He was good with an idea," Helen Schwamborn recalls, "but he ran around so much, he couldn't keep his mind on what he was doing. Someone else had to do the work." He would return from one of his long field trips and want to turn the factory upside down, rip the place up from the roots and rethink everything. His engineers hated to see him coming.

During the thirties, Airstream was only a fledgling operation in a rapidly expanding market. Trailer manufacture had become, according to *Time*, the fastest growing industry in the U.S. More than 300 manufacturers were in operation, and an estimated 250,000 trailers were bouncing along the highways of America. The Covered Wagon Company of Michigan was far and away the largest manufacturer, with the luxury end of the market dominated by Aerocar, whose swank road yachts had been bought by tycoons like Philip K. Wrigley and W. K. Vanderbilt. Trailers had proven useful as Western Union offices, hunting cabins, mobile offices for dentists, and health clinics at Indian reservations. Pop futurists were claiming that within the next fifty years over half the U.S. population would be living and working out of trailers. "A new industry has gotten into swing with a battle cry the like of which has never before been heard in this land," *Harper's* magazine sneered in 1938.

Byam built his trailers in a small building near the Van Nuys Airport in the San Fernando Valley. In December of 1941 the Department of War classified aluminum alloy as a critical material, witholding it from civilian use. Byam was forced to close down the Airstream factory and take a job at United Aircraft (some accounts say he also worked for Lockhead), where he worked nights as a production supervisor. His wartime experience in the aircraft industry would strongly influence his design of future Airstream models.

Byam resumed building Airstreams in 1947, a time when the trailer business was enjoying a tremendous boom. In the postwar housing shortage, trailers were serving as temporary living quarters for newlyweds and college students matriculating under the GI bill. It was during this period that the American trailer began to evolve in two distinct and irreversible directions—recreational travel trailers like the Airstream and semipermanent mobile homes, the "wide load" monstrosities that were ending up, as often as not, in unsightly warrens euphemistically called "trailer parks." A traveler at heart, Byam loathed the whole idea of the mobile home, which he called "our uncouth cousin." "[Mobile homes] have begun to erupt all over the nation like smallpox," he lamented. "The high esteem which the smart little travel trailer [has] earned through its service to vacationers, sportsmen, and tourists [has] faded in the squalor of slum camps."

State and local governments often failed to make the distinction. Legislation designed to battle the growing menace of the mobile home penalized the travel trailer as well. Many localities prohibited the roadside parking of trailers. New statutes restricted vehicle length and outlawed the towing of trailers at night or on weekends. To drive from Los Angeles to New York, the owner of a 35-foot rig had to secure permits from at least six separate states—and stay clear of Iowa altogether.

In 1951, Byam placed an ad in a travel magazine inviting anyone with a trailer to accompany him on a first-ever motor safari through Mexico; all comers were told to rendezvous in El Paso. Byam figured only a handful of sojourners would show up, but on the appointed day, seventy-five trailers awaited him at the border. A second caravan to Mexico drew more than five hundred trailers—producing a convoy so long that as the vanguard reached two hundred miles into Mexico, stragglers were still crossing the border at a rate of one per minute. Startled campesinos thought the caravan was an invading army, but later welcomed the *yanquis* with mariachi bands and tequila.

Originally open to owners of all trailer makes, the caravans had proven so popular that Byam was forced to limit his future trips exclusively to Airstreamers. "I was out to have fun," Byam explained, "to show people how to travel by trailer and to build international goodwill. But the caravans got too big to handle."

The Wally Byam Caravan Club was chartered in 1956—a propitious time for the birth of a society of recreational vagabonds. The Korean War was over. Gas was plentiful and cheap. In an increasingly mobile economy, trailer travel was finally gaining social acceptability, a fact evidenced by the release of the Lucille Ball and Desi Arnaz movie, *The Long, Long Trailer.* And with the passage of the Interstate Highway Act the following year, the largest federal road system in world history was rapidly being blasted from the bedrock.

The club led tours through Canada, Central America, and Cuba, where President Batista personally greeted the caravanners outside his palace in Havana. But it was in 1958 that Byam came up with the most quixotic dream of his career: a trailer caravan through Africa from Cape Town to Cairo.

It didn't take long for the pied piper to find one hundred takers. "He could really paint a picture," says Helen Schwamborn, recalling how Byam charmed his African caravanners. "He made traveling sound so exotic and glamorous. He had a captive audience whenever he got to talking about all the wonderful scenery and the animals and birds. He made Africa sound like a dreamland. The way Wally painted the picture, no one ever stopped to think about all the hardships the trip would involve. Sometimes he'd really stretch things and I'd have to say, 'Now Wally—you know that's not true!' And he'd say, 'Oh, what difference does it make? You can see they're enjoying it!' "

The trek would require a year of planning, including meetings with State Department officials in Washington and Vice President Richard Nixon. Finally in 1959, 41 Airstreams were shipped by sea to South Africa. Heading north from Cape Town, the 101 caravanners traveled for eight months and covered nearly 15,000 miles, often on roads that were so bad, as Byam later put it, "not even the elephants would walk on them." The media dubbed the Airstreamers "the Lost Caravan," because they had a habit of disappearing for weeks at a time. On some legs of the journey, they averaged no more than three miles a day, and on several occasions they even had to build their own roads and pontoon bridges. In the Belgian Congo, the natives mistook the Airstreamers for an army that had come to liberate them from the colonial authorities. A pygmy tribe in Uganda thought they were gods. On the cratered moonscape of southern Ethiopia, the caravan lost twenty-two truck axles in a single day. In Addis Ababa, the Airstreamers were invited to park on Haile Selassie's imperial race track, where late at night packs of hyenas came down from the hills to scavenge their refuse.

Byam looked like Livingstone in his pith helmet and safari khakis, a French interpreter standing by his side. Tribal chiefs often assumed he was a king, so he had to act like one, making up protocol as he went. During his visits with Haile Selassie, Byam was careful to keep his hands tightly clasped together, since he had been warned that touching the Lion of Judah would be taken as a serious insult. The demands of the trip made Byam unusually surly at times; one member who disputed him was left behind in Ethiopia. He spent his evening hours dictating the book *Here and Abroad*. Periodically he sent little green recording discs back to the company engineers with instructions for improvements and modifications in trailer design. Byam was sixty-three and in good health, but in the final months of the African caravan, his eyesight started to fail him.

Back in the United States, he went to see an ophthalmologist, who, in turn, sent him to a neurologist. The diagnosis was grim: Byam had a brain tumor. He underwent several unsuccessful operations, and then was confined to a hospital bed in his Los Angeles house. On July 22, 1962, Mr. Trailer, the man who once said "life begins at sixty," died at the age of sixty-five.

The club kept growing after his death, and the caravans continued unabated. In 1964, over a hundred Airstreamers took an around-the-world hopscotch from Los Angeles to Lisbon that lasted 403 days. An Asian trip had long been the personal dream of Byam, who wrote that one day his followers would form "a mechanized caravan threading the trail that spice-bearing camels once trod, bringing . . . the products, philosophy, and goodwill of a whole new way of life." The trek was documented in a series of travel films narrated by Vincent Price which showed, among other things, elephants pulling trailers from the mud in Siam and Airstreamers baking apple pies in the Afghan desert. The caravan even ventured behind the Iron Curtain, at one point parking its Airstreams on the grounds of Red Square.

By the late 1960s, Airstream had established itself as the undisputed king of the RV industry's luxury-class rigs, spawning a host of look-alike competitors with names like Streamline, Avion, and the Silver Streak. By 1975, the Wally Byam Caravan Cub had swelled to twenty-four thousand members, and the international rallies were drawing ten thousand pilgrims each year. But the oil embargoes during the Carter administration diminished the popularity of RVing, while shoddy construction resulting from new corporate management nearly finished off the Airstream company in the late 1970s.

Thor Industries, Airstream's parent company since 1980, has done much to recover Airstream's prestige, but it hasn't been able to erase the fact that RVing has become a life-style in decline, even as the country ages. Airstream's major competitior, Avion, suspended operations in 1990, and most other manufacturers have been sustaining heavy losses. The club, which has a natural attrition rate (on average 350 WBCCI members pass away each year), has had to redouble its "recruitment and retention" efforts.

Yet unlike many other RVs, Airstream draws committed caravanners who are less likely to drop out with the vagaries of the economy or increases in gasoline prices. Veteran Airstreamers like Frank Sargent of Fort Meyers, Florida, will tell you that the Wally Byam Club appeals to something in people that will never go out of fashion. A retired engineer whose numerous patented inventions include the Porta Potti (a portable toilet), Sargent worked with Byam on the early principles of self-containment and now wears Byam's mantle as the club high priest. It was Sargent who organized a month-long Airstream caravan through China in 1985. "Why do people go caravanning?" Sargent poses. "Well, you might as well ask, Why do people go fishing? Why do people go hunting? It's not for subsistence or survival anymore. No, it's something elemental. The nomadic instinct is something that's deep in us. It's an instinct as old and powerful as our need to stare into an open fire. People for thousands of generations have moved in caravans. Gadding around in groups is a part of what we are. It fulfills the tribal instinct."

It's a bright Thursday morning in South Bend, and the Silver City is rapidly being dismantled. The Byamites are folding up their lawn chairs, ratcheting down their awnings, and packing up their bottles of sunscreen lotion. Wally Byam Control has fizzled off the air. Caravans are heading up and moving out in all directions. Teams from the garbage committee are scouring the abandoned parking lots, picking up litter.

In Blue-7, Jaimie and Susan King of New Bern, North Carolina (#7018), are preparing to shove off for Missouri and parts west. As self-described "youngies" (they are both in their fifties), the Kings represent the future of the Wally Byam Club. A semiretired human physiology professor who wears a zip-up astronaut suit, Jaimie climbs into the driving center of his 28-foot turbo diesel motor home and fires up the big rock-cruncher engine. He then runs down a safety checklist that would probably satisfy the FAA, while Susan scurries around in back securing everything. "How's the refrigerator?" he inquires.

"The refrigerator is locked."

"I got the porch platform, but how about the bomb bay doors?"

"They are closed and locked."

"Countertop?"

"Secured."

"Tables?"

"Secured."

"Bathroom sink all right?"

"Secured."

"And the bathroom mirror?"

"It is . . . locked."

"Water pump?"

"It is . . . off."

"How about the water heater?"

"Off."

"Well okey-dokey," Jaimie proclaims, Notre Dame receding in his side-view mirrors. "That's it. WE ARE ROLLING!"

The Burled Gates
of Nome

The Iditarod Trail, Alaska

I. ANCHORAGE

THE HOWL OF 1,400 HUSKIES is unsettling, a desperate caterwaul that sounds, by turns, like a starved coyote, a snared rabbit, and a cat in heat. The urge to pull ripples in the lean muscles, smolders in the yellow lupine eyes.

"THIRTY SECONDS!" booms the announcer's voice.

The word "sled dog" conjures up a sturdy malamute, but these are small dogs, rangy and fine-boned, with a hint of grey-hound or whippet lurking somewhere in their Siberian genes. Buck, the proud protagonist in Jack London's *The Call of the Wild*, weighed 140 pounds. These dogs are a third that size, but they are deceptively powerful. Once in the traces, the huskies lunge with all their tensile strength, feet clawing the ground, rib cages heaving, hairs bristling, the diamond-patterned harnesses pulled taut on their backs—

"FIFTEEN SECONDS!"

—so that teams of five or more men must hold back the lines to keep the dogs from skittering down the trail before their time has come.

"Five . . . four . . . three . . . two . . . one . . . *Go!*"

At eight A.M. on the starting day of the 1990 Iditarod Sled
Dog Race, the chute at Fourth and D streets in downtown Anchorage is a blare of klieg lights and hot-colored racing gear.
The race officials have trucked in snow by the ton to create a
temporary sled trail on the city streets. Though the Alaskan
interior has been suffering record cold temperatures this week,
it's a balmy 35°F in Anchorage on this Saturday morning in early
March, and the dogs are burning up, their tongues hanging out,
lapping up snow. The starting line is plastered with sponsorship
slogans: Iams Eukanuba Dog Food, Pemmican Jerky, Timberland Boots. Standing before the cameras of ABC's *Wide World
of Sports* is announcer Lynn Swann, former wide receiver for
the Pittsburgh Steelers, a black Adonis in a chic down parka. A
tape of Jimmy Buffett's "Margaritaville" pours over the crowd
of fifteen thousand spectators while beefy bouncers in fox pelt
caps police the barricades.

In back of the chute, several hundred dog handlers are
sorting and stacking Ziploc bags of meat and lard. Nylon harnesses lie in heaps on the sidewalks. Dander hangs in the air.
Every few minutes another pickup truck arrives with a fresh
cargo of huskies, the excited dogs peeping through small round
holes in their kennel compartments. Each musher has an identifying ink stain slathered on his dogs' flanks. Everywhere is the
reek of excrement. Vats of dog gruel cook on Coleman stoves.
Steam rises from a hundred yellow puddles in the snow.

The mushers inch their way to the chute, with a new team
blasting off every two minutes: Greasy-haired Norsemen just in
from the bush. Arctic jocks waddling in their fat mukluks and
vapor barrier boots. Miners in floppy Yazoo hats, grizzled loggers and wildcatters, Yukon River rats. They work in a flurry
of ripping Velcro and slippery layers of Gore-Tex. They hop
on their runners, test their footbrakes, fuss with the stanchions
on their sleds. Tim Osmar of Clam Gulch. Emmitt Peters of
Ruby. Rick Mackey of Trapper Creek. Now comes Joe Runyan, the wonderboy strategist who raises homing pigeons in his
spare time. Now comes Col. Norman Vaughan, the oldest man
in the race at eighty-four, a 1929 graduate of Harvard who
mushed in an exhibition race at the 1932 Winter Olympics at
Lake Placid and accompanied Admiral Byrd on his first expedi-

tions in Antarctica. Then Martin Buser of Big Lake. Lavon Barve of Wasilla. Bill Hickel, the Anchorage millionaire, son of the governor. Two minutes later it's the infamous Poodle Man, John Suter, the dreamer who dares to run a team of standard poodles in place of huskies.

"ONE MINUTE!"

Susan Butcher slides into the chute, and the crowd gives her a hearty salutation. A hyperkinetic woman with rosy cheeks and thick brown hair pulled back in a braid, Butcher has assembled the fastest dog teams in the annals of the Iditarod. But the crowd's applause seems more an expression of awe than endearment. While Susan Butcher is probably the most famous person in Alaska, she is by no means a universally loved figure. A lot of the old sourdoughs think Butcher is a hoyden, the kind of brazen hussy who would trample over her own mother to get to the finish line first. Perhaps her unpopularity is simply a reflection of wounded male pride in a state once dominated by manly men. After Libby Riddles's victory in 1985 and Butcher's three consecutive Iditarod wins in 1986, 1987, and 1988, Alaskan men have good reason to despair for their gender. A popular T-shirt proclaims the bitter truth, "Alaska: Where Men Are Men and Women Win the Iditarod."

"THIRTY SECONDS!"

Butcher lives with her husband, Dave Monson, in a cabin near the Tanana River west of Fairbanks. She works with her 150 dogs every day. Fame has brought her corporate manna. Unlike many of the mushers, who have to piece together paltry sums from local establishments like Homesteaders Hardware or the Alaska Dairy Goat Association, Butcher retains heavyweight sponsors like Purina Dog Food, Timberland, and 7-Eleven Stores. She looks like an F-14 pilot in her black goggles and her high-tech bodysuit by Allied Fibers. Her seventeen huskies are all proud-looking specimens, alert, attuned to her every movement, surefooted in their matching black neoprene booties.

"Ten . . . nine . . . eight . . ."

Susan hugs Sluggo, her trusty lead dog, then mounts her sled. She grips the handlebar with one hand, and waves triumphantly to the crowds with the other.

"Go get 'em Susan!"

". . . five . . . four . . . three . . . two . . . one . . . *Go!*"

Butcher tears out of the chute, her neck slightly whip-lashing from the initial jolt. Her runners scrape through the crusty snow as her dogs bound forward at twenty miles an hour.

"See you in Nome, Susan!" cries the Iditarod announcer.

Now a silver-haired leprechaun edges toward the chute. He is seventy-three years old and has a hearing aid in each ear. He flashes the crowd a sly grin, his gray eyes twinkling mischief. He carefully unsnarls his gangline with the patience of an old fisherman. His small wrinkled face is scratched and studded with gray beard stubble. He wears a blue baseball cap that says "Eagle Pack Premium Pet Food."

"ONE MINUTE!"

His five handlers are locked in a tug-of-war with the dogs. He wobbles over to his sled and calmly parks himself on the runners. In a soft grandfatherly voice that is barely audible, he calls to his handlers, tells them to let go of the dogs. The huskies spring forward, and the sled lurches to the starting line. "Whoa!" he cries.

"THIRTY SECONDS!"

The announcer's voice crackles over the loudspeakers: "Please give a warm welcome to Joe Redington, Father of the Iditarod!"

A deafening cheer wells up from the crowd. Everyone knows Joe Redington. He's a household name from Anchorage to Prudhoe Bay. Alaskans wake up every morning to the sound of his voice on TV ads for Maxwell House coffee and Tang breakfast crystals. Redington is called the Father of the Iditarod because he invented it. It was Redington who in the late 1960s came up with the idea of running a sled dog marathon across the forgotten trails of the Alaskan interior. He saw the race as a way to revive the lost art of mushing, a tradition that had all but died in the tracks of the snowmobile. "When I first came to Alaska, there was a dog team behind every house," Redington recalls. "They was the people's means of transportation, their wood and water. But when the snowmachines come along in the early sixties, people started getting rid of the dogs, because you didn't have to feed that snowmachine. I decided something had to be done. We had to make a reason for keeping the dogs. So we decided on the race."

Not only did Redington concoct the Iditarod, he has raced in it for the last sixteen years, finishing as high as fifth place.

Despite his advanced age, Redington is generally recognized as one of the top twenty mushers in the world.

Redington, who has raised huskies ever since he came to Alaska in 1948, has developed a line of racing dogs with tight feet, tough pads, and an unbridled desire to run. Mushers from all over Alaska speak of "a Redington dog" as if it were a distinct breed. Three quarters of all the huskies that run in the Iditarod race are "Redington dogs," or their direct descendants. And today Redington's Knik Kennel is the largest sled dog operation in Alaska, housing as many as 450 dogs at a time. "I've always had more dogs than the average person," he says.

If Redington had never dreamed up the Iditarod, he'd still be a legend in these parts. In Alaska, of course, legends come a dime a dozen, so you have to discriminate. Every old-timer has a grizzly bear story, or some tall tale about surviving an airplane crash in the Brooks Range. But Joe Redington is the real McCoy. You will find him on every Alaskan's short list of certifiable folk heroes. Never mind that he's a quivery old gnome who stands five-foot-six and is deaf as a post. He is the dean of the Alaskan tough guys. The *Los Angeles Times* once called him "The Toughest Man in Alaska."

People say that Joe Redington has a guardian angel. He's the sort of man who has a knack for getting into fixes from which he then miraculously extricates himself. He's been missing and presumed dead on more occasions than his wife, Vi, likes to recall. Her motto is "Try Not to Worry."

On the Iditarod Trail, he's often tumbling off his sled, smashing into trees, colliding with a snowmachine, or slipping through the ice and getting a bad case of chilblain. But so far he's always made it home to tell the tale. "I don't scare too easy," he boasts. "Maybe I ain't too smart. Because I think sometimes it might pay to get scared."

Redington has lived the Alaskan life with gusto—as homesteader, commercial fisherman, bush pilot, guide, and dog team runner for the Army's Search and Rescue Unit, pulling plane wrecks and corpses from the mountains. Once he and his protégée Susan Butcher took a team of dogs to the summit of Mount McKinley (it had never been done before). On one occasion he crashed his plane in the wilderness, straightened out the propeller between two trees, cut a runway out of an alder stand, and flew out six days later. Once when he was mushing a starving dog team through a blizzard, he had to slaughter his weakest huskies and feed them to the others. In 1981 the Alaska governor sent Redington to Washington, D.C., to "mush" a team of dogs down Pennsylvania Avenue in President Reagan's inaugural parade. In a mysterious caper reported in *The Washington Post*, two Maryland youths stole Redington's dog team, but police found the huskies in a Gaithersburg basement hours before the parade. In the end, Redington's team and his sled (equipped with rollers) made the historic trek down Pennsylvania. "It was good mushing!" he remembers fondly.

Redington bristles at the name some of the younger mushers have given themselves. "I'm not a 'dog driver.' I'm a musher. There are all kinds of damn drivers. Pile drivers. Screwdrivers. Truck drivers. I don't want to be no driver. I'm a dog musher. I don't like the word 'driver' because it sounds like you're driving your dogs into the ground. I mush dogs that loves to go. If I tried to drive my dogs with a whip they'd just look back at me like I was crazy."

French Canadians in the Yukon Territory used to shout, "*Marchez*!" (meaning "Go!"), but few racers today actually use the command "mush." This is a matter of some concern to Redington. "The public loves to hear 'Mush,' " he insists. "They don't want to hear 'Hike' or 'Go,' or something else. They want to hear 'Mush,' and that's what I use. I learned it from an old mail carrier who came to Alaska in nineteen and four. If that's what the old-timers used then that's good enough for me. I say it good and sharp. When I start my dogs out I say, 'Mush!' "

This morning Redington was running so late that he almost didn't make it to the starting line. His truck was acting up again. "Dang fuel pump went out," he complains. Redington is always having trouble with his old Sierra Classic truck. Right now it's parked in back of the chute, a rusted-out behemoth covered in bright orange stickers that say "Tang Breakfast Crystals." The truck's front end wears the evidence of a recent collision with a moose. The front bumper is badly twisted, the hood sprung, the grille mashed and bent. Dried moose blood is spattered everywhere.

"Gentlemen, start your engines!"

"Ten . . . nine . . . eight . . ."

"Well, I gotta go."

"Six . . . five . . . four."

"Tear em up, Joe!"

"Three . . . two . . . one . . ."

"Smoke 'em!"

"*Go!*"

"Mush!" Redington calls to his huskies. He yells it good and sharp.

"Iditarod" is an Athabascan Indian word that means "A Far Distant Place." Once there was a town called Iditarod, a gold mining outpost on a tributary of a tributary of the Yukon River. Iditarod flourished for a decade during the early 1900s, but today it's a ghost town of vacant saloons, a tumbledown rooming house, a brothel of buckled lumber. The race passes through the ruins every other year, but otherwise, the trail has little to do with Iditarod, geographically or historically.

Still, it's a fitting name for the world's longest mushing marathon, for no one really knows how many miles separate the chute in Anchorage from the burled arch in Nome. Some say it's 1,200 miles, some say more. The "official" count is 1,049 miles, but that's a symbolic figure: One thousand, because it's at least that many miles, and forty-nine because Alaska is the forty-ninth state. The oft-mentioned comparison is to imagine a trek from Kansas City to Los Angeles, except without roads. The race crosses two mountain ranges—the Alaska and the Kuskokwim—and some two dozen rivers. Running northwest from Anchorage, the mushers pass through three distinct cultures: European, Athabascan Indian, and Eskimo. Once they cross the Susitna River near Willow, fifty miles north of Anchorage, they vanish from civilization for the better part of two weeks.

The citizens of Alaska follow the mushers' progress across the tundra with keen interest. In bars from Homer to Fairbanks, conversation turns to sled dogs. Every morning the *Anchorage Times* reports the statistics of the seventy mushers as they pass through the race's twenty-five checkpoints. Who's ahead at Rainy Pass? Has Butcher taken her twenty-four-hour layover yet? What was Buser's time between Nulato and Kaltag?

Mushers are Alaska's baseball heroes, Alaska's Hollywood stars, Alaska's astronauts. But they are more than that: They are avatars of the North Country romance of the the strong dog and the beautiful cruel enveloping cold. Alaskans have very definite ideas about what it means to be an Alaskan, and running a team of huskies is one of them. Alaskans call the rest of the United States "Outside," and the term is usually spoken with a note of condescension. Outside is that big parking lot down there where life is artificial and canned and picked over. People don't just drift to Alaska; they come to get away from Outside. Something drives them there. And whatever it is, the underlying reason for their moving to Alaska is never far removed from the land itself, and from an image of the way life ought to be lived in relation to the land. In this sense, mushers are the proto-Alaskans. The musher is to Alaska what the surfer is to Hawaii, what the cowboy is to Texas or Montana. "Coming to Alaska," Joe Redington says, "had always been my dream from the first time I read Jack London's books. I knew that someday I would wind up in Alaska. This is what I was looking for from the time I was born—trapping, outdoor living, mushing. When I came here in 1948, I was probably in the state fifteen minutes when I bought my first sled-dog puppy at a filling station just inside the line. I was always kind of a gypsy. I slept out all my life. I've lived more in a tent than I have in a house. In fact, I hate a damn house."

The days of the Klondike gold rush are gone, and the bush plane has long since supplanted the dog team as the principal carrier of mail and supplies. But it is comforting for Alaskans to know that somewhere in their state people are still mushing dogs, keeping the old arts alive. It is ironic, and perhaps a hallmark of the national culture, that it took a manufactured event—a high profile race with a $50,000 first prize—to save a tradition that originally grew out of necessity. Huskies were once the arctic camels; now they've become the arctic thoroughbreds.

Alaskans like to say that they have three seasons: winter, summer, and Iditarod. It is a preposterous event, audacious, quixotic—a pageant worthy of the vast dimensions of the landscape. The race represents Alaska's rebuke of winter. It is a statewide triumph over cabin fever, that gray malady that descends over the North Country.

The Iditarod is only two decades old, but Alaskans speak of it as though it were an ancient ritual sprung from the hyperborean mist, an event without origins. The Iditarod is simply what Alaskans do, a natural outgrowth of the culture. Alaska is a land of migration, where the rhythms of life are marked by the movement of species across great distances. The sockeye salmon make their trek up the Yukon, the caribou herds tramp the steppes with the seasons, the gray whales migrate with the shifting ice floes of the Chukchi Sea. In the context of Alaska, the Iditarod race is simply another peregrination of the species, an exodus sure as clockwork. Never mind that it's perilous to man and dog alike. You might as well tell the young men of Pamplona to stop running their bulls. As a former mayor of Nome puts it, "The Iditarod is what Alaska lives on for the rest of the year."

The Iditarod race commemorates, and was in part inspired by, an earlier race across Alaska—in this case, a race against death. In January of 1925, a diphtheria epidemic broke out in the town of Nome. The deathly contagion crept from one house to the next, with new cases reported hourly. Serum supplies were exhausted. Authorities were unable to summon airplane pilots to rush the desperately needed medicine to Nome, so a group of nineteen dog mushers, led by the famed Norwegian dog driver Leonhard Seppala, formed a relay across the state. A package of 300,000 units of antitoxin was raced by train from Anchorage to the railhead at Nenana; from then on, the serum was in the hands of the dog mushers, who sprinted westward 674 miles in the dead of winter, passing through many of the same villages that serve today as Iditarod checkpoints. Seppala's mission of mercy made headlines around the world. *The New York Times* ran the story on page one for a week. "BLIZZARD DELAYS NOME RELIEF DOGS IN THE FINAL DASH," one headline despaired. "ALL COMMUNICATION LOST; EPIDEMIC STILL GAINING." Seppala ran the final leg of the relay with his prized team of twenty Siberian huskies. The serum arrived in Nome after 170 hours in transit, and the epidemic was averted. Seppala later made a trip with his huskies to the Lower 48, and received a hero's welcome from San Francisco to Boston. Today a statue of his lead dog, Balto, stands near the arsenal in New York's Central Park. Upon his death in 1967, Seppala's ashes were sprinkled over the Iditarod Trail.

There are other sled dog races of note, such as the Yukon Quest in Canada and the John Beargrease Invitational in Minnesota. But the Iditarod is the world's premier mushing marathon. Designated a National Historic Trail by the Bureau of

Land Management, the Iditarod has become a mythic destination. Dog aficionados from Europe and the Lower 48 come to volunteer at the checkpoints, haul dog food, fly planes, or man the ham radios. This year a group of amateur mushers from Kalamazoo, Michigan, (following Seppala's precedent) has come to Alaska to spread the ashes of a beloved friend over the trail. "He always wanted to run the Iditarod," explains the dead man's best friend. "So we thought, well, this would be the next best thing."

THEY SAY ANCHORAGE IS ONLY a thirty-minute drive from Alaska—the *real* Alaska, the Alaska of the Yukon River, the uncharted wildernesses of spruce and alder. But even in Anchorage, a generic modern city of shopping malls and reflective glass office towers and two hundred thousand tax-paying citizens of the United States of America, you can feel the precarious perch of civilization. To the east, the Chugach Mountains hang in icy silence. Lapping at the southern flanks of the city is the Cook Inlet, a narrow finger of seawater filled with dirty blocks of ice. And to the north, Mount McKinley gleams like rock candy through the dense banks of fog.

It's the real Alaska that has Jack Niggemyer worried. Niggemyer is a rusty-bearded ale keg of a man who looks like Kris Kringle in his youth. As the manager of the Iditarod race, Niggemyer is in charge of this moveable feast of people, dogs, airplanes, snowmobiles, and cargo. Quick-tempered, given to expletives, Niggemyer calls himself the "race manager from hell." Over the course of the two-week marathon, he will have to contend with mushers' egos, overzealous reporters, Humane Society do-gooders, arcane race rules, and the demands of a limited budget. But his chief struggle will be against Nature itself. "You gotta have brain damage to want this job," he contends.

The Iditarod bylaws state that under no circumstances will the race be postponed by weather. But this year Niggemeyer is having second thoughts. "Things are as bad as they could possibly be," he reports. "This is our worst Iditarod nightmare come true."

In addition to the usual vagaries of Alaskan weather—high winds, subzero temperatures, blizzards, and overflow ice—this year there is the matter of the volcano. Mount Redoubt has

Joe Redington, Sr. Father of the Iditarod.

BELOW: Champion musher Leonhard Seppala and his Siberians in 1916.

Iditarod champion Susan Butcher with her lead dog Sluggo.

blown its stack for the third time this week, and a dark canopy of ash has descended over much of southern Alaska. More eruptions are expected later in the week, with possible earth tremors to follow. Much of the Iditarod trail is now coated in brown soot. As Niggemeyer knows, volcanic ash can wreak havoc on a race. It irritates the mushers' eyes and burns their lungs, forcing them to cough up blood. The abrasive granules wear down the slick plastic emulsion on the runners of the sleds. But the ash is hardest on the dogs: It works into their paws and causes their footpads to crack and bleed. When they become thirsty on the trail, the dogs eat the ash-covered snow, and many of them become ill.

"I can't do anything about the volcano," Niggemeyer protests. "Although I guess we could start looking for virgins to sacrifice."

Then there's what Niggemeyer calls the "moose situation." Record snows this year have caused thousands of moose to starve to death. A starving moose is an ornery and unpredictable creature, with a nasty habit of stomping anything that gets in its path. To defend themselves and their teams, the mushers have to pack firearms. Generally mushers don't like to shoot a moose unless they absolutely must; race rules stipulate that if a musher kills an animal on the trail, he has to gut it on the spot and arrange for the meat to be salvaged. Gutting a thousand-pound moose is a particularly bloody affair, and it can take the better part of a day, especially in 30-below weather.

"Do what you have to do, guys," Niggemeyer tells the mushers at a prestart meeting. "But please don't go out there like a bunch of Rambos, shootin' every moose you see. We don't want the trail to be strewn with carcasses."

As for other wild animals, Niggemeyer is optimistic. "Hopefully, we won't have to worry about wolves and bears," he predicts, "though there have been some sightings of killer bison."

II. MCGRATH

A SPECK OF CIVILIZATION at the confluence of the Takotna and Kuskokwim rivers, McGrath is definitely the "real Alaska." It is a mining outpost in the frozen heart of the bush, with a population that is so small that the entire phone directory is printed on one page. This time of year, the only way to get to McGrath is by air or dog team. The few cars and trucks that you find on the streets were flown in by C-130 transport plane. Driving here is like driving on an island: The roads all peter out a few miles beyond the city limits. Until the FAA finally built a fence around the runway, McGrath was famous for being the only place in Alaska where a bush pilot could taxi up to a bar.

The McGrath checkpoint is 415 miles from Anchorage, and about a third of the way to Nome. To get here, the mushers have to cross the Alaska Range and traverse some of the most treacherous landscape on earth. The mushers speak in particularly ominous tones about a certain stretch called the Farewell Burn, a 90-mile ghostland of charred stumps and felled trees that was the site of a major forest fire in the late 1970s.

It's 20 below and sunny on the morning we arrive in McGrath. The town is buried under seventy inches of snow. I am staying with my wife in a tiny apartment attached to the rear of the local Catholic church. Snowmachines race through the streets. The blue sky is aswarm with Cessnas and Piper Cubs. A communications tower winks from a bald mountain in the distance.

The Miners Cafe is a greasy spoon near the runway. The sign out front says NO INTOXICATED PEOPLE ALLOWED. Moose antlers hang over the doorway, and KSKO-AM constantly chirps messages over a little transistor radio: *"A blue mitten was found outside the school this morning . . ."*

The cafe is run by a stout temperamental woman from the Azores named Rosa. A pinup calendar featuring a picture of Rosa's bikini-clad daughter is tacked over the cash register. The reporter from *The Anchorage Times* is sucking on Skoal and hammering out tomorrow morning's story on his Tandy laptop. Lynn Swann saunters into the cafe with a bevy of adoring women from the ABC Sports crew. Next to him, a klatsch of veterinarians play gin rummy and stare into the snowbanks, waiting for the dogs to come in.

For hours and days, we huddle in the wet warmth of the cafe nursing cups of bad instant coffee and bowls of greasy chili, trying to imagine the ordeal that the mushers must be going through right now somewhere to the east, grateful that it's them and not us, and yet vaguely envious of their experience. Every hour or so we hear Jack Niggemyer shouting orders over the radio and then tremble as he storms into the cafe spewing bile in all directions.

Rick Swenson is the first musher into McGrath. An auburn-haired, mustachioed man sponsored by the Iams dog food company, Swenson is a swaggering musher of the old school, the kind of blunt and crusty man you might read about in one of Robert William Service's paeans to the Yukon Territory. Swenson is one of the greatest sled dog drivers in Alaskan history, and the only musher who has won more Iditarods than his arch rival, Susan Butcher. Swenson makes a quick pitstop in McGrath, and then slips out of town under cover of night. But a mile down the trail, he confronts a hungry moose cow and her calf. The moose charges and stomps two of the dogs before Swenson can pull his team around; he sprints back to McGrath with his injured dogs riding in the basket and waits until the break of morning.

Joe Redington lurches into town at eight the next night under a full moon. He parks his team behind the house of an old friend. "Gotta feed my doggies," he mutters as he stirs up a kettle of gruel. The dogs eat ravenously, then curl up in straw beds and fall fast asleep, their muscles still twitching in their dreams. Redington waddles into the house and pulls off his mukluks. He sits down at the dining room table and quietly sips a mug of hot Tang. What he really wants, strangely enough, is an ice-cold chocolate milk shake, but he's out of luck. "I'm afraid McGrath isn't a milk shake town," he grouses.

A combination of stormy weather and volcanic ash has left three of Redington's dogs in sorry shape. He has decided to "drop" them here at the McGrath checkpoint. An official veterinarian will examine the dogs and then they'll be flown back east to a prison near Anchorage, where the inmates will look after them until the race is over.

Earlier in the race, Redington reports, he got into a potentially lethal scrape with a mad moose, but his guardian angel was with him again. He was mushing near the Big Susitna River on a narrow trail when the moose encountered his team. "He come right down the gangline. He never touched a single dog, the sled, or me. It was a nice moose. It didn't hurt anything. But I noticed when it went over the top of me, my headlamp shined right up in his eyes, and they looked as big as eggs. I think it was scared."

What about you? I ask.

"Well, I wasn't really scared. If you'd had something to check my pulse, I don't think it would have ever changed. I didn't feel any different at all. Just went on down the trail."

Redington had another trying experience near Rainy Pass. "It was real windy, and the hillsides were steep. I couldn't find the trail. It was all blown over. There were about a dozen teams out there, and we was going in all directions, the dogs just spinning around and around. We was having quite a time out there. At one point my team got wrapped around a tree." He laughs.

I have to ask him: Given the moose and the ice storms and the sleeplessness and the lashing winds, is mushing . . . *fun?*

"There's times when it's miserable," he concedes, "and I might say, why in the hell am I out here, fighting this cold? But if you've ever run a team on a nice moonlit night with the northern lights flashing out there, you'd see why. When you're out there all alone, and the only sound is the runners, and the dogs are going along at a good clip like they're enjoying it, it's a feeling that you'd have to do to know exactly what it was like."

III. UNALAKLEET

THE FLIGHT BY BUSH PLANE from McGrath to the Eskimo village of Unalakleet takes a little over a hour and costs $500. My wife and I decide on Wilbur Air because Wilbur seems like a nice enough fellow, and he needs the work. He is a taciturn man with an office right on the runway in McGrath.

We leave McGrath on a dazzling cold morning, 10 below. Wilbur takes us over the Kuskokwim Range, then buzzes the Iditarod checkpoints of Takotna and Ophir. From the air, the stunted spruce trees look like beard stipple. The trail appears as a tiny hairline in the blue-gray snow, occasionally cross-hatched with the footprints of a rabbit or wolf.

Between checkpoints, we spot a lone musher swallowed in wilderness. His sled dips into a swale, then scratches across a mile-long mirror of glare ice. He looks up at us and waves. Though much of the trail is marked by tripods and red fluorescent tape, in some stretches it's nothing more than a faint depression in the crusted powder.

From Ophir, Wilbur banks southwest across the Beaver Mountains and flies over the ghost town of Iditarod—not a soul in sight. We pass over the frozen swampland known as the muskeg, a hundred miles of raw country without roads or fences or the subtlest markings of man. Then we come to the mighty Yukon, a ribbon of ice that stretches north and south to the horizons. It is said that no one can call himself a true Alaskan until he has peed in the Yukon. The mushers treat the wide-open river as a superhighway; it is here on the flat ice cap that they pour on the steam for the final dash to the coast.

Now Unalakleet slides into view, a snug village huddled against the floes.

Unalakleet is an Eskimo word meaning "where the sea wind blows," and that is a meet description. The wind in question is strong and cold, and comes directly from Siberia. Unalakleet is where the Iditarod Trail joins the Bering Sea coast. The rest of the race will be run here on the ice shelf; the route follows the Norton Sound, then hooks west for a straight shot down the Seward Peninsula. The mushers dread the winter storms that can develop suddenly along the Sound, with gale-force winds that blow snow horizontally and cause whiteout conditions. In such blizzards, the dogs' eyes have been known to seal shut with ice, forcing a musher to stop every mile or so to pry them apart.

This afternoon Unalakleet is abuzz. Lavon "The Silent One" Barve, the frontrunner, has just blown into town, with Joe Runyan and Susan Butcher in hot pursuit. The town's main drag is choked with snowmachines—Blue Maxes, Yamahas, Ski-Doos. The ABC helicopter has landed, and camera crews are hauling gear up to the Lodge, the town's only inn. It seems that *Wide World of Sports* has booked up all the rooms, so we must sleep in the school gym with the din of the ham radios.

My wife and I spread out our sleeping bags under one of the basketball goals. Then we walk out to the ice to watch the sun sink over Siberia. We see an Eskimo boy with a rifle slung over his shoulder returning from an unsuccessful seal hunt.

There's a ruckus on the main drag. Though it's 20 below zero, Lynn Swann, dressed in Spandex tights and an ABC parka, is out *jogging*. He is followed by a trail of laughing Eskimo kids, many of whom have never seen a black man before—except on TV.

At the Lodge restaurant I meet a young Unalakleet resident named Warren. He wears thick black-rimmed glasses. He confesses he is bored with Unalakleet, wants to move to Anchorage and become a travel agent. "Time to move on," he frowns. "Get something going."

Warren says the Iditarod is the most exciting time of year. So many people, so much commotion. Warren is collecting the autographs of every musher who passes through town. He can talk about the mushers for hours. He knows them by name and number, knows where they live and how many dogs they've dropped and who their sponsors are. He feasts on the incidental details. He listens to the radio for the updates. He wants Susan Butcher to win two more Iditarods to "shut Swenson up."

Unalakleet has a population of 850, most of whom are Eskimos. Social life revolves around bingo at the Igloo Arcade. Many of the Eskimo residents still rely on a subsistence life-style of trapping, hunting, and fishing with the seasons. Unalakleet is a "damp" town, which means that you can drink alcohol, but you can't buy it. Still, alcoholism is rampant. Warren says the black market is brisk. "You want a pint of Gilbey's? Thirty dollars."

Now Butcher skids into town unnoticed. She parks her team behind a house and scatters some straw. She inspects her dogs' feet, then warms up several buckets of food. She works in tiny quick jerks, her hands moving fast over the lines and harnesses, her body wheeling about, her eyelids blinking rapidly in concentration.

Finally the reporters descend on her. "All right, fellas," she relents. "Five minutes."

Are you worried about Barve?

"Well, Barve's got a really good team," she acknowledges. "But I know what I have to do with him. I've already calculated what I can afford to give him. I'm more worried about Runyan. I don't know where he is with his speed. We keep trading off going faster and slower. So I gotta watch him."

What's your strategy from here on?

"I want to shed those guys early and really make a push here on the coast."

As it happens, Susan Butcher used to live in Unalakleet years ago. She worked on a musk ox farm just out of town. It was here in 1975 that Butcher first met Joe Redington, who ran a local fish processing plant in the summer. They discovered that they shared a love for sled dogs and soon became close friends. In the fall, Butcher followed Redington to Knik and lived in a tent on his property for three months, training sled dogs from his kennel. Redington became a mentor for Butcher. "I adore Joe," she says. "And I give him an immense amount of credit for teaching me what a real Alaskan is supposed to be. He taught me the patience to deal with adversity as it comes. I should have been raised a Redington."

THE VILLAGE ELDER OF UNALAKLEET is a ninety-one-year-old man named John Auliye. He is a friendly man whose eyes are clouded with cataracts. He invites us in, offers us a bag of Nacho Cheese Doritos. His modest cabin is cluttered with caribou hides and ivory carvings. A game of solitaire lies unfinished on the dining room table beside a bottle of seal oil. A crucifix hangs on the wall.

John Auliye has witnessed two great episodes of Alaskan history. He served with Colonel Muktuk Marston's Alaskan Scouts when they liberated the Aleutian Islands from the Japanese in World War II. And he mushed a leg of the 1925 serum run to Nome, driving a dog team from Shaktoolik to Moses Point, where he passed the diphtheria antitoxin on to Leonhard Seppala. "I didn't know anything about the medicine," he recalls, "but I was willing to take it even if I didn't get paid. If you help people, blessings come back. That's true, you know. Years later I meet people from Nome who thank me for saving their life."

Auliye hasn't been on a sled in years ("Too old," he protests, "no good"), but he takes a keen interest in the mushers who skip through town every March. He's glad that the Iditarod has revived the sport, though he's not sure about some of the newfangled techniques that the racers use. "They spoil the dogs now. When we raced to Nome in '25, our dogs didn't wear *booties*." He says the word with disgust.

I ask Auliye what he thinks about the prospects for young Eskimos like Warren growing up in Alaska today. He turns somber. "Eskimo boys no longer know how to be an Eskimo. The old life is gone. To hunt and trap. To spear a whale. To call the seal with three scratches on the ice. To kill a bear with one shot only. When I was a young man, I killed with one shot. I hit a brown bear, it dropped."

A look of despair creeps into his face. "But these boys today," he broods. "They have nothing. They can't make it in the Eskimo way. They can't make it in the white man's way. No education. They go to Anchorage. Turn to drink. Watch TV. They are nothing."

THE "WHITE MAN'S WAY" of dog mushing is perhaps best exemplified by the work of Roy Chapman, a "sports medicine" researcher who has set up camp a few hundred yards from Auliye's house. Chapman is a member of the Arctic Sports Medicine Team, a research project loosely associated with the University of Alaska in Anchorage. Chapman and his team of scientists are using the Iditarod as a laboratory to study the physiological effects of extreme cold. The researchers concentrate on such arcane matters as "Vo2 max," "core temperature," and "specific gravity." They follow the mushers' "hydration patterns" and "gastric emptying rates." The Arctic Medicine project has its own musher entered in the race, Greg Tibbitts. An Iditarod rookie, Tibbitts is mushing a team of dogs on loan from Joe Redington. The researchers closely monitor Tibbitts's metabolism at each checkpoint. "The Iditarod is the ideal clinical scenario for studying arctic conditions," Chapman explains. "You couldn't pay people to put themselves through the kinds of things that mushers go through as a matter of course. The cold, the stress to the body, the sleep deprivation. And they like it! That's what slays me. We're testing these guys, they've got blood all over their faces, they can hardly stay awake. And they're saying, 'Oh yeah, I'm having a *good* time!' "

Chapman adds that prolonged sleep deprivation causes some mushers to experience hallucinations on the trail. They may see goblins and ghosts, a nonexistent cabin, a skyscraper in the middle of the bush. "I've had guys come in and tell me some great stories about how they've just had a twenty-minute conversation with their mom. 'How is she?' I'll ask. 'Oh, she's been dead for fifteen years, but she's doing good.' "

I ask Chapman to describe the optimum body type for an Iditarod musher. "The ideal size and shape for a musher is what we call a 'mesomorph,' which means that he is kind of small and round, not unlike the basic Eskimo physique. The mesomorph can retain his heat better. He doesn't look like an athlete at all. But he turns out to have tremendous upper body strength, tremendous grip strength, and a more efficient metabolism. When I think of the ideal musher, I imagine Joe Redington as a thirty-year-old man. Even in his seventies, Redington is tough as nails. You might look at him and think he's a frail little man who stumbles across the dog lot. But I'm constantly amazed by the man's physical strength, by the way he just slings around those hundred pound bags of dog food. He has a handshake that will crush a beer can. If Joe Redington was in his thirties, he'd wipe these guys up."

TWO DAYS LATER, Redington straggles into Unalakleet, looking weatherbeaten and dazed. He's only slept three hours in the past forty-eight. On two occasions, he's nodded asleep and fallen off his sled. I ask him if he's hallucinated on the trail, like some of the others.

"Nope," he snaps. "I've never seen anything that didn't look right to me."

IV. NOME

"END OF IDITAROD RACE—1049 MILES," reads the burled archway in Nome. The arch stands in the center of Front Street, an odd-looking span of knotted spruce timber attached bulb to socket like mastodon bones. Hanging from the burled arch is the "widow's lamp," an oil lantern that stays lit until every Iditarod musher has arrived safely. The trail stops directly in front of the Nugget Inn, where a wooden milepost marker announces, "Siberia: 149 Miles."

It's 15 below and cloudless on the eleventh day of the race, and the town is hopping. The latest word is that Susan Butcher has pulled out of Safety, the penultimate checkpoint, and is barreling toward Nome in record time. Several locals jump on their snowmachines and rumble south to greet her. Though it's only eight A.M., the streets are thronged with race officials, camera crews, veterinarians, and scores of smiling Eskimo children. The taxicabs are lined up at the Nome Airport, where the morning Alaska Airlines flight from Anchorage has just arrived. KNOM Radio burbles from the stores and restaurants, with Iditarod bulletins airing every fifteen minutes. The Alaskan Commercial supermarket is handing out free cups of coffee. Hirsute men with hangovers stand under the storefront eaves, clutching their plastic cups and squinting into the blinding whiteness, as Eskimo artisans hawk baleen baskets and walrus tusk carvings.

Nome is a community of four thousand hardy souls who take pride in their remoteness from . . . *everything*. One of the town slogans is "No Roads Lead to Nome." It is literally the end of the line—not just for the Iditarod Race but for North America. The town is even farther west than Hawaii. From here you could tromp over the ice to the international date line. Next stop: the coastal village of Provideniya, on the Chukchi Peninsula, the Russian Far East.

Nome is a wholly improbable place. The town's name derives from a spelling error. In the mid-1800s an English explorer charting the Seward Peninsula scrawled "? Name" on his manuscript map. A cartographer in London later copied it down as "C. Nome," or "Cape Nome." If yellow metal hadn't been discovered here, no one would have dreamed of pitching a city on this flat, featureless stretch of the Bering Sea Coast. But when word came in 1898 that "Three Lucky Swedes" had found gold in nearby Anvil Creek, the prospectors came in droves. With the Klondike claims beginning to play out, Nome would be the next big strike. In the early 1900s, Nome became the largest settlement in Alaska, a sprawling tent city of twenty thousand people stretched for ten miles down the coast.

There is an abiding sense of the surreal about Nome. At the city morgue, the bodies have been stacking up all winter (the grave diggers must wait until late spring for the permafrost to soften). Sin and virtue are locked in mortal conflict, with saloons and liquor stores currently outnumbering churches fourteen to thirteen. Out on the beach, the town is holding a golf tournament called the Bering Sea Classic, complete with orange golf balls and six "greens" painted onto the snow. The linksmen play in the shadow of a fourteen-story monstrosity of metal affectionately known as the Bima. A floating bucket dredge that looks like Darth Vader's "Death Star," the Bima roves the coast during the summer, churning up the sandy shallows in search of gold; but right now it sits dormant, locked in ice.

Air raid sirens wail in the distance, indicating that an Iditarod musher has been spotted at the edge of town. The announcer on KNOM screeches over the airwaves, "She's here! Susan Butcher IS IN NOME! She's going to win her fourth Iditarod, and it's going to be a record!" Hundreds of Nomites stream out of their homes and businesses and mass at the burled arch. A helicopter hovers overhead. The ABC cameramen flip on their lights. Technical crews unspool endless yards of cable. Lynn Swann tests his microphone levels as makeup people powder his nose.

A red dot grows on the beach. It's Butcher's bodysuit glimmering against a blanket of white. Her trim huskies are trotting at a steady clip. She glides past the Fort Davis Roadhouse and Swanberg's Dredge. She turns onto Front Street, and the crowd lets out a rousing cheer. Butcher jumps off her sled and runs the final fifty yards alongside her dogs. Buried inside her fur ruff is a beaming smile. "Whoa," Butcher cries. The harnesses slacken and the sled coasts to a halt beneath the arch.

The dogs regard the hooting crowds with bemusement. Their heads are wreathed in white cloudpuffs, their own moist breath meeting the cold air. They've run the Iditarod enough times to know that this is the final stop. After 1,100 miles, the dogs still look impressive, but the stress of their odyssey weighs in their faces. Their muzzles are pulled back in quivery scowls, their eyes glassy and glazed, their whiskers grizzled with frost. They look back at Butcher to make sure there are no imminent commands. Then they quietly lie down in the trail and lick the packed snow from their blistered paws.

Butcher signs the Iditarod arrival book. Announcer Leo Rasmussen, a former mayor of Nome, makes it official: "Susan Butcher arrived in Nome in eleven days, one hour, and fifty-three minutes."

Butcher has beaten her old race record by twelve minutes. She will leave Nome with fifty thousand one-dollar bills. (The prize money is paid out in this way for an interesting reason. Because Nome is virtually a marooned city, very little fresh currency enters the local economy. Thus, the town's money supply quickly wears out. Ask for change at a Nome restaurant, and chances are you'll get a handful of ragged bills. So every March the Iditarod winner relieves the town of fifty thousand tattered notes, while the local bank receives a shipment of crisp dollar bills from Anchorage.)

Butcher unhitches four of her dogs—Elan, Tempy, Lightning, and Sluggo—and poses for the cameras. The squirming huskies wag their tails and lick Butcher's face, a sure front-page photo for tomorrow morning's *Anchorage Times*.

Later in the month Butcher will visit President Bush in the White House, then travel to New York on a promotional tour. But right now, all she can think about is getting some sorely needed rest—and a "degreasing" from a local beauty parlor.

THREE DAYS LATER. A fierce blizzard on the Norton Sound has detained the race. For eight hours the mushers were holed up in cabins and roadhouses between Shaktoolik and Elim, waiting for the storm to pass, but now they're sprinting west again.

It's nine-thirty on a blustery Saturday night, 40 below counting wind chill. All told, twenty-four mushers have arrived in Nome. The townspeople are swept up in the carnival atmosphere. The mayor is emceeing a wet T-shirt contest at the Polaris Bar. A drunk Eskimo weaves down Front Street, then pukes in the crusty snow by the burl arch. A hooker beckons customers from a second-story window. In side streets and front yards, the tethered teams of huskies lie on beds of hay and yap at the moon.

The air raid sirens blare again. The word from KNOM is that Joe Redington has been spotted at the Fort Davis Roadhouse on the east end of town. Bar patrons pull on their parkas and stumble onto Front Street to greet Redington. His wife, Vi, is all bundled up and patiently waiting at the finish line.

Redington's headlamp bobs down Front Street, the pale white light silhouetting his dogs. He looks fragile on the sled, his short frame slumped against the drive bow, his boots precariously balanced on the narrow slats. His dogs lope across the finish line, their feet caked in ice up to the fetlocks. Redington dismounts without fanfare. He pads up to the platform and signs his name. He looks weary and pale in the glare of the cameras, but he manages a gritty smile. He can't feel his face and he can't hear a thing: He lost both of his hearing aids on the trail. He drawls into the microphone, "I always like to get here to Nome. I don't even know what I placed, but whatever it was, that's good."

The crowd cheers, "Way to go Joe!"

Leo Rasmussen announces the official time. "Joe Redington arrived in Nome on the seventeenth of March at nine-fifty-eight P.M. with thirteen dogs. Total elapsed time of fourteen days, twelve hours, fifty-nine minutes, and fifty-nine seconds. A hale and hearty welcome to the Father of the Iditarod to Nome."

Redington steps down from the platform and gives Vi a bearhug. Then he instructs his handlers to bed the dogs down for the night.

"This way, Joe! Over here for some pictures!"

Redington turns and faces a wall of reporters. He answers a few questions, but it's too cold for the crowds to linger. The revelers stagger back to their stools at the Board of Trade Saloon. The KNOM deejay spins an old standby called "The Iditarod Song," by an Alaskan folksinger named Hobo Jim. The mayor returns to the Polaris Lounge for the finale of the wet T-shirt contest. And Joe Redington tramps over to the Glue Pot restaurant for an ice-cold milk shake, as the voice of Hobo Jim crackles over the transistor radios of Nome and vanishes with the howl of the huskies into the arctic night—

> Give me a team with a good lead dog
> And a sled that's built so fine
> And let me race those miles to Nome
> One thousand forty-nine
> When I get back home
> They can tell my tale
> I did
> > I did
> > > I did the Iditarod Trail!

Woodstock in Leathers

THE HARLEY BOYS STOOD SILENT at the base of Mount Rushmore, looking up at the granite faces, thinking big.

In a single day, eleven thousand bikers had ridden their hogs down from campsites in Sturgis to marvel at it, shattering the all-time attendance record at the monument. Huge, bedraggled men with deep-baked Conan faces and bloodshot eyes and sour-smelling T-shirts and tattered hanks of oily hair blown back from the road winds. Scarred and blistered men, men with stubs and busted legs, hobbling on canes. Iron-butted men in steel-tipped boots, their faces splattered with the gooey carcasses of bugs. A few biker babes in reptile skin miniskirts and Sleezy-Teez halter tops. All-American outlaws, patriotic in a hard and unsentimental way, revving their unmuffled engines.

The one called Mule stood off by himself, licking a cone of "Teddy Roosevelt Maple-Nut" ice cream. Mule wore spurs on his boots and leather gauntlet gloves on his hands. A tattoo of a buffalo skull ran down the length of his arm. Mule had never seen Rushmore before, and he was searching for words. "What can I say?" he said. "It's awesome. It's class. It's so . . . *big*!"

Craggy old Uncle Abe off to the right, his down-turned

face full of noble doubts. Teddy Roosevelt set back in a shadowy recess, no doubts whatsoever, grinning the bluff grin of Empire. Jefferson aiming high over the plains, a dreamer restless in his rock. And at far left, Washington, just being Washington, telling no lies, his chiseled forehead shining bone-white against the big cerulean skies.

"Those are the dudes who made this country what it is," Mule proclaimed, ice cream tinting his beard. "I don't know about the others, but I betcha Theodore Roosevelt, being a Rough Rider and all, woulda gone for a Harley." With that, Mule hopped on his shovelhead with the Grim Reaper airbrushed on the peanut gas tank along with the words, "IS THERE LIFE AFTER DEATH? FUCK WITH THIS BIKE AND YOU'LL FIND OUT," and shoved off for points north.

ELEVEN MONTHS OF THE YEAR, Sturgis is a somnolent town of six thousand in the Dakota gold country. But in the second week of August, the town holds a motorcycle rally known as the Black Hills Motor Classic, and almost overnight it becomes a Gomorrah of steel and hobnail boots. The population swells to over two hundred thousand, making it the largest city in the state. The road warriors ride in from all over the United States to take part in this rollicking fandango in the prairie. For a week, Main Street is lined with tens of thousands of Harley-Davidson motorcycles, parked at cocked angles from the curbs. Heritage Softails. Cafe Racers. Low Riders. Fat Boys. The air is choked with blue fumes. Day and night, the bikers growl their engines down the strip, their mamas holding on behind. Vendors hawk brass knuckles, switchblades, and endless miles of chain. There are swap meets, sled pulls, and motorcycle rodeos. Advocacy groups meet to whip up support for the *jihad* against helmet laws. Master pinstripers paint gas tanks on demand. The street signs are plastered with fliers advertising "THUNDER KLUNDER'S WALL OF DEATH!" and "BIG DADDY RAT'S CHOPPER SHOW!" The side streets buzz with the reedy sibilance of electric tattoo needles. The bikers gather in open-air beer gardens with makeshift walls of chicken wire and sawdust strewn on the concrete floors. As the parties intensify across the Black Hills, biker evangelist groups like the Good News Riders and the Tribe of Judah hold tent revivals to save their wicked brethren from certain damnation.

Milwaukee is the home of the Harley-Davidson Company, but Sturgis is the capital of the Harley Nation. It is the only town that has a Harley model named after it: "The Dyna Glide Sturgis." For biker purists, the Classic has an aura of religious grandeur, like Cannes for filmmakers or Westminster for dog breeders. Hundreds of bikers get married at the rally (twenty-five dollars and no blood tests required). There is even a beer brewed especially for the season.

The Classic's mystique has spread overseas. Sturgis is a popular destination for Harley owners in Europe and Australia. "I've been hearing about this all my life—I can't believe I'm finally here!" exults John Brodie of Brisbane. Brodie sold his house in Queensland to pay for the journey to Sturgis and arrived with a group of fifty riders from his "bikee" club, Gold Coast Hog. "Jews go to Israel, Moslems go to Mecca, and we go to Sturgis. It's something you have to do at least once in your life."

Sturgis and its environs appeal to the bikers' sense of themselves as heirs to the hard-riding, hard-drinking traditions of the Wild West. The town was named after J. G. Sturgis, a cavalry lieutenant who fell with Custer at Little Big Horn. The Black Hills region, sacred ground for the Lakota Sioux Indians, is widely considered America's finest riding country for street bikes. Highway 385, a state road that runs along the spine of the Black Hills, passes through meadows matted in daisies and high sierra blown dry by the Chinook winds. The bikers roam every inch of the Hills, smelling the ponderosa pines, soaking in the sulfur springs, shooting craps in the same Deadwood saloon where Wild Bill Hickok drew his "dead man's hand" of aces and eights.

From Sturgis, the bikers can make day runs in any direction. To the east are the Badlands, spectral realm of buttes and gulches. To the west, in Wyoming, is Devils Tower, the monolithic shaft of granite that served as an alien landing pad in Steven Spielberg's *Close Encounters of the Third Kind*. To the north is the barren spot that marks the Geographical Center of the United States. And to the south, a few miles beyond Rushmore, is Crazy Horse Mountain, where a local family has spent forty years blasting the hillside into the likeness of the Sioux warrior.

This year—1990—is the rally's fiftieth anniversary, and

the bikers have turned out in record numbers: four hundred thousand, according to one estimate, though no one can say for sure. It is, quite simply, the largest biker rally ever held. The Sturgis newspaper, *The Meade County Times-Tribune*, has called it "Woodstock in Leathers." Bikers here feel they are witnessing a historic moment in the annals of American metal. For months leading up to the rally, national biker magazines have been sounding the clarion call. "What kind of noise would 500,000 Harleys make?" posed an article in *Easy Riders*. "You long-toothed veterans: Only 34,000 of you got ashore at Normandy on D-Day. Woodstock? It only lasted three days and pulled in no more than 350,000. [But] 500,000 Harleys would make a noise loud enough to be heard in every state and in Washington, D.C. itself!"

Practically everyone in the American biker world has trekked to Sturgis for the fiftieth. Peter Fonda has come to sign autographs for fans of *Easy Rider*, and to take grief from Vietnam vets still lathered up about Jane's infelicitous trip to Hanoi. ("I love my sister," Fonda tells them. "She was right in perception, just wrong in delivery.") Neil Diamond has put in an appearance, and unconfirmed sightings of other celebrities have been reported—Clint Eastwood, Mickey Rourke, Silvester Stallone, Jay Leno. The late Malcolm Forbes, who attended the 1989 rally with his famed riding posse, The Capitalist Tools, is here in spirit. His 200-foot hot air balloon in the shape of a Harley looms over the Black Hills.

And then there are the colors: the Bandidos, the Sons of Silence, the Gypsy Jokers, the Hell's Angels. Outlaws have been coming to the Classic for decades, but gang violence is surprisingly low. The Classic is said to be the one time during the year when the gangs agree to a ceasefire.

Still, it's a busy week for law enforcement officers. Every year police issue thousands of traffic tickets and arrest hundreds of bikers for riding under the influence. Bikes with altered serial numbers are confiscated. Police keep a special lookout for the exaggerated "ape-hanger" handlebars on custom choppers. Every year a few lady bikers are cited for public exposure, and fly-by-night tattoo operators are shut down for spreading infections. The local jail fills early in the week, so officials have to transport scores of prisoners to Rapid City.

Every August undercover agents from the FBI, the Drug

Enforcement Agency, and Alcohol, Tobacco, and Firearms descend on western South Dakota. In 1989, the U.S. Attorney's office cited the rally as a major narcotics trafficking center. In past years, leaders of motorcycle theft rings and fugitives have been nabbed at the rally.

The increase in crime has only reinforced what a lot of conservative folks around Sturgis have felt for decades—that the rally has outgrown this little storefront burg. The town fathers have circulated petitions to have the Classic canceled, but the petitions never get very far. Even as they curse the bikers for their filth and nerve-wracking noise, most people welcome their return each August as a relief from eleven months of high plains boredom. The Classic is the town's claim to fame—and the major source of its income. Many residents plan their family vacations around the time of the Classic. Those who remain simply plug their ears with cotton and ride out the storm.

Local establishments undergo a curious metamorphosis. Dean's barber shop becomes a tattoo parlor. Lynn's Country Market opens a studio where bikers can get their pictures taken with a live black panther. Bob's Restaurant sports a sign in the window that proclaims "IMAGES OF ELVIS APPEAR ON OUR FLAPJACKS." At the Shears & Sears Hair Salon, customers can get a buzz cut with the word "Sturgis" stenciled in their scalp. The ladies at St. Francis Church welcome the hordes every morning for huge breakfast "feeds." Chiropractors and ambulance-chasing attorneys come out of the woodwork to offer their services. The Rapid City Hospital, in anticipation of extra orthopedic work, runs an ad in the newspaper showing an X ray of a fractured arm: "We'll Develop Your Unplanned Vacation Photos."

The Harley-Davidson Company pitches camp at the Civic Center in downtown Rapid City, a safe remove from the mayhem in Sturgis. Here, the Harley Owners Group (HOG), a cleaner-cut clan of recreationists sponsored by the company, holds its own rally. The HOG gathering is a kind of Sturgis Lite for riders who seek Harley fellowship without the barbarous excesses. At the company boutiques, fashion-conscious bikers can buy everything from designer leathers to Harley perfume.

Harley's PR people refer to outlaw bikers as "The One-Percenters"; they insist that 99 percent of Harley owners are tame, hygienic, hardworking Americans. The company has worked assiduously to refine its brutish image, and the campaign has paid off: Affluent motorcyclists (known in industry parlance as "Rubbies," for Rich Urban Bikers) have become a big part of the scene.

Rubbies, easy riders, one-percenters—they're all members of the Harley Nation, a society built around little more than love for a big machine. It is a society that has embraced souls as disparate as Evel Knievel and Elizabeth Taylor. It's often hard to guess about the people who come to the Sturgis rally. Appearances can be deceiving. The guy you've got pegged as a bounty hunter just might be a bounty hunter, or he might be a stockbroker going through mid-life crisis. The Classic is a grand masque, a place where alter egos get a workout and old enthusiasms are dragged out of the garage for one week of the year.

Owning a piece of Milwaukee metal is all that is required for induction into the Harley Nation. One man, writing in the letters section of *Easy Riders*, summed up the joys of citizenship this way: "I don't give a shit if you have long or short hair, if you wear a tie to work or coveralls. All that concerns me is the sense of pride and freedom and the innate brotherhood that comes from riding an American legacy."

Like Dante's hell, living quarters at the Classic are arranged in descending circles of depravity. Bikers can seek out their preferred level of sin and settle down for the week. Gentlemen bikers stay in the fancier hotels around Rapid City. Serious gamblers prefer lodgings near Deadwood, where they can be close to the blackjack tables. Gangs like the Hell's Angels stay far outside of town in semifortified encampments. But the great unwashed masses sleep on the outskirts of town in communal campgrounds with names like Wild West, Hog Heaven, and Covered Wagon.

"NO BOOZE, DRUGS, GUNS, OR BAD ATTITUDES" reads the sign outside the Buffalo Chip Campground, but on a typical night you will see all of the above.

The Buffalo Chip is the ninth circle at Sturgis: vats of beer, lakes of puke, acres of bare breasts, and billowy clouds of reefer.

There is a refreshing honesty about The Chip. Its owners set out to throw the grossest, crassest party in Meade County and they've succeeded. It is the only place I have ever witnessed public coitus, or public fellatio, or the public disappearance of a zucchini squash between a woman's legs. Not that any of this is sanctioned by the campground authorities—or the scores of undercover cops who reportedly roam the hillsides. It's just that when you open five hundred acres of ranchland to a hundred thousand bikers, things get out of control.

The Chip is dedicated to fulfilling the biker's four basic urges—grub, swill, tunes, and chest-gazing. Guests at The Chip can get a tattoo, have their knives sharpened, or buy a plate of Indian tacos. They can watch the strippers in the "Soft-Tail Lounge" or browse at novelty shops like Voodoo Hawg Bitchin Biker Gear. The campground has its own currency, called "buffalo chips." It has its own newspaper, *The Buffalo Chip Gazette*, and a one-watt radio station emceed by Wolfman Jack. It even has a Domino's Pizza shop that delivers to the nether reaches of the camp.

Concerts at The Chip have been mythologized in *Spin* magazine. Headline acts that have played here over the years include Bachman Turner Overdrive, the Marshall Tucker Band, Joan Jett, and the Nighthawks. In the center of The Chip is an immense crater that serves as a natural amphitheater. The bikers can ride down into the bowl and watch the concerts from the saddles of their Harleys. To request an encore, they just rev their engines.

I arrive at The Chip around dusk. On the tattered hillsides, thousands of tents and plastic tarps are fluttering in the breeze. In the distance I can trace the outline of Bear Butte, an odd-looking swell in the golden prairie that Custer once used as a landmark for moving his cavalry. (Bear Butte is sacred to the Cheyenne Indians, but to the bikers it is affectionately known as "Bare Butt.")

Utility trucks have been sprinkling the land with water to keep the dust down, and now the camp is a mud bog. I slither over to the money exchange booth and get a stack of buffalo chips. Then I stop at one of the open-air bars for a glass of the camp cocktail—"Purple Passion," a stout concoction of pure grain alcohol and grape syrup. Down in the crater, a warm-up band is playing an obscure biker tune called "Boozin, Cruisin, and Losin."

One of the hundreds of people milling around the campground bar is Pam, a hard-core biker chick from New Mexico. Pam is a wild cat of the desert, wiry and watchful and tough as nails. She has a permanent sneer and a nest of dishwater blond hair. Pam says she roams the Southwest with a posse of outlaw bikers. She's been coming to Sturgis for eight years in a row. "It's the granddaddy of them all," she states, her sneer melting for a moment into a look of earnest sincerity. Pam is especially proud of the fact that she rides a "hardtail," a bike without shock absorbers. Riding a hardtail means that her body "wears" every groove and pebble and hapless varmint she's ever hit on the road, the knocks and shakes transferred directly from asphalt to flesh like the vibrations of a jackhammer. "Hardtail is the only way to go," Pam boasts.

At the Electric Pen Emporium, tattoo artist B. J. Sloan is doing Thor the Viking on the biceps of a young man from Oregon. "It's not just convicts and drunk sailors that are into tattoos," Sloan points out. "A tattoo is all about commitment. A good tattoo tells the life story of a person. It's an allegory, a progression of symbols. It's dermagraphics, man. Skin art."

Late that night I walk to my rent-a-car, which is parked on a remote hill. I throw open the hatchback, crawl into my sleeping bag, and fall asleep to the sound of a thousand campfire orgies dotting the landscape.

At dawn I am awakened by two loud voices:

"So I took the motherfucker's arm like this, and I broke it over my knee."

"I did a guy in prison like that once, 'cept it was over a locker room bench. Wham—broke it clean in half! Asshole had stolen my smokes."

I look up from my sleeping bag to see two Visigoths leaning against my rental car, oblivious to my presence inside. Their chopped hogs are parked a few yards away. The two bikers have bugged-out Benzedrine eyes, and they are sharing a fifth of Jack Daniel's. One of them turns to relieve himself on my front tire. I keep my eyes closed and try to play possum. Occasionally the conversation stops, and I can hear the sound of chemicals shooting up nostrils.

". . . so I took out my blade and cut him up bad. Turned out the fucker died, man! I *killed* the son of a bitch!"

"Hey look!" the other voice interrupts. "There's someone inside this thing!" I hear a tap on my window. "Jeeeezus—you think he's a narc?"

There is a long silence as the bikers inspect me.

"Should we fuck with him?"

"Hmmmm."

"Naw. Look at him. He's crashed. He didn't hear nothin'. Let's get outta here."

I hear them kick-start their engines, but I don't budge. I'm shaking in my sleeping bag. I hear them blasting off across the field. A bright orange sun has risen over Bare Butt.

ALTHOUGH THE CULT OF HARLEY now rules the Black Hills Motor Classic, the gathering actually began as a rally for one of Harley's principal competitors, the Indian. The late Clarence "Pappy" Hoel, a motorcycling enthusiast who ran an Indian dealership in town, started the Classic in 1938. For fifteen years Indian was king, but when the company folded in 1953, the Harleys took over. Today you can still find plenty of vintage Indian Scouts and Chiefs parked on the strip, their Art Deco chromework glinting in the sun. The Harley boys treat the Indians deferentially, like village elders.

Other motorcycle makes are welcome in Sturgis, though not with open arms. Britbikes like Triumphs or BSAs are taken in as distant cousins from across the pond. BMWs get respect but little love. Motor trike owners, known as Brothers of the Third Wheel, are regarded as colorful sideshow freaks; their weird-looking rides, imaginatively fashioned out of hearses or welded to look like the space shuttle, fetch a lot of stares.

Japanese-made bikes, on the other hand, are *non grata*, dismissed as "Jap Crap," "rice grinders," and worse. Occasionally a Honda owner will have the temerity to park his Goldwing on Main Street, but he is inviting trouble. In the early eighties, when the Harley company was getting clobbered by the Japanese, vandals in Sturgis made a sport of burning Jap Crap in the public park at the edge of town.

Until the sixties, the Classic remained a regional affair, dwarfed by older rallies in better-established biker meccas like Daytona and Laconia, New Hampshire. The Jackpine Gypsies, Pappy Hoel's riding group, ran the rally on a shoestring budget. Visiting motorcyclists pitched tents in Hoel's backyard. There

Bikers gathered at the base of
Mt. Rushmore.

The Sturgis Strip, 1990.

The original Harley, 1903.

was a race, a buffalo feast, and a beauty pageant in the park. On the final day, Hoel would lead a tour to Mount Rushmore, where his wife, Pearle, would fix a picnic for the men.

Pearle Hoel, now in her mid-eighties, is a sweet lady with watery eyes and a high quavery voice—not the irascible old hellion you'd expect as the grandmother of the Harley Nation. She still keeps Pappy's tarnished racing trophies in the basement. "I was never into motorcycles," she confesses, pronouncing the word motor*sickles*. "I just rode behind Clarence. It's hard to believe how this thing has just grown and grown and grown. There's really no accounting for it. A lot has changed over the years, that's for sure. For one thing, the ladies don't wear clothes anymore.

"I look forward to all of this, you know," she says, the Harleys thundering outside. "But I guess I'm like everybody else—I'm kind of glad when the week is over."

It's EIGHT O'CLOCK IN THE MORNING, and the Sturgis Strip is already a solid bank of Harleys—six blocks long, four rows deep. Through the morning haze, I can faintly see the town's name spelled in white boulders on a distant hill, except the first two letters are missing—"U R G I S."

Tens of thousands of bikers are out posing and profiling. Guys with names like Iceman, Lizard, Bandit, and Lurch. So much reverence on the faces of so many bad seeds, or at least people trying to look like bad seeds, all roistering in their riveted concho vests and latigo belts. Sultry mamas in leather chaps but no underwear, their bare cheeks exposed. Some are fiddling with their engines, packing for day runs to the Badlands. A few are snoozing on their bikes, their bodies draped over the seats and gas tanks, their feet pitched over the handlebars. Others are riding down the center lane of Main Street, flashing the crowds hungry looks that say, "If you don't check me out, I'll kill you."

The crowd is a wall of T-shirt slogans—

INJECTION IS NICE BUT I'D RATHER BE BLOWN
WHO DIED AND LEFT YOU IN CHARGE?
KILL 'EM ALL AND LET GOD SORT 'EM OUT
FLATHEAD, PANHEAD, KNUCKLEHEAD, GIMME HEAD
JUST BEND OVER AND TAKE IT LIKE A MAN, LADY!

BURN THIS FLAG AND YOUR ASS IS MINE
IRAQ SUCKS
THE SUPREME COURT SUCKS
DAYTONA SUCKS
YOU SUCK

It doesn't take long to realize that biker men are truly mammary obsessed. "Show your tits!" they cry day and night, and whenever a woman obliges—which is surprisingly often— all the men in the vicinity are duty-bound to rush to the scene and pay homage, as if every bared breast were a little miracle to be savored.

This morning there is a commotion in front of Gunners Lounge on Main Street. A gang fight here last night ended with one man shot in the neck and two others stabbed. Miraculously none of the three combatants died. Yellow police tape is marking the scene, and the sidewalk is still stained with blood. A dozen Hell's Angels are standing outside Gunners, garnering stares. So far, the Gunners incident has been the only reported gang activity this week, although rumors of a major showdown between the Angels and the Outlaws have been circulating. (A story in the Rapid City newspaper has warned that gang members have bought all the baseball bats on sale at an area Kmart.)

Eleven people have died during this year's rally, nine of them in highway accidents. One woman was instantly killed when her bike, traveling seventy miles per hour, struck an antelope. Another woman died of carbon monoxide poisoning in her tent. Police killed an Australian biker after he went on a rampage with a bowie knife.

But the topic of death is seldom heard on the sidewalks of Sturgis. This is a celebration, a time of rejoicing. On the streets, the huge men (where do they grow people this big?) are bearhugging, weeping like babes, welcoming lost prodigals back to the fold. Everyone wears the smile of Harley brotherhood.

And everyone wears the same clothes. For people who pride themselves on individualism, Harley boys look remarkably alike, as if they'd all bought their threads from the same mail order catalog. Bikerdom is a fossilized culture. The uniform hasn't changed in thirty years. As always, only three clothing materials are acceptable: Denim, leather, and metal.

Instead, bikers pour their originality into their "scooters."

Each machine has a slightly different look and feel. Every detail on the bike speaks worlds about its owner's personality. Enormous attention is lavished on the gas tank pinstriping, the airbrushed cameo on the fender, the custom chrome work. The length of the front fork or the shape of the cylinder head reflects one's chosen caste; it is through these details that bikers pledge their fealty to the smaller clans (such as the "panheads" or the "knuckleheads") that delineate the Harley cosmos.

Bikers also express themselves through their proximity to various kinds of animal flesh. They like being around dead stuff. Everywhere you look there's carrion—rooster claws, bear heads, elk antlers, horse skulls—anything that was once alive or was once part of something that was alive. People sit on street curbs gnawing turkey drumsticks. Vendors sell bobcat tails, bull scrotums, and fox pelts. The air is filled with the gamy smell of alligator, wild boar, and venison sizzling on open grills.

Live animals are popular, too. People like to bring menacing-looking beasts for shock effect. Like the biker from Nevada who has two pit bulls riding in his sidecar. Or the muscle-man outside the Fireside Lounge with the python wrapped around his body. Farther down the strip there is a tarantula in a Mason jar, an iguana on a chain, and a timber wolf curled up in a motorcycle trailer, his yellow eyes full of doom.

After walking the strip for a while, the animals, live and dead, begin to blur together—the hides and fangs, the hairy arms, the smell of meat, the throaty grumble of engines, the tattooed dragons, the serpents and spiders and hellhounds. The whole dark menagerie begins to coalesce in the mind, and what emerges is the Harley Beast, a human animal thing, pure and stripped down, a creature of basic urges, predatory and mean but also natural and therefore good.

BIKERS OFTEN REFER to the Harley itself as a beast—"a hog," "a steed," "a steer." Or, as Willie G. Davidson calls it, "an iron horse."

Willie G. is the grandson of one of the company founders and perhaps the biggest celebrity at the Classic. People wait in line for hours to shake the hand of the scraggly-bearded man in the black beret. A formally trained designer who once worked as a stylist for Ford, Willie G. is given much of the credit for recapturing the company's sense of itself when it went astray during the dark days of the 1970s. Today he is known as the "keeper of the company soul."

Willie G. talks a lot about things like "the Harley essence" and "the Harley mystique." He understands that a Harley isn't meant to be a sleek or particularly fast machine; nor is it a sputtering little tin can for getting around town. The Harley is your mother's greatest nightmare: a hefty bike for the open road, a living thing with a big braying engine. It is a long, low, sagging chunk of metal with lots of exposed parts. It is tail fire, chrome and rivets, Western saddlebags, and endless folds of lustrous black leather. While the Japanese companies race toward a sleek modernity, rigging their machines with aerodynamic shells and liquid-crystal instruments, Harley reaches back in time, to the days of the Wild West, to a wide-open era when manners were coarser and men lived closer to their impulses. While the Japanese try to tame the Beast, Harley aims to keep the Beast alive.

In 1901, the year the E. R. Thomas Motor Company produced the first commercial motorcycle, William Harley and Arthur Davidson, two boyhood friends, were working in a Milwaukee manufacturing plant. Harley was a draftsman, Davidson a pattern maker, but their real love was tinkering with gasoline engines. They thought they could make a better motorcycle than the Thomas model, and that summer they got to work building motors in their backyard. It was a primitive operation. They fashioned the first carburetor out of a tomato can; an old leather belt served as a drive chain. But with the help of Davidson's two brothers, William and Walter, they unveiled their first prototype in 1903. It was a benchmark year in the history of mechanized travel: In Detroit that year, Henry Ford incorporated a new motor company, and at Kitty Hawk, the Wright Brothers had gotten off the ground at last.

Volume was low the first year: Harley-Davidson produced a grand total of three motorcycles. The early models were known as "Silent Grey Fellows," the name referring to the flat gray paint that became the company's standard color. The H-D bikes were clunky and loud, but they earned a reputation for toughness. One of the original bikes racked up over 100,000 miles. By 1907, Harleys were being used for police work and postal deliveries. In 1916, the U.S. Army used Silent Grey Fellows in Texas border skirmishes with Pancho Villa.

Harley saw more than 150 competitors come and go during the first half of the century, among them: Yale, Pope, Merkel, Henderson, Thor, Excelsior, and Indian. Harley survived through a combination of hard work, close customer relations, and perhaps most critical of all, the procurement of lucrative Army contracts. During the Great War, the Allies ordered 20,000 motorcycles, most of them Harleys. H-D changed its standard color from gray to olive drab. In World War II, 90,000 Harleys were built and shipped to the allied armed forces.

The Harley's good service as a wartime workhorse ensured its success back home. The company had wrapped itself in the flag. Thousands of returning servicemen wanted civilian versions of the bikes they'd ridden at the front.

The H-D company got a further boost from the 1953 release of *The Wild One*, a film about a roving band of bikers who ride into a small town not unlike Sturgis. Marlon Brando was actually riding a Triumph, but people commonly assumed it was a Harley. And with the Indian Motorcycle Company closing its plant in Springfield, Massachusetts, Harley was the only American bike left. Old-fashioned motorcyclists feared *The Wild One* would give their fair sport a bad name. But for a restless breed of young rebels, riding an iron horse seemed a fresh antidote to the prevailing prissiness of the Eisenhower years. Among the thousands of teenagers who grew up trying to perfect the Brando sneer was a kid in the slums of North Memphis named Elvis Presley. In 1956, Presley was pictured with his new Harley on the cover of *The Enthusiast*, the official H-D magazine.

Harley thrived in the 1960s, but when American Machine and Foundry (AMF) bought the company in 1969, things went awry. AMF expanded production threefold to meet the rising demand for motorcycles. Quantity replaced quality, and Harleys developed a reputation for shoddy construction. Oil leaks were a perennial problem. (For years, Harley loyalists defended the embarrassing oil splotches under their bikes with lines like, "Oh, he's just marking his spot.") The company was getting savaged by the Japanese invasion, and by the late seventies even Harley loyalists were abandoning ship in favor of the cheaper, quieter, better-built Kawasakis, Suzukis, Hondas, and Yamahas.

The Japanese companies not only dominated the market for small and medium-sized bikes, but with the introduction of models like the Honda Goldwing, they were also making inroads into Harley's once inviolable turf—heavyweights with 700-cc displacement and above.

In 1981, Harley-Davidson came within hours of declaring bankruptcy. But in a desperate move to save the company, a group of senior Harley executives (including Willie G.) pooled their personal fortunes and bought it back. The tale of how the company pulled itself from the abyss became a well-chronicled rust belt success story. The new management lobbied the Reagan administration to approve protective tariffs on heavyweight imports. The tariffs worked their magic: In four years, Harley had reclaimed the heavyweight market and plugged the oil leaks.

Perhaps the most promising sign of the company's renaissance came in 1984, when the California Highway Patrol formally returned to the Harley fold after ten years of flirting with Japanese models. In 1987, President Reagan, smelling an All-American photo opportunity, visited the Harley plant in York, Pennsylvania. "We're on the road to unprecedented prosperity," he told the employees gathered at the plant. "And we'll get there on a Harley!"

AMONG THE THOUSANDS of Harley owners who waited until the fiftieth to make their first pilgrimage to Sturgis were Peter Morrochelio and Paul Ganno, two Italian-American friends who grew up together in the Boston area. Both in their mid-thirties and still single, Peter and Paul live on separate floors of the same house in Stoneham, Massachusetts. Peter is a stout fellow with a salty Boston accent. He looks as though he could hold his own in a barroom brawl, but there is a gentleness in his face that suggests he isn't the fighting type. Because Peter has a "responsible" job (he's in charge of the trucking fleet for the New England division of Grossman's Lumber Company), he wears short hair and trims his mustache. "My boss asked me, 'Peter, do you want to be a biker or do you want to be an executive?' I said, 'Well actually I want to be Malcolm Forbes and have the best of both.' "

Paul is shaggier, shorter, more withdrawn. A self-taught

mechanic, he owns a motorcycle repair shop, Ganno's Machined Assemblies, in the heart of Stoneham. "Complete Harley-Davidson Motorcycle Service," his business brochure advertises. "Repairs—Rebuilding—Maintenance. NO JAP CRAP." Paul looks a bit like Robert DeNiro with a smear of oil on his face and black grime under his nails. He is the intuitive sort of grease monkey who can spot a rebuilt shovelhead at twenty paces and quickly sniff out the archeology of every magneto and carburetor spring.

Peter and Paul are as devoted to Harleys as anyone you're likely to meet, but they have never been "bikers" in the stereotypical macho sense of the term. Neither of them has a tattoo. As Peter sees it, "God did a good enough job." Neither of them has ever worn a gang patch. Peter explains, "I ride to get *away* from rules and regulations!" And they never went for badass biker garb, preferring the straight look of denim and boots, which they say is not a "look" at all, just what they had always worn growing up. For Peter and Paul, riding a motorcycle isn't a social statement. It is pure freedom. A rush. An escape hatch. "Motorcycling is the cheapest form of therapy I know," Paul explains. "It clears the mind. Like if you get mad at your old lady—you just hop on your scoot. It's just you and it."

"When you're in a car," says Peter, "you're numb to what's going on around you—the wind, the temperature, the heat of the asphalt, the bird on the wire. You miss all of that. The thing that the car manufacturers are after is 'The Quiet Ride.' You put up the window and you're sealed inside this little tomb. But on the bike you're on the edge. You're not just observing this pretty little picture. You are *in* the picture. That's what makes life worth something, to me at least: to smell and feel and touch everything that's around you, to be enveloped."

Which is exactly why Peter, like most Harley riders, is so adamantly opposed to state helmet laws. "Hell, why ride a bike if you're going to lock your head in a steel tank? A helmet takes out all the rawness. The sounds get muffled and the peripherals get blurred."

As they grew up, Peter and Paul kept postponing the trip to Sturgis. Money concerns, girlfriends, family troubles—something always got in the way. They made treks to other rallies, like the big spring blowout in Daytona, but for them, Sturgis was the real McCoy. And with the fiftieth looming on the calendar, they decided 1990 was the year. They might not get a chance to make a cross-country trip again, they thought. "Riding a Harley across the country is a fantasy that has played in my mind ever since I saw *Easy Rider*," recalls Peter. "The older I got, the more important it became to me. And so when the fiftieth came along, we said to ourselves, 'We're finally going to pull this thing off!' "

So Peter and Paul rounded up a group of four other local riders, among them a former butcher who goes by the name "Captain Coldcut." Captain is a lanky character who wears Harley jewelry and an air cleaner cover for a belt buckle. A Vietnam vet, his bike is stickered with POW-MIA slogans. "I've got all the vices except gambling," Captain freely admits. He is now a member of Mean and Clean, a national biker organization for recovering substance abusers.

The trip to Sturgis took four days. The group hopped the Massachusetts Turnpike heading west out of Boston, crossed the Berkshires into New York, then took Interstate 90 through the wrinkled steel country and the sulfurous mill towns of Pennsylvania. For the next five hundred miles it was perfect flatness—the lulling farms of Ohio and Indiana giving way to the pastureland of Wisconsin and southern Minnesota. Two hours into South Dakota, they were jolted awake by the precipitous drop to the Missouri River. Suddenly they had slipped into an entirely new landscape: buttes and dusty ranchland, the first faint suggestions of the West.

As they crossed the Cheyenne, they could see a dark mass hanging in the distance, a wave of dark pine and granite rising from an ocean of gold: the Black Hills. "It's such an awesome experience to be riding out there and to look over at your friend on his Harley, and to be living out this dream that you'd been talking about ever since you were kids," Peter exclaims. "Here we were, two old friends, Peter and Paul on the road to Damascus. We're traveling in the Plains and then suddenly we come to these mountains. We're no longer in the Midwest; we're in the *Wild* West. It's then that you realize that you aren't just going to a motorcycle rally. All of a sudden names you remember as a kid come rushing back to you. It's like, so *this* is where all that history happened."

* * *

SOME NEW HISTORY is about to happen tonight at The Buffalo Chip Campground. Twenty thousand people have come to hear Steppenwolf, perhaps the greatest biker band of all time.

The crater is brim full of cycles. The smell of beer and vomit mingles with the motorcycle fumes. The stage is a mountain of Marshall amps and liquor billboards. Spotlights comb the skies. The Miss Buffalo Chip pageant is in progress, and the biker beauties are parading the stage clad in string bikinis and high heels. Someone in the audience tosses a cucumber onto the stage and yells, "Make it disappear!"

At the far end of the dustbowl, a dozen bikers are playing Chickenshit Bingo, a game of chance that involves a rooster defecating on a large bingo card.

Nearby, a group of friends from Canada are doing the "wienie bite"—a traditional agility test in which a biker rides beneath a foot-long hot dog dangling on a string while his woman kneels on the back of the seat and attempts to bite off a chunk of meat.

I wander along the ridge above the crater, peering at the long rows of vendors. The Bone Factory is selling artificial human skeletons that are "anatomically correct." At Bondage Goods, there are nipple rings, slave bracelets, and harnesses. A carnival barker named Crazy George is collecting bail money "for all our brothers stuck in jail."

Now Steppenwolf has taken the stage—haggard dinosaurs with tubercular-blue skin, their scaly forms mailed in black leather. The band belts out oldies like "The Monster," "The Pusher," "Magic Carpet Ride." The crater is now a boozy pulsing mass of bodies. Women are perched on shoulders, hurling their halter tops into the air.

I'm standing with a catatonic biker who calls himself Nemo. "Biggest fuckin' party on the planet!" he raves, tossing back another cup of Purple Passion. "Gonna remember this one the rest of my life. Makes Woodstock look like a friggin' dress rehearsal."

An hour passes, and Steppenwolf leaves the stage. The crowd revs for an encore, creating a mighty din that carries twenty miles across the prairie. A galaxy of butane lighters speckles the floor of the crater.

"Born to Be Wild!" Nemo screams. "They gotta play 'Born to Be Wild!' "

Finally, Steppenwolf slinks back on stage.

Now the whole crowd is chanting: "Born to Be Wild! Born to Be Wild! Born to Be . . ."

"Ladies and gentlemen!" announces the low, rheumy voice of Steppenwolf's lead singer, John Kay. "Please remain standing for our national anthem!" Suddenly a typhoon of guitars, and then Kay is screeching—*Hitchin' for a running. Hare out on the highway.* Nemo is filled with raucous joy. He lets out a caveman scream and shakes a fist in the air. When the chorus comes, he bellows the beloved lines—*like a true nature child, we were born, born to be wild*—and the Black Hills tremble with the contented roar of the Harley Nation.

PART III

GOING TO GRACELAND

So he passed over, and the trumpets sounded
for him on the other side.
—John Bunyan, *The Pilgrim's Progress*

Jerusalem on the Mississippi

Memphis, Tennessee

"SATAN IS A LIAR!" shrieks the girl from Detroit, the tears welling in her unblinking eyes. "Satan is a liar and we have a victory NOW!!"

Onstage, the swaying choir has reached a crescendo, singing "Yes Lord, yes Lord, completely yes!" and now the Saints have broken out dancing, strumming washboards and pounding tambourines to the mounting frenzy of the gospel anthem. "From the bottom of my heart, to the depths of my soul, Yes Lord!"

"Satan is a liar!" the girl from Detroit keeps saying. "Satan is a liar! Liar! Liar!" She turns and hugs her sisters crowded in the aisle, taking care to step over the elderly lady in the white sequined dress who has dropped to the floor for a conversation with the Ghost:

"Baabaabaawambidawambiooooobaybaabaawangwongbaa!"

"Get it!" the sisters scream, gathering around the woman and locking arms in a formation called a "tarrying circle." "The tongue is here!"

"Baawooooodoingdoingwoooobaabaahangeeeeeeeeeeeee!"

"Feel it! Feel the fire!"

"Dlangdlangdlangdlangdlangdlangdlang!"

At the height of the fever, the Presiding Bishop gathers the flowing skirts of his robe and rises to survey his flock of twenty thousand believers crowded inside the Memphis Cook Convention Center. "Sweet Jesus!" he declares, extending his hand over the crowd. "Look at all that Saint Power out there! This thing getting hotter by the minute! We are positively having us a Holy Ghost explosion! Somebody gonna think we're drunk! But we're not filled with gin! We're not filled with Old Crow! We're filled with the Holy Ghost!"

The energy of the crowd is constantly changing force and direction. In some other setting, twenty thousand people losing control like this would be called a riot. But here there are subtle economies of emotion that keep the scene from flying into chaos. Some people are jogging in place; the woman ahead is speaking what sounds like Greek, an old man is seizuring in the aisle, and the lady two rows back is shouting something about how the Good Lord—*Praise His Holy Name!*—has just shrunk the goiter off her neck. "Was big as a cantaloupe, but now it's gone!"

"Gratitude can change your attitude! Hey, brother, get some Love! 'Cause Love don't make you puff up!"

Everywhere souls are being saved and backsliders are returning to the fold. The choir is hitting notes in the stratosphere, the glorious refrains underscored by the vibrato screech of a Hammond organ pushed through Leslie speakers. People are holding tape recorders in the air as if to capture the room's energy field and take it home.

"He's a good God! Sweet Jesus! He's got the power over sickness! He's got the power over the sickle cell! God is here to help you deal with all your isms and your schisms!"

Standing next to me is Teressa, the determined girl from Detroit with the deep brown eyes, still giving the Devil his due: "Satan is a liar, liar, liar!" Teressa is a coltish girl with smooth ocher skin. She wears white gloves, a white linen dress, white high-heel shoes, and a white hat. She cannot be more than fourteen years old. She throws her arms around me and hugs me tightly. Then she steps back and looks deep into my eyes. "You *know* he is a liar," she proclaims. "But we have a victory now!"

"We didn't come all this way, we didn't come all these thousands

of miles, to be entertained by show business! We came to hear the Master's business!"

The bishops have marched onto the stage, wearing vestments swathed in multicolored clerical stoles. A sign language translator stands in the wings, her hands working frantically to capture all that's going down. Nurses in starchy white medical uniforms sit in one corner of the hall. Ushers march down the aisles in white gloves and tuxedoes, directing the flow of humanity with the exaggerated movements of a mime troupe.

The Bishop's speech is traditionally a joyous occasion, a final drenching in the Holy Spirit before the Saints' long journey home, and this year is no exception. Yet there is a sense of foreboding in the air, a new uncertainty about the future. For by now everyone here has heard the grim reports that have made front-page news in the Memphis paper this week: The Bishop is dying of cancer of the pancreas—inoperable, they say—and may have only a few months to live.

A hush descends over the hall.

"Not long ago," the Bishop begins, his voice ominous and quavering, "I went to the doctor. And he said, 'Cancer' . . ."

Why, Lord, why.

"And he said the treatment is chemotherapy."

Lord save ya' sweet Bishop.

"But I didn't want no chemotherapy, because I'd heard it makes your hair fall out . . . and I didn't want to be buried bald! No, I want to look *pretty* when I die!"

Praise the Lord!

The Saints begin to stir again as the Bishop's voice opens up, the pace quickening, the old Pentecostal fire gathering inside him. "So . . . instead of going to the hospital . . ."

Preach it!

". . . I checked into the *Saints'* hospital!!"

Say it, Bishop!

"Because I *know* the treatment of prayer . . ."

Uh-huh, uh-huh.

". . . is better than the treatment of chemotherapy!!!"

Sweet Jesus-God-ah-Mercy!

"And I want you all to know today . . ."

Preach it!

". . . that I'M NOT MAKING NO FUNERAL ARRANGE-MENTS!!!!!"

Pandemonium.

Teressa, tears streaming down her cheeks, raises her hands to heaven and starts to quiver, a power rumbling inside her. "We have a victory!" she cries out. Then she, too, feels the tongue coming on and drops to the floor for a bout with the Ghost.

"Issshawambiflogishyishyidwangolowaogowambologi!"

WHEN I WAS A BOY growing up in Memphis, the Chamber of Commerce frequently used to boast that our city had more churches than gas stations. I doubt this was really the case, but Memphis certainly earned its title as the "Buckle of the Bible Belt." Sometimes on Sunday afternoons, after our family had returned from the Presbyterian church, I'd take out my transistor radio and scan the stations for baseball games, only to discover that the airwaves were still being hogged by religious broadcasts. Every pulpit in town was competing for air time: Southern Baptists, Primitive Baptists, Freewill Baptists, Reformed Baptists, Two-Seeds-in-the-Spirit Baptists, United Methodists, Seventh-Day Adventists, and a great yodeling slew of free-lance revivalists. The farther up the dial you got, the freer and livelier the worshiping became. The radio needle would sweep over the polyester prophets of the white suburbs, past the local Jerry Falwells and the latter-day Elmer Gantries, and then it would enter the more expressive realm of the black faiths.

Finally you got over to the very end, to a scratchy little low-watt station that played the liveliest broadcast of them all— three or four uninterrupted hours of keening, whooping, and Delta stomp music. I didn't know it at the time, but these were the black Pentecostalists, the ones who spoke in strange tongues and laid their trembling hands upon the sick. The largest Pentecostal denomination in the world was based there in Memphis, its headquarters just a few blocks from the Mississippi River. It was called the Church of God in Christ (normally written COGIC, but pronounced "*Ko*-jik"). Here was a church where people stood up whenever they pleased, and where hardly anything was written down. It was another culture on the other side of the city—the other end of the dial. But even then, I was bewitched by the mysterious rhythms, the triumphant music, the un-Presbyterian energy of it all. It may not have been "Onward Christian Soldiers," but one thing was unmistakable: *This was worshiping.*

My hometown is known the world over as a pilgrimage city, fabled in song and film for the legions of Elvis Presley fans who come each August to gaze on the King's tomb at Graceland and purchase relics. But every November, the Church of God in Christ hosts a substantially larger gathering of pilgrims that makes the scene on Elvis Presley Boulevard look like another day at the mall. For more than eighty years the church's believers have returned to the Mother City. The Memphis riverfront becomes a tent revival, and the autumn air stirs with some of the most beautiful, gasket-blowing gospel music in Christendom.

The Holy Convocation is an around-the-clock festival of religion that touches on every corner of the city. Shelby County's fourteen thousand hotel rooms are booked six months in advance. Radio stations broadcast hourly COGIC bulletins. The parking lots by the convention center are clogged with merchants selling Jesus pins, fur hats, and sorghum molasses from the beds of pickup trucks. Tag-team street evangelists stand on corners, shaking Bibles and howling jeremiads through electronic bullhorns. *"The middle letter of sin is 'I.' The middle letter of pride is 'I.' And what about the middle letter of guilt? 'I,' isn't it? . . . Tells you something, don't it?"*

On the Mid-America Mall, young acolytes sell boxes of "fund-raiser candy." Paperboys hawk fresh copies of *The Whole Truth*, a newspaper with such a loyal following that Saints have been known to place it under their pillows as a medium of divine healing. At night, the Saints creep up and down Front Street in their polished Cadillacs and Olds 98s, tooting their horns at friends on their way to the midnight gospel concerts at the Orpheum Theatre.

They come here from Bedford-Stuyvesant, Watts, the East Side of Cleveland, the South Side of Chicago. They come from Kosciusko, Mississippi; Tuscumbia, Alabama; and a thousand one-mule towns across the South. They come from COGIC missions deep in the shantytowns of Soweto, South Africa; Monrovia, Liberia; and Port-au-Prince, Haiti. The Holy Convocation is a pilgrimage in the truest sense—a retracing of ancestral footsteps. The Saints go to Memphis the way Mormons go to Salt Lake. "Jerusalem on the Mississippi," they call it.

Memphis is the church's international headquarters and

burial place of founder Charles Harrison Mason, the beloved prophet who reigned over the COGIC kingdom for sixty-five years. It was Mason who, in 1907, conceived the idea of holding an annual revival following the cotton harvest each November. Mason predicted that the Holy Convocation would grow so large one day that Memphis wouldn't have a place large enough to hold all the pilgrims, and his prediction more or less came true. Today, COGIC has to stretch the fire codes each year to pack in all of the returning Saints.

Bishop Mason lived long enough to see much of the tremendous growth he'd predicted for COGIC. He died in 1961 at the age of ninety-five, and is buried in a marble crypt in the foyer of Mason Temple, a cavernous, quonset-roofed auditorium in the projects of downtown Memphis where Martin Luther King delivered his "Mountaintop Speech" the night before his assassination.

Today the church that Mason built claims a membership of 3.7 million souls worldwide (the World Council of Churches puts the figure at a more conservative two million), yet little is known about this mysterious denomination born nearly a century ago in a cotton gin. COGIC kept such a low profile throughout its history that the federal government didn't officially recognize it as a religious body until 1975. The members call themselves "Saints," believing that their special holiness "separates" them from the wider society. The church leaders seem to cherish COGIC's obscurity, regarding the outside world as a fanciful distraction from the more serious business of praising the Spirit. Over the years COGIC has developed its own rules and arcane customs: Women aren't allowed to wear lipstick or rouge or any sly adornment that might contribute to what is called "the false look of Jezebel." On Sundays the ladies come to church in modest white dresses, while the men wear simple black suits like the Amish. Church ushers wear white gloves and are required, in a protocol of murky origins, to fold their left hands behind their backs. The Saints do not drink, smoke cigarettes, or attend movies. They discourage marriage outside the faith, regarding all marital unions with non-Saints to be "unequally yoked."

The church's byzantine internal affairs are a continuing source of intrigue to local reporters, who have long suspected that the national organization is woefully mismanaged, if not outright corrupt. Shadowy reports of misplaced funds and political dissension have surfaced from time to time, but the national church has generally kept a lid on leaks. Official documentation on COGIC is scarce: The church has few public financial records, no open business meetings, and no reliable statistics on membership or growth. The national church didn't even get around to installing an accounting system until 1986. COGIC ministers and bishops have no fixed salaries, relying instead on voluntary cash donations called "love offerings." The church has generally avoided taking public positions on political and social issues. And unlike many fundamentalist churches, COGIC never fully entered the high-exposure realm of TV evangelism.

Yet quietly, almost clandestinely, COGIC has grown from a ragtag religious sect of Delta sharecroppers to a major international denomination, with missions in forty-seven countries on four continents. Today, COGIC calls itself "the fastest growing church in the world," with especially rapid growth in developing countries from Africa to the Caribbean.

The Church of God in Christ is a Pentecostal body, which puts it in the same spiritual tradition as televangelists like Jimmy Swaggart, Oral Roberts, and Jim and Tammy Bakker. Like all Pentecostals, the Saints believe in the inerrancy of Scripture and the imminent Second Coming of Christ. They view the Ghost as an active force in their lives. The Ghost can be responsible for such paranormal phenomena as faith healing, the gift of prophecy, slayings in the spirit, and glossolalia (speaking in tongues). "The Holy Spirit," reads the COGIC statement of faith, "proceeds from the Father and Son, is of the same substance, equal in power and glory, and is . . . to be believed, obeyed, and worshipped."

The name "Pentecostal" derives from a passage in the second chapter of Acts that describes the supernatural gifts and strange utterances that descended upon the Apostles as they were staying in Jerusalem on the Day of Pentecost, an ancient harvest celebration. "And they were filled with the Holy Ghost, and began to speak with other tongues," the passage reads. "And [the townspeople] were all amazed, and were in doubt, saying one to another, 'What meaneth this?' Others, mocking, said, 'These men are full of new wine.' "

Pentecostalism is a uniquely American tradition, born of a

series of evangelical revivals that swept the United States in the late nineteenth century and culminated in the historic Azusa Street Resurgence of 1906, a spiritual jamboree that energized a Los Angeles ghetto for more than three years. All Pentecostal groups trace their origins to the Azusa Revival, where it was reported that thousands spoke in tongues and were washed in the healing powers of the Spirit. Among the thousands of pilgrims who traveled to Los Angeles that fateful year was COGIC founder Bishop Mason, who was utterly transformed by the experience. "Getting back to Azusa" is a common refrain in Pentecostal churches, carrying with it the notion of returning to an era free of the cynicism of the scientific age, when the supernatural powers of the Ghost spread like a contagion among the believers.

Theological beliefs aside, COGIC is vastly different from its white Pentecostal brethren. COGIC was founded by a black man, the son of slaves, for black believers. COGIC customs grew directly out of the cotton fields and shotgun shacks of the Mississippi Delta. As machines forced the sharecroppers off the land, and the black families migrated to the smokestack cities of the North, the Church of God in Christ became a source of solace, a means of preserving the spirit of the old rural ways in the face of urban life. So a COGIC service is in some ways going back in time, back to the roots of slave culture in America. The echoes of Africa can be heard in the sermons and prayers, in the spontaneity and lyrical sweep of the service. Something powerful has been preserved here, some raw idiom faithfully passed down.

Ethnomusicologists have marveled at the pure distillation of African-American culture emodied in COGIC's hymns, Negro spirituals, and call-and-response gospel music. In the early 1950s, COGIC churches across America were the first to incorporate electrified instruments and drums into church services, thus pioneering the pop-gospel tradition. COGIC-affiliated gospel groups such as the Hawkins Singers, the Clark Sisters, Andre Crouch, and the Grammy Award–winning Winan Family are considered among the heavyweight talents of black spiritual music today.

It is a source of some embarrassment to the church publicity directors that the Reverend Al Sharpton, New York's racial gadfly, got his start preaching in a Brooklyn COGIC church at the age of nine. Sharpton is no longer associated with the church, but his scrappy style still bears many qualities of the COGIC pulpit tradition—mistrust of the written word, reliance on theatrics and sheer volume to advance an argument, the street preacher's dogged championing of the underclass. The live-wire spirituality that runs through the COGIC experience has long appealed to the poorest and most desperate segment of the American black population, the same class that Sharpton has sought, in his own way, to represent. "The Church of God in Christ traditionally viewed itself as the church of the unlettered black masses," notes Lawrence Jones, dean of the Howard University Divinity School. "It offers a highly emotional faith that is unadulterated by Western intellectualism."

THE SUPREME LEADER of the Church of God in Christ for the past twenty-one years has been Bishop J. O. Patterson. Church literature describes the seventy-seven-year-old clergyman as "the man who fathers three million sons and daughters around the globe." Patterson is the son-in-law of founder Mason, and only the second presiding bishop in the eighty-three-year history of the church. His full title, if you're a stickler, is "The Most Reverend James Oglethorpe Patterson, Sr., Presiding Bishop, President of the Corporation, Chairman of the General Board, Chairman of the Board of Directors, General Overseer and Chief Apostle of the Church of God in Christ." Others just call him "Big Daddy."

Patterson is an affluent funeral parlor executive and pastor of the city's largest COGIC congregation. He presides over the all-powerful Executive Board of the national church, a body of twelve bishops that meets behind closed doors inside the COGIC world headquarters, based in a dilapidated former luxury hotel near the Mississippi River. Patterson's tenure as presiding bishop has been marred by intense controversy, but his ultimate authority is unquestioned. "God selects the leaders in this church," he once said at the Holy Convocation. "This church is not a democracy. It's a *theo*cracy."

Pancreatic cancer is a particularly deadly disease; few of its sufferers have been known to live more than a year after diagnosis. Yet most of Patterson's congregation seems to believe him when he says he's cured: Faith healing is one of the hallmarks of the COGIC experience. And Patterson has made testimonials of dramatic recoveries before, such as the time he claimed the Spirit saved him from a dangerous allergy that had caused him to swell up "twice my normal size."

The Bishop's illness has left him gaunt and sallow, but he is still a commanding presence in the pulpit. He is a tall, mustachioed man with a baritone voice and steely eyes that methodically scan the room. He wears a white robe with a purple stole. Swinging from his neck is a hefty crucifix of gold and rubies. When he preaches, Patterson doesn't flail and prance around in the hyperactive style of most Pentecostal ministers; he clenches his teeth and hunches slightly forward, dropping his head down like a bull moose. One senses that Patterson, a mortician by trade, is a man distrustful of motion.

The Official Day speech is one of the Bishop's rare personal appearances during Convocation Week; Patterson is a master of the well-timed stage entrance, and knows how to build suspense simply by keeping himself scarce. His photographed image, however, is everywhere. For months prior to the Holy Convocation, his likeness has been plastered over the slums near Beale Street. You can see him staring out from the diesel-blackened ads on the rear panels of city buses. You can see him glowering down from billboards pitched high above the red-light districts, his dour image competing with the Kool cigarette and malt liquor ads. "The Saints Are Coming!" the signs announce, a seemingly incongruous message of hope next to the bishop's austere face. For in these billboards, as in all his official photographs, Patterson never smiles. There is only a scowl and an inscrutable fisheye stare that registers its abiding disapproval over the litter of downtown Memphis.

The church treats Patterson like royalty: He rides in a black Fleetwood limousine with a license plate that reads "COGIC-1," and is escorted by a coterie of minions who wear black suits with white gloves and constantly shield his movements. During Sunday services at his church in Memphis, Patterson sits quietly on a large throne known as the Apostolic Chair and sips coffee from a silver chalice, occasionally picking up the phone to confer with the sound engineers. He lives in a plantation-style mansion near Graceland with a wrought-iron gate and a permanently manned guardhouse. On his travels abroad, his schedulers book first-class flights and accommodations, carefully choreographing red-carpet receptions at foreign airports.

Bishop Patterson rarely meets with members of the press. Arranging a personal interview with him, I'm repeatedly told by his office, is "out of the question."

The Bishop's prestige extends beyond the church. For years *Ebony* magazine has included Patterson in its annual list of America's most influential black leaders. Presidential candidates such as Jimmy Carter and Jesse Jackson have flown to Memphis seeking Patterson's endorsement. NAACP Director Benjamin Hooks, who grew up in Memphis and is a personal friend of Patterson's, has sought the Bishop's support for various causes. At the church headquarters in Memphis, the walls are crowded with photographs of the Bishop shaking hands with various international leaders, including Ronald Reagan, Tip O'Neill, Shimon Peres, and Brazilian President José Sarney.

The Patterson family has become a kind of a theocratic political dynasty in the black community of Memphis. The Bishop's only son, attorney J. O. Patterson, Jr., is a former state senator and long-time city councilman who in 1981 served as interim mayor of Memphis, the first black man to occupy City Hall. Bishop Patterson's nephew, Gilbert E. Patterson, is a charismatic COGIC minister with his own popular following in Memphis. The Patterson family runs one of the largest funeral parlors in Memphis, Patterson Mortuary, and a lucrative insurance company that specializes in burial policies.

Bishop Patterson and his son are joint pastors of the Pentecostal Institutional Church, a modern 3,000-seat temple off Beale Street. The church has plush coral blue carpeting, two white baby-grand pianos, and a closed-circuit television system owned by Patterson Ministries, Inc., which distributes cassettes and videos all over the world. In the rear of the church is a stained-glass window, designed by Bishop Patterson himself and built at a reported cost of $4 million, which depicts Jesus Christ as a black man.

For all the regal trappings that surround Bishop Patterson, his followers insist that he is still a man of the people whose tastes and views haven't strayed far from his simple origins in rural Mississippi. Patterson wears blue jeans and flannel shirts around the house, they say, and his culinary tastes run in the direction of beans and molasses-soaked cornbread. For his vacations, he still likes to fish for crappie in the muddy oxbow lakes of the Delta. One of his common refrains in sermons is "Thank

God for the ignorant folk!" He has a habit of sprinkling his sermons with barnyard parables about mules, milk pails, and the slaughtering of hogs. He is always careful to show that he hasn't lost touch with the workaday concerns of the predominantly poor people who make up his congregation—concerns about illness, grocery bills, and paying rent. "I don't care if beefsteak goes up to ten thousand dollars a pound," he'll say, "every now and then, God's going to send you a hamburger!"

Patterson does not issue formal encyclicals in the grand style of the Vatican, but he's quite adept in his own way at getting his doctrinal ideas across. He once summed up the full sweep of his theological views in one sentence: "I am not frigidly formal or foolishly fanatical, but I am fervently fundamental, earnestly evangelical, and purely pentecostal." His positions on specific matters of national church protocol or vice can usually be found in one of the many informal pronouncements that he has delivered at Holy Convocations over the years:

On cigarette smoking: "Smoking is wrong. I've never seen anybody get the Holy Ghost while they were smoking!"

On premarital cohabitation: "The Holy Ghost don't believe in shacking. We've got to stop dragging Holiness in the dust."

On clerical attire: "I don't believe that preachers ought to be wearing skin-tight suits and high-heeled jitterbug shoes."

On homosexuality: "God put us here to replenish the earth. God made Adam and Eve, not Adam and Steve."

On tithing: "Are you giving God a tip or a tithe? I have never in my life seen a U-Haul trailer hitched to the back of a hearse."

On alcoholism: "They say it's a disease, but I know it's a lie, because you can't buy disease by the pint. It's a sin! It's a sin!"

Patterson was elected Presiding Bishop in 1968 after a rancorous eight-year feud, still referred to within the church as "The Wilderness Wanderings," that followed the death of founder Bishop Mason in 1961. As Mason's son-in-law, Patterson was considered a popular choice for successor, but technically the reins of the church were left in the hands of Bishop O. T. Jones, Sr., of Philadelphia. Patterson's controversial election came after a prolonged court battle and resulted in a schism in the church hierarchy. In 1969, fourteen COGIC bishops loyal to O. T. Jones bolted and established their own organization, COGIC International, moving their headquarters to Kansas

City. (Most of the dissenting churches have since returned to the fold.)

From the beginning, there was grumbling about Patterson's secretive and often dictatorial style. Many members grew concerned, for example, when Patterson refused to disclose his plans for an extravagant renovation of the old Mason Temple in Memphis, calling the project "a military secret." In the early 1970s a bitter feud erupted among members of the Patterson clan over the operation of the family funeral home; it was reported in the Memphis papers that during legal negotiations to resolve the dispute, Bishop Patterson, in a pique of rage, hurled the lawyers and their briefcases out of a conference room. A few years later, another family feud made local headlines when the Bishop's nephew, Rev. Gilbert E. Patterson, openly accused his uncle of squandering denominational funds, ignoring church bylaws, and using "scare tactics."

Meanwhile, stories about unorthodox business dealings and rampant disorganization emerged. In 1972, a prominent white Memphis family, with no known connections to COGIC, suddenly announced that its estate was giving the church a $1 million no-strings-attached gift in the form of a 400-room luxury hotel in downtown Memphis, the Chisca, which had fallen on hard times. No explanation was offered. Though opposing factions in the church called the Chisca a "white elephant," Patterson accepted the gift and promptly turned the hotel into COGIC's world headquarters.

In 1975 the IRS threatened to withdraw the church's tax-exempt status because it was unable to confirm what it suspected were COGIC's grossly inflated membership statistics. The church said its estimate of 3.5 million members was based on "human computers," but it was clear no one in the national organization really had a handle on church growth. In the mid-seventies a concerted effort to reach all COGIC ministers by mail was answered by two thousand returned envelopes reading "address unknown." Patterson was more than a little cavalier about the IRS dispute. "Statistics are not important to me," he said at the time. "When the Ghost comes, you find that the rest of the world is just a passing fancy. I'm not concerned about how many members I have. I'm only concerned about how many *Saints* I have."

Throughout the early 1970s, several challenges to Patterson's reign were raised in anonymous pamphlets circulated surreptitiously at the Holy Convocation, forcing Patterson to make cryptic public speeches in which he lashed out at invisible "enemies" of the church. But in 1978, two courageous COGIC elders came forward with a package of twelve signed resolutions to make the church more "democratic." The elders argued that the church had become "a one-man show," and that the national organization was "threatened with insolvency and financial mismanagement." Among their reforms, the two men suggested that the church hire a CPA, make the minutes of the General Assembly public, limit the Presiding Bishop's office to three terms (twelve years), establish a separate judiciary commission to review grievances, and open up the editorial pages of the church newspaper, *The Whole Truth*, to a wider spectrum of opinion. After initially receiving permission to present their proposals at a public meeting one evening in Memphis, the two elders were physically dragged off the stage and taken to the office of the general secretary, where they were handcuffed by policemen, interrogated, and threatened with arrest. Their ultimate punishment was never reported, and my repeated attempts to reach them, some twelve years after the controversy had vanished from the newspapers, were unsuccessful. Bishop Patterson, for his part, was unequivocal in describing their reforms as a dangerous heresy. "The Devil wants the Church of God in Christ," he told his followers. "The Devil wants to infiltrate the church with rebellious people and spiritual hecklers."

But the spiritual heckling continued. In 1983 the General Assembly, COGIC's legislative body, issued a report accusing Patterson and his executive board of, among other transgressions, "mismanagement, conflict of interest, excessive honoraria, misleading information, and excessive and unwise spending." Church contributions, it was alleged, were routinely going unreported and understated in official records, and large sums had been transferred without authorization or proper documentation. Nepotism was rife within the national organization. Seven members of Patterson's family, including his wife, Rose, were on the COGIC payroll, and his son J. O. Jr. was handling all contracts and legal affairs. In 1983, Bishop Patterson used a Convocation speech to promote his son's bid for Memphis City Hall, even going so far as to pass out envelopes soliciting campaign contributions.

Most controversial of all has been Bishop Patterson's ambitious dream of building a $30 million Pentecostal village to be called The Saints' Center. The national church has acquired twenty-three acres of downtown real estate on which the Bishop plans to build a 2,000-car garage, a publishing house, a domed convention center, a wax museum, a hall of fame, and an outdoor arena to be called the James Oglethorpe Patterson Performing Arts Amphitheatre. At the heart of the proposed complex will be All Saints University, a Pentecostal college and seminary. Patterson's dream is to make ASU a place so holy that even the campus police will carry Bibles. "If all the people of the world were students at ASU," Patterson once mused, "Memphis wouldn't need a police department or a locksmith, and all the liquor stores would go out of business."

Patterson has been roundly criticized for trying to establish the Saints Center as a personal memorial to himself. More than a few have suggested that the plan is all too reminiscent of Jim and Tammy Bakker's ill-famed Heritage USA theme park. The national church has collected undisclosed millions in the name of the Saints Center, and has resorted to such fund-raising schemes as selling hand and body cream (Saints' Center Formula IV Lotion). Though the first phase of the university was scheduled to be completed as early as 1984, not a single building has been erected on the barren, weedy site. "The church has collected millions over the last twelve years for the university," charged COGIC elder Milton Jackson in a 1987 *Commercial Appeal* article. "But it's all disappeared. You might as well be putting money in a bag with a hole in it."

Bishop Patterson has remained unfazed by the dissension over his pet project. "You can't get the approval of everybody when God gives you a vision," he once remarked. "The Saints Center is not for me. It's for God!"

THE GREAT RELIGIOUS SECTS OF THE WORLD are frequently the products of two men—a visionary and a builder. Before Brigham Young could establish his Mormon kingdom in the salt flats of Utah, he needed the grand spiritual design laid out by the prophet Joseph Smith. So it has been with Bishop Patterson, who has used his political strengths to consolidate the church structure, turning a loose-knit organization of some four hundred thousand believers into a modern denomination of more than three million souls worldwide. But there would have been no church for Patterson to build without the compelling vision and charismatic personality of his predecessor, Bishop Charles Harrison Mason.

The Saints speak of founder Bishop Mason as if he were alive and well, watching over them with a sweet grandfatherly vigilance. At the 1989 Convocation, one bishop referred to him as "that great prophet of God, greater than a Moses, greater than an Isaac, greater than a Jacob!" An oil portrait hanging at the world headquarters depicts Mason as Jesus in a reinterpretation of da Vinci's *Last Supper*, the Messiah breaking bread with his twelve black disciples. Tapes of Mason's sermons reverberate through the halls, his ominous voice crackling in torrents of brimstone. You can buy collections of Mason's prayers, selections of his quotations, hagiographies, and innumerable photographs of his stern image (like Patterson, Mason never seems to smile in official portraits). The church leaders often invoke his name when floating new ideas to the congregation. "Bishop Mason would want it this way," they'll suggest, or, "Do it for the founder."

Bishop Mason was a short, spry man with close-cropped, grizzled hair, leathery brown skin, and a pencil mustache. "The Diminutive Holy Man," the Memphis papers dubbed him. Every day he wore the same uniform: a black serge suit, a white broadcloth shirt with removable collars, and a black bow tie. He had a disarming habit of closing his eyes for minutes at a time, like a Buddhist monk in meditation. His only vice was chewing gum.

Despite his humble demeanor, church accounts describe Mason as a "militant." He prayed two hours on his knees every morning before breakfast. He advised his church members to keep a Bible in every room of their house, even the bathroom ("Don't waste your time in there!" he'd admonish). He made a practice of speaking to Satan directly, as in "Satan, I rebuke you! Get out now! Let loose of my little ones!" Some Saints will tell you that Mason actually raised people from the dead and turned away tornadoes by the sheer muscular force of his faith. In 1918, federal authorities arrested Mason for his opposition to World War I. The FBI suspected Mason of collusion with the Germans, and maintained a secret file for decades, hoping to build a case against him for treason.

The late Bishop Charles Mason, founder of COGIC, posing with
his beloved roots in 1953.

Official Day at the Holy Convocation.

Bishop Patterson's funeral procession outside Mason Temple, January 1990.

During his sixty-five-year reign, it was unheard of for church members to disagree with Mason. He ruled by quiet example, establishing a church government that was essentially a benevolent dictatorship. He was a pious man. Unlike Patterson, he never had personal servants or bodyguards. The church structure grew out of a few simple principles set down in his *Book of Discipline*.

His sermons were usually unplanned, spoken in a peculiar stream-of-consciousness style that bounced around good-naturedly as the Spirit moved him. Sometimes, though, he'd strike a topic that would cause him to erupt unexpectedly in a withering barrage of words, like this discourse on pride taken from a sermon he delivered in 1926:

> . . . Short dress pride, low-necked pride! Men PROUD over their success over others! Lawyers PROUD over their arguments in sentencing someone for gain! Judges PROUD over their power to send men into custody! Men and women PROUD of their fine homes and automobiles! Women PROUD of their power of attraction that BEWITCHES a man, turning him from his home, his wife, and his children. Man PROUD in his WICKEDNESS in taking to himself another man's wife, and bringing shame and disgrace to himself! The rich man PROUD of his ascendancy over the poor, having gathered his gain by FRAUD and keeping back the hire from the poor! National PRIDE in bringing forth wars and polluting the land, causing blood to touch blood—all of these forms of pride God will work with in storms, earthquakes, and with flames of devouring fire!

The son of slaves, Mason was an untutored mystic who instinctively turned to Nature for signs of the Holy Ghost. His was a kind of Christian animism. The Ghost was everywhere— in that cypress stump over there, in the pecan groves, in that ornery old mule. It was said Mason could divine God's will by studying the freakish shapes of certain twisted roots and petrified vegetables which he had pulled out of the black soil. He liked to haul his gnarled specimens into the church and use them as visual aids. "Mystical wonders of God," he called them.

There was a root that resembled a crippled human hand, a
branch that vaguely resembled a serpent, a gourd that had the
"exact likeness of an animal's head." A tree limb that looked
like a crippled dog would form the basis of a sermon on how
to establish a better spiritual footing. "Take heed, my brethren,"
he'd say, "this dog is on three legs! You may now be standing,
but soon you are to fall because there is something lacking in
your foundation!" Mason could slice open a watermelon and
augur a drought or a war based on the configuration of the
seeds. And if signs of the Ghost could be found everywhere in
nature, even inside a melon, then He could be inside you, too.
You just had to want Him bad enough.

But getting the Ghost was not some clean doctrinal exercise
of the mind; it was a raucous, sweaty affair, a tumble on the
mat, like Jacob's wrestling match with the angel. You had to
feel the pulsing presence of the Spirit inside your body, had to
taste Him on the buds of your tongue. Strange things could
happen, just as they had on the day of Pentecost—rushing
winds, cloven tongues of fire, visions. And once you got Him—
or rather, He got you—all your workaday troubles, all your little
bruises and fevers and arthritic pains, would appear suddenly
insignificant, and you would want to spend the rest of your days
celebrating God's grace.

Charles Harrison Mason was born a year after Appomattox
on a Tennessee cotton plantation not far from Memphis. Even
as a young boy he showed a spiritual predilection. Often he
would walk into the woods alone and pray for hours at a time.
He liked to sing the old slave hymns with his parents and their
friends in the Missionary Baptist Church. As an old man he
always used to say that his life's work had been to recapture the
simple vitality of the "slave religion" he'd learned at the knee
of his parents. It was a religion short on doctrine and long on
prayer, a religion of song and unvarnished emotion. It was a
spirituality that suffused one's whole existence and was connected to the daily rhythms of rural life—the thunderstorms
and droughts, the births and deaths of the livestock, the ebb
and flow of the harvest and planting seasons.

In 1878, a yellow fever epidemic hit Memphis, decimating
the city's population. The Masons fled west to Arkansas to escape the mosquito-borne plague, but not soon enough: Within
a year, yellow fever had claimed his father's life, and young

Charles fell ill a few months later. (Some accounts claim his illness was tuberculosis.) His chills and delirious fevers persisted for several weeks, and his mother feared for his life. But one morning, in what church literature describes as a miracle of the Spirit, the fourteen-year-old boy suddenly recovered. It was his dramatic healing that would clinch his decision to pursue the ministry. In the following years, the young Mason made a name for himself as a lay preacher, offering testimonials of his miraculous cure at tent revivals and summer Bible camps. He was ordained as a Baptist minister at the age of twenty-five. The same year, he married a young Arkansas woman named Alice Saxton. His new bride took a dim view of his chosen profession, however, and within two years they were divorced. Mason, distraught and on the brink of suicide, enrolled in an Arkansas Baptist college, thinking "an education might help my preaching."

The headstrong Mason lasted only three months in seminary, but it was a crucial experience for him all the same. One version of the story was that Mason was expelled for expounding radical ideas. By his own account, Mason dropped out, finding that the curriculum and the bookish ways of his classmates had no relevance to his ultimate goal of resurrecting "slave religion."

"The Lord showed me that there was no salvation in schools and colleges," Mason later wrote. "For the way they were conducted grieved my soul. I packed my books, arose, and bade them farewell. I decided to follow Jesus with the Bible as my sacred and only guide."

So in 1895 Mason set out on his own as an itinerant preacher. He worked the gins and sharecropper shacks of the Cotton Belt, following the railroad tracks from town to town. He preached in brush arbors and carnival tents. He conducted all-night revivals from the beds of haywagons. At the outset, he attempted to work within the Baptist and Methodist traditions. But everywhere he went, Mason found the established churches rejected his teachings. Some local ministers were uncomfortable with all those weird roots and rotten potatoes he doted on, and were alarmed by the way his free-lance evangelizing stirred the people's emotions.

Others were troubled by his theology. Mason had begun to preach a radical definition of "holiness" that was derived from the teachings of John Wesley. He held that the true believer can achieve a state of perfect holiness, or "sanctification," that is very nearly Christ-like; the "sanctified" Christian is not of this world, and should therefore take pains to "separate" himself from society. Mason's otherworldly message threatened the authority of established black ministers, who served not only as spiritual leaders, but also as the de facto political heads of black communities throughout the Jim Crow South.

In 1897, after he was run out of Jackson for preaching his "radical" definition of holiness at a revival, Mason landed in Lexington, Mississippi. Here he established his own church in an abandoned cotton gin. During the church's first meeting, as the worshiping reached a frenzied pitch, someone fired five pistol shots and two blasts from a double-barreled shotgun at close range into the crowd. Several of the worshipers were injured, but miraculously no one was killed. "The Devil stirred someone to shoot into the congregation while we were shouting and praying," Mason later recalled. "This wonderful catastrophe was reported by the newspapers, and served more as advertisement than as a hindrance. People came as never before!"

Mason incorporated the new denomination and called it the Church of God in Christ. The name, he said, had come to him in a divine inspiration.

Today Lexington is a drowsy county seat shaded by magnolias and a dozen grain silos that rise over the rusty hills and gulches to the east. To get there, you take Highway 61 out of Memphis and head south through the Mississippi Delta, the Mesopotamia of the blues. It is a stark landscape still haunted by the ghosts of slavery which seem to lie low in the languorous bayous, in the piney woods swallowed by kudzu, in the endless rows of cotton plants drooping in their black furrows. Little has changed in the nearly one hundred years since Mason first arrived. Cotton is king, though the soybean has made a considerable dent in the order of things. Mason's church, the St. Paul Church of God in Christ, is still here, newly renovated and drawing large crowds on Sundays. COGIC also owns a seminary in Lexington, called Saints Academy, but when I visited the 300-acre campus, it was closed down for lack of funds, the buildings shuttered. The road out of Lexington was lined with trailer bins piled high with cotton to be ginned. For miles the white whisps fluttered in the air and blanketed the roadside ditches like a deep winter's snow.

IN 1906, NEWS OF A FIERY SPIRITUAL REVIVAL in southern California was reaching evangelists back East, and Mason decided to investigate. In 1907, he took a train to Los Angeles and made his way to a downtown ghetto, where at 312 Azusa Street the revival was running day and night out of a livery stable. A *Los Angeles Times* report, which happened to appear on the day of the San Francisco earthquake, spoke of "wild scenes" and "the weird babble of tongues." Witnesses said a strange electric force suffused the room. As a pastor from Pasadena put it at the time: "The power of the Lord was so great in the auditorium, it seemed to tingle your spine, and your hair stood up on end."

Inside the sweaty hall, packed crowds sat on wooden planks laid across nail kegs. Sawdust was sprinkled on the floor, and a stack of wooden shoeboxes formed a makeshift pulpit. Blacks, whites, and Chicanos shouted and prayed together. "The color line has been washed away by the blood!" one participant marveled in his diary. Women and even children were free to preach, and anyone present could stand up and testify as the Spirit moved him. Hymns were sung a capella. Worshipers plucked saws, banged cow ribs, and strummed washboards with thimbles. One man who brought a fiddle was thrown out for playing "the devil's music." Some people went upstairs to the "tarrying room" for more intimate sessions with the Ghost. The walls of the tarrying room were lined with canes and crutches left behind by cripples who claimed to be healed. Tobacco pipes and liquor bottles were piled on the floor as proof that sinners had abandoned their vices.

The revival was led by a stout holiness preacher from Houston named William Joseph Seymour. An account at the time described Elder Seymour as a "plain, common-looking man with a short beard and a glass eye, not given to great outbursts." But there was nothing plain or common about Seymour's methods. Like Mason, Seymour was a black man who had been expelled from a number of churches for advocating radical notions about "holiness." It was under Seymour's patient direction that Mason was "slain in the Spirit," and for the first time in his life, he spoke in tongues. "The Spirit came upon me,"

Mason later said. "All of my being was filled with the glory of the Lord. When I opened my mouth, a flame touched my tongue which ran down to me. My language changed and no word could I speak in my own tongue. My soul was then satisfied."

The Azusa Street Mission was demolished in 1928, and the site served as a city parking lot for fifty years. Today the entire block is occupied by the Japanese Cultural Center of Little Tokyo. Perhaps out of deference to history, there is still a sign that says "Azusa Street," but the street itself is gone. All that's left of the revival is the private home where Elder Seymour held the first meetings before the crowds grew too unwieldy. It is a bungalow at 214 North Bonnie Brae Street in a predominantly Hispanic section downtown.

It was raining on the morning I visited there, two days after Easter. From the front porch, I could look back through the gathering storm and see the HOLLYWOOD letters stretching across the ridge. "We Dedicate This Site to God—The Birthplace of the Pentecostal Movement in America," announced the plaque out front. A Filipino Pentecostal named Jun greeted me at the door and gave me the standard tour.

"Seymour preach here."

Jun pointed toward the front porch. "But it collapse from too many people. Then move to Azusa."

The guestbook in the front hall was filled with names of visitors from as far away as India, Germany, and Australia. Jun said that every spring on the Day of Pentecost (fifty days after Easter Sunday), several thousand believers from the Los Angeles area march from here to the Azusa site. "This where it all began," he said as I was leaving. "You stay here long enough, and you feel the power too!"

Bishop Mason stayed five weeks in Los Angeles. His experience in the tarrying room was so intense that he was struck dumb for a month. He returned to the Delta a changed man, brimming with a new enthusiasm for the mystical powers of the Spirit. But many of his followers were skeptical of his strange descriptions of the miracles he'd witnessed at Azusa. Some members split off from the main church, thinking their beloved pastor had finally ventured too far afield. In 1907, Mason rounded up the remaining faithful and moved the church headquarters to Memphis. In the newly constituted COGIC, Mason assumed the title "General Overseer and Chief Apostle."

The same year, Mason struck upon the idea of holding an annual revival in Memphis to bring the Saints together. The original Day of Pentecost in ancient Israel had been a feast to celebrate the end of the harvest season, and that's how Mason envisioned the Holy Convocation. It was to be held a week after all the cotton had been picked and the sharecroppers had received their season's pay. Mason wanted the Convocation to be a purely spiritual celebration, a time to recapture the fire of Azusa; there was no place here for church politics or tedious doctrinal disputes. The gathering lasted twenty-one consecutive days, with services running around the clock.

The Convocation was a much more intimate affair in the early days. The Saints ate common meals of beans, cabbage, and cornbread served in the basement of the church. Jim Crow laws prevented the pilgrims from staying in the Memphis hotels, so most made arrangements to sleep in the homes of local church members. Others camped on the floor of the church.

In 1918, Mason's opposition to World War I put the church on a collision course with federal authorities. In a sermon entitled "The Kaiser in the Light of the Scriptures," Mason urged his congregation not to "trust in the power of the U.S., England, France, or Germany, but trust only in God." COGIC's official doctrine was unequivocally pacifist. "We are opposed to war in all its various forms," a church statement read, "and we believe the shedding of blood and the taking of human life to be contrary to the teachings of our Lord Jesus Christ." In 1918, a COGIC pastor in Blytheville, Arkansas, was tarred and feathered after he made what local authorities described as "seditious remarks concerning the President and the white man's war." The same year, federal agents in Los Angeles identified several white followers of Mason to be "of German extraction," and that was enough for the FBI to start building a case. Mason was arrested in Lexington and jailed for preaching against the war, but a U.S. District Court in Jackson dismissed the case. FBI agents had confiscated Mason's briefcase as primary evidence, but the most incriminating items they found inside were a Bible, a handkerchief, and a bottle of anointing oil.

In fact, the agents were less concerned about Mason's con-

scientious-objector status than they were with his "interra-
cialism." Bishop Mason had ordained scores of white
Pentecostal ministers throughout the South, and, for a short
time, white COGIC congregations nearly outnumbered black
ones. "It is clear," the 1918 FBI file snidely reports, "that Mason
and his followers felt it to be of far-reaching significance that
one of the great religious movements of the 20th Century was
founded by a member of the African race."

BY WORLD WAR II, THE CHURCH OF GOD IN CHRIST was prosper-
ing. Hundreds of new COGIC churches were spawned in the
North and Midwest as blacks migrated to find wartime factory
jobs. Meanwhile, the national organization in Memphis had a
new home: Mason Temple. The city paper boasted that the new
church in downtown Memphis was "the largest convention hall
owned by any Negro church group in America." Built at a cost
of $400,000, Mason Temple was designed to be the "Mother
Church," COGIC's equivalent of St. Peter's basilica. The temple complex was a self-contained universe for the returning
pilgrims. It had its own rooming house, barbershop, shoeshine
parlor, mailroom, Western Union office, hospital, and cafeteria.
A $1,600 neon sign proudly hummed the church name outside.

For decades Mason Temple served as a kind of town hall
for the city's black community. In 1968, striking sanitation
workers made the Temple their headquarters, and Martin Luther King, Jr., delivered a rousing speech from Mason's old
pulpit. King was killed by an assassin's bullet the next day at the
nearby Lorraine Motel.

Today, Mason Temple is still an imposing edifice, but it has
fallen into sad disrepair. The tubed lettering on the old neon
sign has been ripped out of its sockets. A beautiful stained-glass
window bearing the saintly image of Bishop Mason is covered
in black soot. Drug dealers sell crack cocaine down the street.

Still, Mason Temple remains the sentimental home of the
national church. During Convocation Week, many Saints continue to sleep on the grounds. Pilgrims stream in at all hours of
the day to get the Ghost in a darkened upstairs chamber called
the Prayer Room. On the day I visited, a distinguished-looking
man who had evidently just recovered from a vigorous slaying
in the Spirit was adjusting his silk necktie and mopping his brow
with a handkerchief. On his way out of the Prayer Room, he

thanked the Ghost for healing an old "hernia condition" and dropped a ten-dollar bill into the box marked "In God We Trust."

Behind the temple stands an old brick manse where I had the good fortune of meeting Mason's widow. Elsie Mason is now in her late seventies and lives in Los Angeles, where she still keeps her husband's collection of roots and gnarled branches. "People from COGIC look at me like I'm something out of a museum!" Elsie protested.

Elsie sat in the manse on a warm afternoon and reminisced about her life with the "Diminutive Holy Man." She and the Bishop traveled extensively together in his waning years, including one glorious trip to a conference in London, where Mason was received as the elder statesman of the world Pentecostal movement. "Oh, London was heaven on earth!" she remembered with a smile.

Our conversation turned to the scandals that had recently rocked the world of TV evangelism. "I knew something didn't add up with those two—the Bakkers," she asserted, referring to the defrocked PTL Club televangelists Jim and Tammy Bakker. "They never got that Pentecostal feel, somehow. You know, if you've got the Spirit, you don't emphasize 'Me' and 'Mine' all the time. You don't care about this world. You forget you and it's all God. And you certainly don't need to have an air-conditioned doghouse! I tell you right now, we didn't even have air-conditioning in our *own* house."

Bishop Mason died in Detroit in 1961. His daughter, who was with him at his deathbed, claimed she heard a choir of angels singing as he passed away. Mason was buried in a copper coffin inside a marble vault placed in the foyer of Mason Temple. More than twelve thousand people came to the memorial service, which was handled by J. O. Patterson Funeral Home. The fifty-fourth Holy Convocation began the next day.

"Back to Pentecost at any cost" is one of Bishop Patterson's trademark expressions, and it seems an especially appropriate slogan for the Holy Convocation. For getting souls back to Pentecost is big business. The Chamber of Commerce estimates that the Saints sink more than $16 million into the Memphis economy each November. Radio and TV ads are dominated by businesses seeking COGIC patronage—

TACO BELL WELCOMES COGIC
GOLDSMITHS INVITES COGIC LADIES TO
MEMPHIS' GREATEST HAT SHOP
"This is FM 107, K-FAITH, Your Convocation Connection!"

Many Saints go on spending sprees in the Memphis department stores. The pilgrims are known for buying fancy suits, jewelry, perfume, and luxury cars. Business is brisk at the Madison Cadillac dealership downtown. A salesman there remembers one COGIC bishop who used to trade in his used Fleetwood for a new showroom model each November. It has long been a tradition for COGIC women to buy fur coats and hats during Convocation Week. At Memphis Furs, full-length red foxes are going for $3,600, Blackglamas for $3,995.

But food is probably the hottest seller. At the convention center, sour pickles, peanut brittle, yams, and new-crop pecans are the big items. A nearby congregation is offering plate dinners at the church cafeteria for $8.99; the entrées include chitterlings, neckbones, oxtails, hamhocks, pig's feet, and buffalo fish. Preaching on a corner near an outdoor concession stand, a thin, dour-faced holy man—clearly put off by the ubiquitous talk of eating—brandishes a Bible and hollers at the swarming crowd: "This here's the only food you be needing! Now stop being tourists, y'all, and let's have church!"

The mezzanine of the Cook Convention Center serves as an agora where all manner of religious paraphernalia is on sale: vestments, gospel records, wheat wafers, hymnbooks, large-print Bibles, collection plates, even church pews. One booth is occupied by a Nashville company that specializes in disposable communion cups ("Crystal Clear Cups," the ads declare, "The Best Cup, the Right Price"). At The Gospel Rack, "Home of the Jesus Pin," silkscreened T-shirts read "BLACK BY NATURE, COGIC BY THE GRACE OF GOD." Another popular silkscreen design proclaims: "ITS A BLACK THING—YOU WOULDN'T UNDERSTAND." Not far from the Gospel Rack, a nattily dressed salesman is peddling sets of sermon outlines for $300. "You can't get this in bookstores!" he insists. "Now look here—fifty-two sermons. That'll keep you covered every Sunday of the year." One of his prefab sermons bears the unironic title, "Counterfeit Christianity: What Is It?"

J. O. Patterson Ministries, Inc., has set up a flashy multimedia display by the main escalator. Here there are $25 videocassettes of the Bishop's sermons, which are continuously flickering on four large color television sets. Throughout the day, wide-eyed young preachers cluster around the monitors, soaking up Patterson's pulpit style, mastering the subtle cadences the way hungry young boxers might study old footage of an Ali bout. "See the way he do?" one of them whispers to a mesmerized colleague. "Listen how he's always sneaking up that volume." This is the closest many of these Pentecostal understudies will get to formal seminary. COGIC does have a small seminary on the campus of Morehouse University in Atlanta, but most of the church's ministers still rise through the ranks in the traditional way—establishing a grass-roots following at the local storefront church, learning the Pentecostal idiom in the desultory way that jazz musicians pick up their licks. Bishop Mason didn't think much of book learning, and in that respect little has changed: COGIC is still firmly rooted in the oral tradition.

Other rooms at the convention center are lined with secular goods. Gillette is promoting its new line of black hair toiletries. Fannie's Sales is offering panty hose and five-hundred-dollar silk suits. The racks at Bea's Custom Millinery are overflowing with ladies' designer hats, all netted and ribboned and outfitted with purple ostrich plumes. Mary Kay Cosmetics has a pink and peach display down on the first floor. Studio photographers have set up booths where Saints can pose for family portraits against a backdrop of a quaint Victorian set piece.

Then there are the snake-oil salesmen, rummaging through their black bags full of weird powders, tinctures, and five-dollar cure-alls.

A persistent saleslady on the first floor is pushing something she calls the AcuVibe Foot Massage, a "revolutionary" new podiatric remedy. "C'mon, brothers and sisters," she coaxes. "You been standing on those feets all day long. Let me put the AcuVibe on you!"

A smooth-talking paraplegic in a silver zoot suit who calls himself "The Wheelchair Preacher" is hustling a special "convocation" issue of *The Mt. Resounders Gospel Tidings*. The two-dollar tabloid, published out of California by Elder Jymmy Mathis II, D.D., purports to be the "official" organ of The Church of God in Christ—a boast that borders on the sacrilegious, given the devout following enjoyed by the older, better-established *The Whole Truth*. The *Mt. Resounders* masthead calls Elder Mathis the "founder, publisher, and world editor," but I later learned that he is widely considered a pariah who circulates his vanity newspaper without authorization from church officials. Among the stories in this month's issue of *Mt. Resounders* is a lengthy feature by Elder Mathis about a "miraculous" new one-handed golf swing technique that, he claims, has won him numerous tournaments—with a little help from the Holy Ghost, of course.

CARRIE DATSON, THE MARY KAY SALESLADY, lives in Cleveland, where she has been a member of the Church of God in Christ for thirty years. Standing proudly over her toners and skin creams, she can scarcely contain her enthusiasm for the Dallas-based direct sales company. "I don't put anything before God," she hastens to note, "but I'd say that after my church, Mary Kay is the best thing that ever happened to my life." Carrie has sold Mary Kay cosmetics for ten years, and though she typically puts in just twelve hours of saleswork a week, she's done extraordinarily well for herself. A few years ago, she won a brand-new car—a cream-colored Olds Firenza—as a prize for her high sales figures. She was given the car keys on stage at the annual convention in Dallas.

Carrie points out the parallels between the Mary Kay and COGIC philosophies of life. "Mary Kay is a Christian herself, you know. She believes in personal growth. She is a stickler about having her salespeople be faithful people, people who observe the Golden Rule. Her philosophy is 'God first, family second, *then* your career.' The company teaches you how to have enthusiasm for life. It teaches you how to set goals. We're programmed to be positive people."

Actually, there are several Mary Kay sales counters at the COGIC convention, but Carrie's booth is the only one "authorized" by the official church hierarchy. This is because Carrie, in keeping with strict rules governing the modesty of women in the church, has agreed not to sell what are called "glamor or vanity items." In a sense, all cosmetics are vanity items, of course, but the church draws distinctions. Blushes and mascara, for example, are definitely contraband, considered nothing more than vulgar face paint to seduce men. But toners, astringents, cleansers, and perfumes are deemed "non-glamor," and thus enjoy the church's sanction. I ask Carrie about perfume, which, it occurs to me, might also be used to lure men. "You know, I've thought about that," she admits. "I guess it's true that Jezebel could just as easily seduce men with her smell as with her looks, but I don't know. Those are just the rules."

The church comes down hard on women members who persist in wearing vanity items. One of the common punishments, Carrie points out, is a practice known as "silencing"— the offending Jezebel is simply not allowed to speak in church. She is shunned by her friends, ignored by her preacher, and forbidden from giving public testimonials or offering even so much as a prayer. "Not supposed to be any parading around in our church," Carrie explains. "The preacher has got to put those kind of women in order."

Keeping women "in order" seems to be one of the ongoing concerns of the COGIC leadership. Though women form the backbone of the church, constituting well over 70 percent of the national membership, the equal rights movement has had no apparent effect on the fiercely patriarchal customs of the COGIC universe. COGIC women are forbidden from wearing "gaudy attire," including pantsuits, short skirts, and all short-sleeved clothing. Women are not allowed to train for the ministry and are forbidden from holding any office that does not fall under a broad category which the church literature unabashedly calls "women's work." Women's work includes service on the Hospitality Committee, the Ushers Unit, the Food Division, the Nurses Unit, the Minister's Wives Circle, and the Sewing Circle. ("Sewing is important for the concentration and relaxation of women," a church pamphlet explains.) At the Holy Convocation, the church holds a sexually segregated Women's Day that is reigned over by a stern matriarch from the San Francisco Bay area named Mother Mattie McGlothen, general supervisor of the Department of Women. Mother Mattie's position on femininity is concisely presented in an official manual, written under her direction, that is circulated among all new women members. "The holy woman," the manual advises, "should be temperate, disciplined, self-controlled, chaste, a homemaker, good-natured, adapting, and subjecting herself to her husband."

Carrie Datson sees no problem with any of this. "The Bible says that men should lead," she reasons. "A woman has no business being a pastor because then she'd be in a position of authority over men. She'd be totally out of order. That's not the way God planned it."

Aside from her saleswork for Mary Kay, Carrie works full-time as a registered nurse at a Cleveland hospital. She spends many of her free hours caring for her husband Ollie, a retired truck driver who is a diabetic requiring kidney dialysis three times a week. Since Ollie became disabled in 1981, Carrie has been the breadwinner in the household, but in no way does she consider herself in charge. "As long as there's breath in my husband," she declares, "he's the authority in our house."

A few months after the Holy Convocation, I visited Carrie at her home in Cleveland. The Datsons live on the city's East Side, a crumbling precinct that bears the telltale scars of the crack wars. When I arrived, a winter storm had just blown off Lake Erie, dumping a half-foot of wet snow on the ground.

The Datsons are members of the East 105th Street Church of God in Christ, the second largest COGIC in Cleveland. Carrie and Ollie have six grown children spread over the Midwest. Her youngest son is a student at Kent State University, where he sings in a COGIC choir. As Carrie and I talked, her son Herman, a recruiter in the U.S. Air Force, was outside the house shoveling a path in the snow for her Olds Firenza.

Carrie is a strong woman with a broad, motherly smile full of pearl-white teeth. She is fifty years old but looks forty. There is the simple strength of pragmatism in her eyes, an inner placidity that seems at odds with the stoked fires of her church doctrine. Yet Carrie speaks convincingly of her firsthand experience with the supernatural, of the glorious white-hot emotion that surges through the believer when the Holy Ghost comes. "Can you remember when you were a child," she endeavors to explain, "getting something that you really, really, really, really wanted real bad? And one day you finally got it, and you were surprised? There's nothing that can be compared to it, but that's sort of the feeling. You just want it so bad, and then you finally get it, get the Ghost. You feel like you can conquer the world. You feel totally free. It's something you have to know for yourself. It's joy unspeakable. You're just totally happy. Something takes hold. You feel like you're really going to float, going to fly away. You can try to govern it down, but you can't. You go to uttering. It just comes out of your mouth. You don't black out or anything. You are still in control of your faculties. The Holy Ghost is a perfect gentleman—he doesn't make anybody go crazy."

Carrie quarrels with skeptics who say that "slaying in the Spirit" is nothing more than superstition, or who suggest that the phenomenon is somehow induced by peer pressure or intimidation from a minister. "The Spirit of God is real," she stresses. "He's whatever we want Him to be to us—whatever we allow him to be. Some people don't know how to give in or surrender. Men, especially. They have this macho image, you know. They are always trying to resist. They're so scared they're going to cry."

Carrie's life story in many ways typifies the COGIC experience, tracing as it does the exodus of black sharecroppers from the rural South to the industrial cities of the North. Carrie was born in 1940 and grew up on a Delta plantation not far from Forrest City, Arkansas, just a forty-five-minute drive west across the Mississippi River from Memphis. (Forrest City was named after Nathan Bedford Forrest, the Confederate lieutenant general who later became one of the founding fathers of the Ku Klux Klan.) Carrie came from what she describes as "a huge, huge" family. Throughout her childhood and teenage years, she picked and chopped cotton ten hours a day during harvest season for thirty cents an hour.

Her family rarely left the plantation, and was too poor even to make the short trip to Memphis. Once her mother bought her a new dress and took her to a photography studio in Forrest City. In the photograph, which now sits in Carrie's living room, you can see in her beaming young face that this little daytrip was the rarest of treats. "Forrest City," rues Carrie, "was as far as we ever got."

Like Bishop Mason, Carrie was reared in the Missionary Baptist Church. There was a Church of God in Christ congregation in Forrest City, and what little she knew about the Saints she didn't find very appealing. As it happened, the family of Carrie's high school sweetheart, Ollie Datson, were members of the Forrest City COGIC. "At first I thought the Saints were stuck-up people," she recalls with a wry smile. "They thought they were better than everybody else—uppity, uppity! They were strange. They didn't go to the movies. Some of them wouldn't take a caffeinated drink. No jewelry, no neckties. They didn't prowl around with the other boys. They didn't socialize with the other women. They kept to themselves, you know. They'd say, 'A Saint has no business going to an unsaved wedding, where there might be alcohol, dirty dancing, cigarette smoking, and profane language used.' Just uppity! But I did notice that they were always the ones who, if someone got sick or died, would come visiting the family, bringing along baskets of food, helping out in small ways—that sort of thing. They had a full-time religion. They didn't take no vacations."

Carrie didn't have a high opinion of her own church, either. "When I was a teenager, I really tried to be active in my church, which was Baptist. But the way people lived really bothered me. Church was an hour on Sunday. Then everybody'd go out and drink, gamble, play the lottery, chase women. And us kids would go to church on Sunday morning so we could go see the movies they showed there at night. See, the Baptist church did not really teach you how to *live*. It was part-time religion."

In 1958, Carrie and Ollie got married and moved to Cleveland, hoping to find work and the promise of a better life outside the Jim Crow South. "I didn't want to bring my children up sharecropping," she explains. But times were just as tough in Cleveland, the young couple soon discovered. "We came here looking for the pie in the sky, only to find there was nothing but beans here too."

Carrie spent several years looking for a church that felt right. Although Ollie had grown up in COGIC (and is now a member), he was reluctant to commit himself to the church as a young man. "He always said COGIC was the true church, that if you really want to go to heaven, you must be saved, sanctified, and filled with the Holy Ghost. He always put off joining. He'd say: 'I'm not ready to live that strict yet.'"

In 1961 Ollie's sister was visiting from Arkansas, and the two women went to hear a young COGIC preacher who was making waves at a spiritual revival in Cleveland. "I was so impressed by him," Carrie remembers. "He was the same age as I was—twenty-one—and yet he had such a powerful presence. I didn't want to get too close. I thought I'd sit back and watch. But as I listened to him, I started thinking about my life. I knew I didn't want to die and go to hell. I wanted to be saved. So when the minster called on me, I went up to the altar. I had always been afraid to ever disobey a minister or do anything wrong inside a church. It was my fear of God, you know. At the altar I asked to be saved, and I suddenly had this feeling of wanting to praise God. It was joy unspeakable!"

TERESSA, THE GIRL FROM DETROIT, has just finished her talk with the Ghost, and the energy inside the Cook Convention Center has begun to dissipate. Suddenly an aide to Bishop Patterson rises to the podium and shouts at the Convocation crowd:

"He's the most unselfish leader in the WORLD! Every time you see him you're seeing a walking miracle! I don't want you to even THINK about giving your leader anything less than ten dollars!"

Everyone knows the cue. It is time for the annual cash gift to the Presiding Bishop, a ceremony known in the COGIC argot as "The Love Offering." The ushers pass around bright orange plastic pails that say "COGIC Finance Department" (in previous years, the church simply used large Kentucky Fried Chicken buckets), and the Saints dutifully drop their bills into the growing piles of cash. Some $200,000 will be collected in under fifteen minutes. The recipient of all this largesse, Bishop Patterson, quietly rocks in a Naugahyde office chair behind the podium.

"Don't be shirking an offering now!" the speaker shouts in a vaguely menacing voice. "You just don't come before God empty-handed! Look around you—EVERYBODY's giving! We'll take traveler's checks, personal checks! C'mon now, let's see that ten-dollar bill. Hold it up high so EVERYBODY can see who's giving and who's shirking his responsibility! Ten dollars is the LEAST you can give. God's kept your body well all through the year. Give your ten dollars to the KINDEST, HUMBLEST, most UNSELFISH leader in the WHOLE world!"

Finally Bishop Patterson rises to acknowledge his followers' generosity. "There's no church in the world like the Church of God in Christ," he brags. "Because our church is rooted and grounded in the spirit of Jesus!"

Then his voice becomes grave. "Now at one time we may have been a little fanatical. Everything was wrong in the early days of our church. Dental work was wrong. Neckties were wrong. Everything was wrong! But now . . . *something's* got to be wrong. Something's got to be wrong today when little fourteen-year-old girls are becoming mothers! Something's got to be wrong when we see the ladies of our church going around looking like Zsa Zsa Gabor. God has given you a natural beauty, but you're worshiping hats and wigs! You're wearing lipstick like the proverbial Jezebel! Something's got to be wrong when some of our preachers are riding around in cars that look like pimpmobiles! That's too vain. Preachers got no business looking like members of the Mafia. What's wrong with Zion?"

The Bishop is already short of breath. He is clearly a frail man, not the marathon preacher he was in his days of twenty-four-hour road show revivals. "Who knows why God gave me the strength to stand here and talk to you today? Who knows? If my illness can do anything this week, I would hope that it could clean up this church's political ambitions, and bring us hastily to judgment. There are people clamoring for this job! Well, to them I say, 'I ain't gonna die, and I ain't gonna resign!' "

Hallelujah, good Bishop!

"Whoever clamors for the job don't get it. See, promotions don't work that way."

That's right!

"To hold this job you've got to love people, not dollars!"

No Sir!

"I hope that in some way, my illness can lead our church back to Old Time Holiness . . ."

Preach the word.

"Back to the kind of Holiness that makes people call us fanatics!"

Yes, yes, good Lord!

"All the way back to Azusa, where God was real! Back to a church where women dress modest and men act like members of the masculine gender. Back to Pentecost at any cost!"

Postscript: Bishop J. O. Patterson died of pancreatic cancer two months later in a Memphis hospital. The funeral at Mason Temple on January 4, 1990, was attended by some ten thousand people—including Benjamin Hooks, Oral Roberts, and U.S. Senator Jim Sasser of Tennessee. President George Bush sent a message of condolence that was read aloud at the memorial service. A horse-drawn carriage, bearing the casket, led a cortege through the rainy streets of downtown Memphis. The funeral arrangements were handled by Patterson Mortuary.

Bishop L. H. Ford of Chicago assumed the leadership of the Church of God in Christ. At the funeral, Bishop Ford left no doubts about the direction in which he would lead the church. "I was trained in the old school, as a foot-stomping, hand-clappin' Holiness preacher!" he declared. "And that's the way it's going to be. When the Holy Ghost got you, formality and protocol don't mean a thing!" Then Bishop Ford began to shake and dance on stage. "This here," he shouted, "is the Holy Ghost protocol taking over!"

Sisters of the Bowl

Kissimmee, Florida

To GET TO OUR WORLD, you head south out of Orlando on the Orange Blossom Trail, past the outlet malls and the strip joints and the Gatorland Zoo, until you come to a white pavilion surrounded by water fountains and cypress swamps. If you happen to arrive in early August, you will find the parking lot packed with thousands of identical minivans with bumper stickers that say, "When I Work, It's a Party," or "Go Ahead, Make My Day—Throw a Party" or "I'm a Party Machine," or "I Don't Believe in the Two-Party System—Two Parties a Week Just Isn't Enough."

This year, 1989, Our World's auditorium is filled with helium balloons and zippy tunes by the Tijuana Brass. A mirrored disco ball sprays shards of light over a crowd of two thousand hysterical women: Stout suburban homemakers with beehives. Valley moms in inch-thick mascara. Corn-fed hausfraus with midwestern accents and thick ankles shoved into high-heel shoes. New Age southern belles seeking self-esteem. A smiling army of Carol Merrills and Vanna Whites. Tri Delta sorority girls in color-coordinated suits and pumps, impossibly together, impossibly precise. Our Ladies of Containment, Sisters of the Bowl.

The women are bouncing in their seats, shaking pompons, forming human "London Bridges" in the aisles for their friends to march under. Others parade across the stage holding placards from their local distributorships, or "ships," as they're called in the parlance of Tupperware Home Parties—

. . . SOUTHBAY PARTY SALES SAYS HELLO TO OUR WORLD!
. . . THE ANGELS ARE HERE!!
. . . *FIESTA PARTY SALES*

The women are growing restless. They want to see "product"—the unveiling of the season's new merchandise—and they will not be denied. "Give us product!" they demand. "We want product! Product *now!*"

Near the stage, forty-five ladies from Pinnacle Party Sales, a ship in Rockville, Maryland, are swaying arm-in-arm to the Tijuana Brass. Pinnacle has much to celebrate this year: They've had a record-breaker summer, thanks in large part to a hot streak by their perennial top seller, Sheila Looney. A jolly redhead of forty-seven from Bowie, Maryland, Sheila manages a sales unit called the "Looney Tunes." This year she made "Top Category" and is ranked Number 56 in the nation in personal party sales. She averages five parties a week and moves $7,000 worth of merchandise every month. Formerly a buyer for the Murphy's dime store chain, Sheila has sold Tupperware for fourteen years. Every Monday night she makes the hour-long drive to the Pinnacle sales rally, often listening to tapes by popular American motivational speakers like Rita Davenport and Zig Ziglar who emphasize, as Sheila puts it, "the importance of surrounding yourself with happy people."

This week Sheila has won loads of awards, including a new dining room furniture set, which the company will ship to her home in a few days. A trail of ribbons reaches down to her knee. "We have a high energy level," Sheila boasts of her ship. "We get very excited. It's like being in camp all year long. And we make money doing it! And prizes! And trips! We're always running into people who say they can't understand why we're having so much fun. They're asking, 'What is the deal?' They look very perplexed."

Over the years, Sheila has won eight company cars. Her latest one, a Lumina moonvan, is parked in the Tupperware lot.

"It's my trophy on wheels," she beams, noting the advantages of Tupperware's car plan over that of direct sales rival Mary Kay Cosmetics, for whom her sister has worked for years. "We have the best car plan in the direct selling industry. See, I didn't have to sell ten thousand Mary Kay lipsticks to get it! And it doesn't come in pink!"

Sheila and her husband Bob drove down from Maryland on I-95, and checked into Orlando's swank Peabody Hotel. Bob, who is a carpet and flooring salesman, has accompanied Sheila to many of the rallies and seminars this week, but today he's spending the afternoon at Sea World; he told Sheila that if he heard another motivational talk his brain "was going to explode."

The chanting has grown louder: "Product, PRODUCT, PRODUCT!"

"New products always excite us," Sheila explains. "When I get back home the hostesses are going to be calling me up and saying, 'What's new?' Because these people are truly Tupperholics. They'll want at least one new piece of Tupperware for their kitchen, and one for their bathroom. They want *new, new, new!*"

Standing at centerstage is Gaylin Olson, a swarthy young exec with smoothed-back hair and a Pepsodent smile. As president of sales, Olson is the Bert Parks of Tupperware: the emcee, the cheerleader, and keeper of the harem. All the women call him by his first name. "Isn't he wonderful?" Sheila burbles. "He's not some far-off executive. You can *talk* to him. Gaylin's a Tupper child, you know. His mom sold Tupperware. So does his sister! He's one of us!"

Gaylin is wearing a *Ghostbusters* getup with a plastic orange flamethrower holstered to his side. He holds a wireless microphone in his hand. "We're going to recognize you like we've never recognized you before!" he promises. "There's lots of deserving people out there who really SOCKED it to us this year. Boy, you've really wowed us! You've broken ALL the records! You're moving your way to GREATER levels of success. It's such a privilege to be a part of this great family. I feel one heart beating in this room right now, and it's called . . . *Tupperware!*"

"Product! Product! Product!"

Gaylin: "What's that? You wanna see WHAT?"

"PRODUCT!! PRODUCT!! PRODUCT *NOW*!!"

Gaylin: "Okay, okay. You want product? Are we going to show you some product! We're VERY excited about this new item and we want to share it with each and every one of you today. Because you're SPECIAL people. Because you're TUP-PER people. Get ready folks! Hold on to your seats. 'Cause we're going to show you a WHOLE NEW LINE of Tupperware that we just know you're going to love! This is a company of DREAMS! So close your eyes and DREAM with us! We want you all to say hello to the NEW . . ."

          . . . *drumroll* . . .

". . . sixteen-piece . . ."

          . . . *screams, squeals, gasps* . . .

". . . TABLETOP LINE!!!!"

"Way to go Tupperware! Way to go!"

A projector flashes a misty image on an overhead screen—the soft pastel bowls and plates pictured alongside fresh fruit spritzed with tiny beads of moisture. The Tijuana Brass pours out louder than ever.

Gaylin: "You *like* it! It's BY FAR the best material in the world, and it's EXTREMELY scratch resistant!"

"Sock it to me, Tupperware!"

Gaylin: "It's made of plastic but it looks like the finest china IN THE WORLD! And it comes in Desert Peach, a color so rich that Donald Trump picked it as the base color at one of his Atlantic City hotels."

Now Gaylin is passing out free samples of the new Tabletop Line, fresh from the factory in Hemingway, South Carolina. Thousands of the brightly wrapped packages circulate through the crowd. The ladies frantically rip the wrappers off, tear at the cardboard boxes. In a few minutes, the auditorium is a romper room strewn with ribbon and plasticware parts. They juggle the lids, balance the plates on their heads, dangle spoons from their noses.

"Love that Tupperware! Love that Tupperware!"

Gaylin: "There's NOTHING that Tupperware can't do! We've designed a mug that's not for sissies. Can you feel that? Just FEEL the heft! And see, that's a man-sized cereal bowl. This is some VERY special plastic!"

The Harem is satisfied. The Tupperware Spirit is gathering in the crowd and suddenly everyone is singing the company anthem. Sheila and her colleagues from Pinnacle Party Sales sing along, and most of them do the accompanying hand signals that everyone in Our World knows by rote—

I've got that Tup-per feeling up in my head,
Deep in my heart,
Down in my toes,
I've got that Tup-per feeling all over me,
All over me
To stay!

YES, THEY'RE STILL MAKING TUPPERWARE. And they're still selling it the old-fashioned way: on the party plan. The lids now come in mod colors like "mesa red" and "poppy," but the fabled seal still keeps the lettuce from turning brown.

Tupperware sprang fully formed from the mind of Earl Tupper, a Du Pont chemist and one of the early apostles of plastic. In the half-century since he unveiled his first cups and bowls, Tupperware has molded itself to the national psyche, and has become one of the enduring corporate trademarks of domestic life, in the same league as Kleenex, Crisco, and the almighty Thermos. Ninety percent of all U.S. homes have at least one piece of Tupperware. Both the Smithsonian and the Museum of Modern Art have samples in their permanent collections. High-tech companies in Silicon Valley use the stuff to protect their most sensitive instruments from moisture. Urologists buy Tupperware containers to house urine specimens, and the Boy Scouts have used them as buried time capsules.

The Tupperware party has proven to be a surprisingly resilient ritual of commerce. It has weathered the equal rights movement and the rise of the Ziploc threat. It has been the butt of jokes on *Cheers* and *Late Night with David Letterman*. It has endured the lampoons of columnist Dave Barry. After forty years of choreographed camp, the Tupperware party retains a mysterious appeal, blurring the lines between work and play. Although the early 1990s brought hints that Tupperware is inching toward national catalog sales (the company set up a 1-800 number and fully automated its central distribution system for credit card charges and UPS home deliveries), the party still works its magic. Tupperware outsells its largest retail rival, Rubbermaid, three to one. Every 2.7 seconds another Tupperware party is starting somewhere in the world. One quarter of all American Women over eighteen have attended one.

Business school professors have scratched their heads in bewilderment at the whole strange dance, and wondered why the company won't just sell the stuff in stores. The party plan runs on irrational principles that can't easily be parsed into graphs and charts for a Harvard case study; the obstacle of the party puts psychological distance between the product and the buyers. They can't just have a Tupperware bowl. They have to seek it out. They have to *want* it. And in the wanting, they think of other, deeper, wants. So many shapes to choose from, and so many colors. Why should they chase a dill pickle around in a clumsy jar full of brine when it could be neatly lodged in a Pick-A-Deli canister? What bright, accessible, compartmentalized worlds their kitchens could be, if only. . . . When their turn finally comes to kneel at the Tupperware altar, they positively crave it. They must have it! And once they have it, they keep wanting more.

As always, Tupperware is a sure barometer of the national zeitgeist. And the 1990s are looking good for the plastic container business. As any Madison Avenue adman will tell you, the values that Tupperware has long championed—community, frugality, kitchen continence—are fashionable again. After an anemic performance in the Reagan years, Tupperware is poised for a comeback. The company's sales were up 7 percent in 1990, to just over $1 billion retail. The company's products are available in more than forty countries, with especially brisk sales in Germany, Japan, and a number of developing nations. Today there are more than 100,000 Tupperware salesladies in the United States alone. Though men are encouraged to sell Tupperware, the sales force is still overwhelmingly female, about 98 percent. However, the distributorships are usually owned by husband-and-wife teams, and most of the upper-echelon executive positions in Kissimmee are filled by men.

Tupperware is publicly traded on the New York and London stock exchanges under the name of its parent operation, Premark, Inc., but it's vastly different from most stocks your broker might suggest. Tupperware is a "direct selling company," the nation's third largest, after Avon and Amway. Direct sales (DS) is a curious phenomenon from the margins of American commercial history, one of those dimly understood folk practices they won't teach you about in business school. DS companies are commercial families with their own peculiar logic and their own measures of success. "It's a very different culture," concedes Gaylin Olson. "Direct selling is a phantom industry. We have our own language and our own automatic checks and balances out in the field."

A tradition descended from the itinerant peddlers of nineteenth-century New England, DS is still an enormously popular pursuit in the United States, particularly among women. The Washington-based Direct Selling Association estimates that close to five million Americans are involved in DS, generating about $12 billion in retail sales every year. Well-established DS enterprises include Mary Kay Cosmetics, Home Interiors & Gifts, the Fuller Brush Company, Encyclopaedia Britannica, Nu Skin International, Princess House, Inc., and the Shaklee Corporation, and thousands of lesser-known regional companies still go door to door, hawking everything from plants and lingerie to burglar alarms and vacuum cleaners.

Direct sales is by its nature a loosely regulated arena, and over the decades it has been a breeding ground for fly-by-night companies that push illegitimate products—melting cookware, phony gemstones, bogus cure-alls. Disreputable DS enterprises have often been organized on "Ponzi" or "pyramid" schemes, classic scams in which a few initial investors make inordinate profits off the earnings and recruitment efforts of lower-level dealers. (The Federal Trade Commission vigorously prosecutes corporations that employ pyramid schemes.)

Tupperware's public relations people are quick to insist that the company does *not* follow a pyramid scheme, and never has. They prefer to call it a "multi-level scheme." Tupperware does place great emphasis on recruiting, and managers make a percentage of the sales of their subordinate "units." But unlike most pyramid schemes, when a Tupperware sales unit grows to a certain size, it automatically "promotes out," which means that it splits into two smaller units, each one independent from the other. Tupperware's growth pattern thus resembles a kind of cell-division, with the lines of authority extending horizontally, not vertically.

Still, the company constantly has to fight the unsavory, foot-in-the-door image that surrounds much of the DS world. Says Erin Anderson, a marketing professor at the University of

Pennsylvania's Wharton School: "Direct sales is a fringe world of business that is viewed as downright disreputable in the academic community. The whole industry has a tinge of the con artist using unsuspecting people who have obsessive emotional needs and who believe they can get rich quick. Many of these companies get people to milk their friends and exhaust the largess of their families. You constantly have to wonder whether they're on the up-and-up."

Modern DS organizations are often led by a charismatic founder—like Mary Kay Ash of Mary Kay Cosmetics—who inspires an almost religious devotion to the company. Most are female-dominated realms that encourage cooperative relationships among saleswomen who, in more conventional corporate scenarios, would find themselves in direct competition with each other.

As Sheila Looney explains, the culture of Tupperware, at its essence, is not a monetary culture, but an emotional one. Tupperware employs familial terms—such as "mother manager" and "daughter dealer"—to describe company ties. A Tupperware saleslady works in a secure world that is delineated by concentric spheres of loyalty: first to her unit, then her ship, then her region, and finally to the national company. Goals are neatly etched into the calendar and given catchy names like "Record Breaker Week" or "The Sock-It-to-Me Challenge." The women know where they stand from week to week. Sheila claims this abiding sense of order helps women achieve a level of self-confidence they never dreamed possible. "I've seen some major personality transplants," Sheila recalls. "I've seen women blossom into such warm, bubbly, whole people again. We get women who are just an extension of their husband and their children. They need a little pat on the back. They need to know that they did something right this week besides carpool the kids and wash their husband's socks. And then all of a sudden, a few months of selling Tupperware, and they get their identity back. Here they are, buying themselves new clothes. It's a very powerful feeling to know that we can give that to people."

Those unacquainted with the saccharine rituals and proselytizing techniques employed by direct selling companies are tempted to dismiss them as cults, albeit relatively benign ones. "To an outsider, life in a direct selling organization is surprising, sometimes even bizarre," writes University of California sociologist Nicole Woolsey Biggart in her book *Charismatic Capitalism*, an exhaustive study of direct selling organizations in America. "It is as though the activity of a traditional [business] firm were viewed in a funhouse mirror. Nearly every familiar feature of corporate life is either distorted or missing. They are businesses run very much like social movements. They have organizational ideologies that are missionary in character. . . . They are run as 'metaphorical families,' and distributors are encouraged to see themselves as having familylike bonds."

EVERY SUMMER FOR FORTY YEARS, Tupperware Home Parties has assembled its "metaphorical family" for an emotional sales rally called the "Jubilee." It is one of the largest corporate reunions in the world, an elaborate pageant of treasure hunts, musical skits, and car giveaways that costs the company upwards of $4 million a year. More than ten thousand salesladies come for the three-day event. Attendance is so large that the company can't handle them all at once, so the ladies arrive in five successive waves over a two-week period. "It's our way of thanking the sales force for a job well done," Gaylin Olson explains. "They all go home with something—gifts, prizes, vehicles. We're totally committed to them. We have to show a lot of enthusiasm up there. At Jubilee, we set the emotional tone for the whole year."

The ladies flock here from all over the globe to wash themselves in the spirit of "Our World," as they call their milieu (*Our World* is also the name of the company magazine). They attend candle-lit induction ceremonies. They stay up late at night in their Orlando hotel rooms for pillow fights and wine-and-cheese parties. On the final evening of Jubilee, called "Fun Night," they dress up in costumes and attend performances by headline acts. In past years the company has booked, among others, Andy Williams, Dinah Shore, Rich Little, and the Osmonds.

But there is also business to attend to at the Jubilee. Each morning the women dutifully lug their bulging spiral notebooks to seminars entitled "How to Increase Your Party Average" or "Friend Finding for the Holidays," where accomplished salesladies share their wisdom—

". . . Smiling changes the whole sound of your voice. Put a

mirror in front of you during phone interviews to make sure
you're always smiling."

"... If your Tupperware gets smelly, stuff the container
with newspaper and place it in your freezer overnight. The
carbon in the newspaper will draw out the odors."

"... Always remember that our chief competitor isn't Rubbermaid. It's that gal who uses twisty ties and aluminum foil,
the gal who says, 'That's good enough! Let it spoil a little!' She's
the person we have to go after!"

The Kissimmee headquarters is the emotional home of Our
World, and it exerts a powerful pull. The three-pavilion facility
was designed by Edward Durell Stone, architect of the Kennedy
Center in Washington. The brightly lit corridors are spic-and-
span, and the toilet water in the company bathrooms is kept
a refreshing Ty-D-Bol blue. Outside the main building is a
thousand-acre park of manicured gardens and meandering
sawdust trails where the pilgrims can go on inspirational walks.
The air is scented with rosebushes. Japanese footbridges cross
palmy lagoons where blue herons stand vigil. Everything on the
grounds is neatly labeled and has a "The" in front of it: The
Wishing Well. The Opportuni-Tree. The Friendship Fountain.
The Walk of Fame.

But the most remarkable attraction at the Tupperware
headquarters is a million-dollar art exhibit called the Museum
of Historic Containers. The museum traces man's epic struggle
against staleness in all its grim forms. The tour begins with an
Egyptian earthenware jar from 4000 B.C. and proceeds more
or less chronologically, displaying objets d'art from the Babylo-
nians, the Greeks and Romans, the Incas, and so on. There
are containers made of shells, reeds, and horns. There are
compotes, cruets, and ewers. There are urns, tankards, and
Delftware bowls.

Having seen the history of containment, you are then invited to gaze upon its future. The tour moves to a second room
that is filled with the latest runs from the Tupperware factory.
The products are neatly arranged on the display tables—
shrines of plastic, ziggurats of polyethylene. Modular Mates.
Servalier Bowls. Super Crisp-It Containers. The wisdom of six
thousand years has led mankind directly *to this room*. For a few
moments you can hold in your hand a little piece of victory—

the triumph of freshness over the microbe and the cockroach and the mold spore: the paragon of packages.

"WELCOME TO A LAND OF FANTASY," the sign greets the incoming pilgrims at the company headquarters. "Welcome to Your Over-the-Rainbow Jubilee!"

This year's Jubilee is based on an Oz theme. The company has decorated the grounds with an eighty-foot-high rainbow made of sixty-four thousand Tupper seals in bright colors, each seal autographed by a different salesperson from around the world.

The Oz theme is fitting, for as a businessman, the late Earl Silas Tupper, the company founder, was not unlike the Wizard. Cranky, paranoid, flustered around people, leery of unions, Tupper ran his company from the shadows. He cultivated an image of quiet, unapproachable omnipotence. His flinty personality demanded complete control: He was president, general manager, treasurer, and sole stockholder. From a dark office in his Massachusetts plant, he followed the minutest details. He kept his movements a secret. He often hinted to people that he was working on something new, something big, but would never say what it was. In his later years, he carried around a black box which held, he claimed, his "greatest invention ever," but he refused to open it. He was obsessed with quality control, and constantly worried that competitors were stealing his patents or attempting to sabotage his company. When he gave tours at his factory, he'd nervously look over his visitor's shoulder, constantly locking and unlocking doors. Tupper called himself a "Yankee trader." He was pure New England—a killjoy, a fuss-budget, and a tireless tinkerer. He married his housekeeper and prided himself on the fact that his Massachusetts home had once been the county poorhouse.

Tupper hated to attend sales conferences; all those squealing women upset him. Few Tupperware salesladies ever met him or even knew what he looked like. Tupper was more interested in things than people. He came alive when asked to explain the *process* of making the molds, the chemical principles involved, the machinery of extrusion and lamination, the injectors and vegetable dyes. Tupper's hyperactive mind was forever looking for ways to streamline, to economize, to shave off waste. Once when Tupper was being wheeled into an operating room for surgery, the doctor found him scribbling notes on how to improve the hospital gurney he was lying on.

Born in 1907, Tupper grew up on a farm near Berlin, New Hampshire. As a boy, he dreamed of sailing in the merchant marine but found instead that he had a knack for business. He discovered he could make more money buying and selling other people's vegetables than growing his own. Later he ran a mail order outfit, dealing in toothbrushes and combs. Tupper never went to college; after taking a few correspondence courses in chemical engineering, he formed his own plastics company at the age of thirty-one. Working as an independent "custom molder" for Du Pont, Tupper set out to make "tomorrow's designs with tomorrow's substances," and in the mid-1940s, tomorrow's substance was polyethylene, a byproduct of petroleum refinement that had recently been produced in England. At the time, plastic was still a new and vaguely frightening material. It looked bad, it smelled bad, and it was slimy. It had a tendency to split. And it had a habit of exploding into flames if you set it on a stove. The most common plastic trademark at the time, Bakelite, had been successfully used for decades in electrical insulation. But at the close of World War II, plastic's possibilities seemed limited.

Earl Tupper was bullish on polyethylene. Working out of a brick plant in Farnumsville, Massachusetts, he kept fiddling with his polymers and monomers until he found a way to purify the stuff, to make it tough and yet pliant: a substance that would remember its own shape. He made it tasteless, odorless, greaseless—not to mention pretty. He called his refined substance "Poly-T."

Tupper's advances came at a pivotal point in the history of plastic. "There was a real ambivalence in the public mind about whether plastic was something you could put confidence in or whether it was just cheap ersatz stuff," says Jeffrey Meikle, associate professor of American studies at the University of Texas at Austin and author of a definitive history of plastic. "Before Tupper, plastic was considered something of a novelty item. During World War Two, when the Army classified brass and other metals as restricted materials, a lot of cheap plastic products suddenly came out on the market, and they were notoriously flimsy and crude: mixing bowls that would crumble in hot water, buttons that would disintegrate at the dry cleaners, polystyrene toys that would break an hour after the kids opened them on Christmas morning. Plastic had a bad name."

Tupper peered into that petrochemical ooze and foresaw a new science of food storage. In 1945 his first product appeared in the stores: the seven-ounce Bell Tumbler. It was perfect. It was so perfect that he gave it a lifetime guarantee.

Tupper then loosed his engineer's mind on the spatial economics of the American icebox. In the late 1940s, most containers for refrigerators were made of ceramic, glass, or enameled metal. They were heavy, cold, cumbersome, and clammy. They took up too much space and were prone to chipping and breakage. But a plastic bowl could work wonders in the refrigerator, Tupper thought. His wife was skeptical. "Oh Earl," she would tease him. "What are you talking about? 'A bowl that can bend.' "

The trick was to devise a secure lid. In 1947 he found the answer: a double-grooved lip that worked like a paintcan lid in reverse. The patented "burpable" seal made its debut later that year in the Wonderlier Bowl, which is still featured in the company catalogs.

Among Tupper's first customers was the director of a Massachusetts mental institution, who found plasticware far superior to the noisy aluminum cups and plates the hospital had been using. He marveled that the only way his patients could damage Tupperware was by "persistent chewing."

Though a 1947 article in *House Beautiful* magazine favorably compared Tupper's containers to jade and alabaster sculpture, the general public was still not warming up to plasticware. Tupper tried to market it in department stores like Macy's and Bloomingdale's, but people shied away. They couldn't figure out how the seals worked. They didn't understand the rigmarole about "burping" out the air. And they were sure their macaroni and cheese was going to come out of there tasting like an oil filter.

Then a divorcée from Dearborn, Michigan, named Brownie Wise entered the picture. Wise was an impossibly perky woman with razor-sharp business instincts and prematurely gray hair clipped in a "poodle" cut. She was precisely the salesperson Earl Tupper needed.

At the time, Wise was working as a secretary at the Bendix

Earl Silas Tupper in his laboratory.

Saleslady Sheila Looney at a Tupperware party in Silver Spring, Maryland.

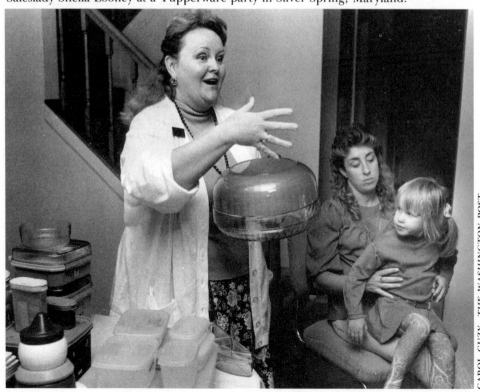

Corporation. Her only child, Jerry, had a congenital heart defect, and to pay the mounting medical bills, Wise moonlighted as a saleslady for a New England–based outfit called Stanley Home Products, selling scrubbing brushes and detergents on the party plan. Stanley Products, whose founder Frank Stanley Beveridge is generally credited with originating the home party plan, is the Ur-company from which Mary Kay Cosmetics, Tupperware, and a host of other direct selling enterprises sprang.

One day in 1947 a friend gave Wise a new set of Tupper's Wonder Bowls. She didn't know what to make of them at first. "It took me three days to figure out how they worked," she recalls. Her baptism in plastic came a few days later. "I was putting one of the bowls in the refrigerator, and I dropped it on the floor. I said, 'Can you beat that?' The bowl didn't break! It bounced! The seal held! You see, bowls didn't do that in those days."

Wise understood that the home was the logical place to sell Tupper's bowls—a nonthreatening environment in which she could explain the seal and the burp and the delightful unsliminess of Poly-T. "It was a demonstrator's dream," she told Charles Fishman of the *Orlando Sentinel*, in a rare personal interview. "There was a classical shape to the bowls, but they needed active demonstration to show a person how to snap the seals in place. You could turn it sideways and upside down. You could show its flexibility. You could show how it would fit in the empty spaces in your refrigerator. It was full of action!"*

For her son's health, Wise moved to the warmer climes of Florida in 1949. There she actively sold Tupper's products along with her Stanley cleaners and brushes. (Though Earl Tupper was still marketing his wares in department stores, he was also experimenting with distribution to various wholesale "jobbers," whose dealers went door to door.) Within a year, Wise had twenty dealers working for her distributorship and was moving more plasticware than anyone in the nation. One week her shipment from the Tupper Corporation was two days late, and she hit the roof. "I called the Tupper Corp., and I

---

*Unless otherwise indicated, all quotations attributed to Brownie Wise that are not taken from my own phone conversations with her are adapted from the transcribed notes of Charles Fishman's in-person interview with Ms. Wise on February 14, 1987, for the *Orlando Sentinel Florida Magazine*. © Charles Fishman, with his permission.

asked for Mr. Tupper. I didn't know if he even existed. I was just assuming there was one. Earl Tupper got on the phone and introduced himself. I said, 'This is Brownie Wise in Florida,' and he said, 'I know who you are.' I said, Mr. Tupper, my order is late for the second time. I wonder if you have any idea how serious a problem this is. It is a very serious problem! It is a disgrace that such a fine product should be sacrificed on the altar of disorganization.' "

Tupper promised her there'd be no more late deliveries. Then he summoned her and a handful of other Stanley dealers to Worcester, Massachusetts, for candid advice on how he might increase his sales. Wise urged Tupper to make a leap of faith: Sell *only* on the party plan.

Tupper capitulated. He may not have understood all the emotional shadings of the direct selling business—the weekly pep rallies, the rites and rituals, the religious atmospherics of the annual meetings—but he was willing to give it a try.

Tupper was impressed with Wise. "You talk a lot and everybody listens," he told her. "How about helping me build a company?" He put Wise in charge of the entire sales division and set her up in a palatial $1 million headquarters in the vacant swamplands south of Orlando. Tupperware Home Parties opened in 1951, and Earl Tupper's products came off the retail shelves for good.

Kissimmee was little more than a cowtown in the early 1950s, but Wise sensed that the Orlando area would one day become a thriving crossroads for tourists. (Disney wouldn't start buying up real estate for another fifteen years.) Wise picked the thousand-acre site for the headquarters and sketched the plans for the original building on a napkin. She claimed the design came to her in a "vision."

Wise's army of salesladies took suburbia by storm. Tupperware Home Parties started out in 1951 with only two hundred dealers in a few isolated pockets of the country; three years later there were nine thousand dealers coast to coast, and annual retail sales soared to $25 million. Tupperware was the right product at the right time, and the party plan was the right way to sell it. In 1950, 70 percent of the nation's households had a working husband and a stay-at-home wife. During the postwar boom, the modern notion of "domestic engineering" came into vogue; women wanted to bring the fruits of the technological age into their kitchens. Earl Tupper's products had an aura of science and a sleek futuristic look that fit the times.

For eight years, Wise was the reigning queen of Tupperland. She spun a corporate confection of hugs and tears and sorority high jinks. She made the cover of *Business Week* in 1954. *Cosmopolitan* called her "Florida's Most Amazing Business Woman." Nicknamed "Sunshine Cinderella," Wise wore white gloves and frilly hats, and drove a pink convertible with green leather upholstery. Her office at Tupperware headquarters had three telephones and was as big as a basketball court. She lived in a rambling, Spanish-style villa with an indoor swimming pool and owned an island covered in citrus groves in the middle of Lake Tohopekaliga.

Wise understood the art of motivation. Pentecostal ministers came to her sales meetings to study her techniques, and would often request copies of her speeches. She was given to uttering inspirational bromides. "Think as big as a house!" she'd say, or "Put hop in your hope!" Wise knew how to use props for dramatic effect. She carried around an ugly blob of plastic which she dubbed "Poly" (she claimed it was the first piece of polyethylene that Earl Tupper ever saw). At conventions she'd ask her salesladies to close their eyes, rub Poly, and make a wish.

Tupperware Home Parties accepted women of all creeds and faiths, but the sales force was overwhelmingly Christian. Wise began all her sales meetings with a musical rendition of "The Lord's Prayer" sung by Perry Como. She said she preferred that her salesladies have a religious faith of some kind. As she put it, "I don't have any confidence in people who believe there is no force in the universe that is more powerful than they are."

Although she was certainly no equal rights ideologue, Wise espoused a veiled feminism that was unusual for the early 1950s; her inspirational message of female empowerment and business success had a potent effect on a generation of women who had been living in the shadows of their husbands. "Far too many of the women in our world are shirking their positive obligation of happiness!" she wrote in her book, *Best Wishes, Brownie Wise*. "And they seem to have thrown their influence down the stairs with their bridal gowns." Wise's den-mother optimism spread like a contagion. For thousands of women,

Tupperware became a form of secular faith. "I don't know how it is," one Tupperware convert told a national magazine in 1954, "but Tupperware has become a religion with me." Said another: "Yes, dear God, I believe in Thee, but now at last I believe in me."

Anna Tate, a retired Tupperware distributor in Gaithersburg, Maryland, still has vivid memories of Wise's speeches. "I'd never seen anything like it. When she came out on stage, people were spellbound. She gave people faith in themselves, which is a magical quality. She inspired women to attempt things that they never thought they could do." Tate remembers a business trip Wise once made to St. Louis. More than 150 Tupperware salesladies greeted her at the airport, and someone rolled out a red carpet. "These women acted like a bunch of bobbysoxers waiting for Sinatra. It was hero worship!"

The hero worship sometimes took odd forms. At a 1952 sales meeting in New York, Wise invited a woman to the podium and asked her to select a prize from a huge assortment of gifts piled on the stage. "Choose anything you like," the woman was told, "anything at all."

"In that case," the woman answered, "I'll take the dress Brownie is wearing."

Wise promptly repaired to her hotel room, removed her outfit, and emerged with a fresh change of clothes. Thereafter, winning Brownie's clothing became an established tradition at Tupperware gatherings. She would attend rallies in $150 dresses and $35 hats, knowing that every thread—petticoats included—would be given away as prizes.

Wise never forgot the First Law of Direct Sales: The dealers are always paramount. Shower them with gifts, smother them with praise, offer them the clothes off your back—whatever it takes to keep them happy. "Build the people," her sales motto ran, "and they will build the business for you."

One way to "build the people," of course, was through national sales conventions. Thus, in 1953 the Jubilee was born. Wise got the idea from Stanley Home Products. For decades, Stanley had held a sales rally called "the Pilgrimage" at its headquarters in Westfield, Massachusetts. Wise took the basic theme of the Pilgrimage, gave it a more feminine cast, and then turned up the volume. She borrowed rituals and techniques from Pentecostal revivals, social clubs, and sorority initiation rites.

From the beginning the Jubilees were extravagant affairs that attracted national attention. *Life* covered the Jubilee two years in a row. They were built around themes like the Wild West or *Around the World in Eighty Days*. One year $19,000 worth of prizes, including mink stoles and diamond rings, were buried on the Tupperware grounds. The ladies were then given shovels and turned loose for an hour. Another year the company gave away two Cadillacs and five Fords. In 1956, the Tupperware salesladies received a questionnaire in the mail that asked, "If dreams were for sale, what would you buy?" The questionnaire instructed the women to write down their "dreams" and promptly mail the wish list back to Kissimmee. At the Jubilee a few months later, a Good Fairy roamed through the audience and tapped seven lucky winners with a magic wand. One woman who had asked for a new wardrobe was treated to an hour-long fashion show and then learned that all of the clothes would be hers. Another woman's wish was to visit her son, a Marine stationed in Japan, on his birthday. Tupperware sent her a round-trip ticket to Tokyo and a one-hundred-pound birthday cake for her son and his whole company.

To facilitate the annual orgy of giving at the Jubilees, Wise knew that the Tupperware headquarters had be to more than a convention site; it had to be a mecca of enchantment, a dollhouse world that would draw the women back, year after year. Every detail contributed to the magical effect. Wise had a silver pattern designed for the company and gave place settings away as prizes. She commissioned a noted horticulturist to raise a breed of "Tupperware" roses (at night when the ladies returned to their hotel rooms they would find their sheets turned back and fresh Tupperware roses lying on their pillows. She landscaped the grounds with gardens and dug numerous lakes, one of which was named "Poly Pond." On the opening day of the headquarters, Wise "christened" the lake by tossing in a Tupperware container filled with polyethylene pellets. Poly Pond was supposed to be the Tupperware Blarney Stone: Anyone who dipped her hands in its waters would enjoy good luck all year. "There's an alligator in there, too," Wise warned the salesladies, "for dealers who don't work!"

For all her shenanigans, Wise was gravely serious about the company's public image and had little tolerance for people who found Tupperware funny. Once the company's public relations firm called Wise to say that it had succeeded in getting Tupperware written into a script on the *I Love Lucy* show. As Wise remembers it, "I said, 'Oh no!' I did not want anyone to make fun of Tupperware. One wrong word could throw the whole thing off. Lucy was going to have a Tupperware party at her home. I said, 'It won't help us. I won't allow it.' I was just afraid it would end up with a Tupperware bowl upside down on Ricky's head."

FOR THE BETTER PART OF EIGHT YEARS, Earl Tupper left Brownie Wise to her own devices. Ensconced in his Massachusetts factory, he kept churning out new designs and new materials, and stayed out of sales altogether. It was said that in all those years, Tupper went to Kissimmee only three times.

Tupper and Wise didn't like each other. "I could not say I liked Tupper as a person," she says. "I don't think I even knew him as a person. He was the most impersonal person I ever met. I never once called him 'Earl.' It was always 'Mr. Tupper.' The man was a stone wall. He gave the impression that he didn't want anything to do with people."

The two kept each other at arm's length, each grudgingly acknowledging the other's talents. "As a business person, I respected Mr. Tupper," Wise concedes. "I respected his ability. That man was a genius with plastic."

Still, Wise didn't automatically endorse his new plastic prototypes. On one of his rare trips to Florida, Tupper unveiled a new product, a flour sifter. As Wise recalls, "I looked at it and I said, 'Mr. Tupper, we will not sell this. It's too hard to clean. And the holes are not fine enough to do a good job sifting.' I called Elsie from the test kitchen. I said to her, 'Elsie, what would you do with this if someone gave it to you?' And she said, 'Whoever made this one didn't know much about sifting flour.' Mr. Tupper was crushed, mad, and offended."

Dour New Englander that he was, Tupper took a dim view of all of Wise's corporate tomfoolery. He didn't like the way she had turned his company into a sorority house and was worried that Tupperware Home Parties had become a one-woman show.

In 1958 the fairy tale of Tupperware nearly came to an end. Wise left the company after an acrimonious dispute with Tupper that she still declines to recount in full. The precise circumstances of her departure remain shrouded in speculation. The official company line is that Wise and Tupper simply "butted heads," but clearly their relationship had been festering for years. "Tupper was truly pissed and vindictive," remembers Gary McDonald, a former executive vice-president for Tupperware and now president of Rachael Cosmetics in Winter Springs, Florida. "Brownie was making all sorts of personal demands. She had become a real prima donna. She had started to believe her own publicity and thought Earl Tupper couldn't get along without her. 'The Queen of the May,' I think Tupper called her."

Wise says that one day in early 1958 Tupper stormed into her office and coolly informed her that he was selling the company to an as yet unnamed corporation that planned to market Tupperware in retail stores. He presented it to her as a *fait accompli*. As Wise well knew, this spelled doom for the party plan and the Tupperware saleslady. She quickly got the message: Tupper was firing her. "It was very well thought out apparently," she says. "I asked him, 'Is that it?' And he said, 'Yes, that's it. It's already been decided.' I got up and walked out and never came back. I was just heartsick. It nauseated me to think of all the work so many women had done and that that man could sit there and just lay those facts on the table—plunk! It was horrible!"

Wise was so furious that in June of 1958 she filed a $1.6 million lawsuit against Earl Tupper and the company executives, charging that they "unlawfully, wickedly and maliciously conspire[d] . . . for the purposes of harassing plaintiff and ruining her reputation in the business world." Earl Tupper's response to the news of Brownie's suit was printed in the *Orlando Sentinel* the next day: "I [am] shocked and bewildered," he professed, "because she hasn't had anything but kindness and consideration from us." The suit was later settled out of court for an undisclosed amount.

While the court case simmered, a rival direct selling concern calling itself Cinderella International announced that it had hired Wise to run its sales force. Wise brazenly chose to base her sales headquarters in Kissimmee, in Tupperware's backyard. In a desperate power play to win back her lost flock of salesladies, Cinderella International placed a full-page ad in the Kissimmee *Gazette* inviting all comers to join Brownie Wise in an exciting new venture. The ad was a thinly disguised call for mutiny. Cinderella would sell cosmetics and cleaning aids on the home party plan, with a system of independent dealers and distributors patterned directly after Tupperware Home Parties. The ad was timed for maximum impact: It appeared on July 4, 1958, during the week of Jubilee, so thousands of visiting Tupperware salesladies would see it. "Cinderella International is delighted to announce the election of one of the outstanding businesswomen in America to head its widespread operations," the ad read.

> Under the leadership of Brownie Wise, our real future now begins. Her inspiring knowledge of the party plan will provide an opportunity for thousands of American women to obtain their individual goals with unequaled sales success! We can well be proud that of the many avenues open to Brownie Wise, she has chosen this one.

It was a classic showdown. Wise was gambling on her personal capital, assuming that the sales force was devoted to *her* and not to Earl Tupper's molds. But her scheme backfired. Instead of ignoring the Cinderella ad, Earl Tupper bought one thousand issues of the *Gazette*, and placed a copy on every seat of the auditorium. When the salesladies arrived on the first morning of Jubilee, the Tupperware executives addressed the issue of Brownie's subversive new company as the first order of business. Tupperware Home Parties president Hamer Wilson asked the ladies to turn to the ad and patiently waited at the lectern while they read every word. In a masterly reading of group psychology, Wilson asked them to cast their loyalties then and there. "Anyone who wants to join Brownie can leave right now," he told them. No one budged. Wise's mutiny failed, and Cinderella never got off the ground.

Later that year, Tupper sold the company to Justin Dart's Rexall Drugs for a reported $9 million. Tupperware had grown too unwieldy for him to manage alone. His son Glenn Tupper, now a coffee grower in Costa Rica, puts it this way: "He was never going to get into a situation where he had to sit down and discuss with a board of directors what he wanted to do with *his* company. If he could no longer have it his way, then he preferred to have nothing to do with it."

Originally Justin Dart was interested in selling Tupperware in his Rexall drugstores. But like Earl Tupper before him, he soon realized that he had underestimated the phantom strengths of direct sales. "I don't know anything about selling plastic pots on the party plan," he told the Tupperware executives. Dart was wary of upsetting the fragile order of things, so he left the company's direct sales approach intact. The party continues to this day.

In his retirement, Earl Tupper became fascinated with islands. He lived in the Bahamas for a time, then acquired a large island off the Pacific coast of Panama. He once had a harebrained scheme that involved digging a channel through his island and turning it into a tourist resort to be called "The Panama Canal." Tupper gave away most of his millions to the Smithsonian Institution (the Smithsonian's Tropical Research Center in Panama City is named after him). He spent his last ten years living as a hermit in Costa Rica, where he became a citizen. Some say Tupper had soured on America. Others say he was only trying to avoid Uncle Sam's taxes. He claimed he'd invented a revolutionary new container that would render his patented "burping" bowl obsolete, but it never materialized. He died of a heart attack in 1983 and was buried near San José. It is often asked, but the answer is no: He wasn't interred in Tupperware.

Brownie Wise still lives with her son Jerry in Kissimmee, only a few miles from the Tupperware headquarters, but she has been estranged from the company for thirty-three years. She has visited the grounds only once. Until the mid-1980s, Wise was a nonperson at Tupperware. Her name was never mentioned at Jubilee, and the company's public relations department gingerly avoided the subject of her departure. She was relegated to what one retired Tupperware executive called "The Black Hole." The company's revisionist history was so successful that today most Tupperware salesladies have never even heard of Brownie Wise. "The company took her right out of the corporate history," retired distributor Anna Tate remembers. "It was like those Communist history books where they take a guy they don't like and just erase him. It was as if Brownie Wise never existed."

In the intervening three decades, Wise says she's done consulting work for Fortune 500 companies and dabbled in real estate. She's often ill and difficult to reach these days, but she still has a disarmingly radiant personality, and plenty of advice to impart to a new generation of Tupperladies. "I see too much of women complaining and not enough doing," she says in her scratchy septuagenarian voice. "You won't find me complaining about woman's lot in life. I say, 'Get it up out of the chair, sis, and get to work! Move it!' "

Though Tupper and Wise left the company within a year of each other, the enchanted corporation that this odd couple built has remained largely unchanged. The company retains much of Tupper's obsession with secrecy and quality control. Tupperware's two manufacturing plants in the U.S., in Halls, Tennessee, and Hemingway, South Carolina, are closed to the public, and the headquarters keeps all plans for new products a tight secret. Every August the pilgrims still make the trip down to Tupperware headquarters. Every Monday night the local salesladies still attend rallies at any one of the three hundred distributorships scattered across the country. And the Tupperware magazine, *Our World*, arrives in the mail once a month.

INSIDE THE HOUSE AT 13102 Broadmore, deep in the coves and cul-de-sacs of Silver Spring, Maryland, eight women are gathered around the beveled-glass coffee table nibbling hors d'oeuvres from one of those sectioned trays with the molded dip well in the center and the little triangular compartments that prevent the carrot sticks from trespassing on the kiwi fruit.

Tonight's hostess, Patty Betz, is a cosmetology teacher and mother of two. Unseen kids are squealing downstairs, throwing things, bouncing off walls. Three-year-old Danielle is crawling over the potted plants. Muffin the miniature Maltese is digging tunnels in the wall-to-wall carpeting. A video game called "Gauntlet" is parked conspicuously in the dining room, a permanent piece of the furniture. "It's awesome," one of the neighborhood kids raves. "You can't die!"

Through all the pandemonium, Sheila Looney remains calm. She is wearing a white lab coat with a gold-plated name tag. "Let's play a little word association game," she suggests. "See if you can think of a food item that starts with the first letter of your name."

Leia picks "lasagna."

Santha goes with "sweet potatoes."

Mary Carol: "M&M cookies."

And so on. With games like this, Sheila claims she can master twenty names without error. "And people love to hear their names called out!" she adds.

Just for showing up, everyone gets a party favor made of Tupperware plastic—an orange peeler, a cookie cutter, or a little coin holder that clips onto the sun visor of your car. "We're the only party plan that gives people something just for being there!" Sheila points out. And for hosting the party tonight, Patty will win ninety dollars in free Tupperware.

Now Sheila is ready to get down to business. On the dining room table, in the shadow of "Gauntlet," the products are stacked and nested in their multitudinous shapes and sizes. "*This* is your salad bowl," Sheila begins, holding it high so all can see. "It's a really pretty piece to have. It isn't *just* a salad bowl, of course. It can also be a cake dish. And the dome-top can be turned upside down and used as a pedestal for a punch bowl. See? And it's a great place to keep your fruit. The dome-top creates a little hothouse effect in there. It'll ripen your bananas in no time! Isn't that marvelous!"

Sheila then points out a little-known distinction about Tupperware lids; only the round seals, she says, are actually burpable. "If it's round, you make the sound," Sheila explains. "If it's square, it keeps the air."

Another distinction: Tupperware gatherings like this one aren't actually called "parties" anymore. Too goofy-sounding. Too homemakerish. The marketing people who ponder these matters down at Tupperware headquarters have been toying with a more contemporary term for years. Now it's official. In the 1990s, parties are known as "classes."

Sheila Looney elucidates, "Time is the most precious commodity these days. To come to a Tupperware gathering, a mother has to leave the kids at home with the father. She can't very well say, 'Oh by the way, honey, I'm going to a party.' But if she says, 'I'm going to a class,' well, that sounds more impressive. It takes on a whole new psychological look. She's not going to play around. She's going to *learn* something."

Sheila has come tonight to spread a new environmental message. Tupperware, the company that buys more than one billion pounds of polyethylene pellets a year, is going green. It seems the manufacturing plant is now melting down the little uglies that come out of the mold wrong and is recycling them into a new line of large-size storage containers. "They come in this pretty forest green color," Sheila demonstrates, "to remind you of the ecology."

But the most dramatic development in Tupperland, Sheila announces, is a new generation of cookware that promises to do for the American microwave what Modular Mates did for the refrigerator. A few years ago the Tupperware technicians took a look around and realized that 85 percent of all American homes had microwaves. But Americans were microwaving Neanderthals, practically roasting their meat on a stick. People had no idea how to use the magic oven. They were guessing at the times and zap-strengths, sizzling the outside of their chicken while leaving embarrassing cores of frozen meat on the inside. This was not good. This was inefficient.

So the Tupperware technicians, whose mission in life is to stamp out inefficiency, invented "Tupperwave."

Tupperwave is a complete cooking system for the Micro Age. It features a "stack cooker" that allows you to microwave three separate dishes simultaneously. You can cook a square meal for six in under twenty-five minutes. All you have to do is follow the recipes and plug in your food groups according to the simple tier system. Error-free nuclear food science, cooking by numbers. "It's marvelous!" Sheila gushes. "The dish on top has your most concentrated heat. That's where your raw vegetables go. In the middle is your entrée. And on the bottom is your most delicate heat. That's where you're going to have your rice. It takes the mystery out of microwaving."

In fact, Sheila proclaims, a sample meal is baking in the kitchen right now. "Can you smell the apples cooking?"

Ten minutes later, the meal from the microwave, the three piping hot dishes flawlessly presented in their separate compartments: Fluffy rice, tender chicken with broccoli, and sweet apples. "Doesn't that look appetizing?"

* * *

IT'S BEEN ANOTHER GOOD NIGHT FOR SHEILA LOONEY. By the end
of the evening, she has sold close to $300 in merchandise, and
dated two more parties. And the new stack cooker has been a
big hit. Three of the women are considering buying it for the
holidays.

Santha (a.k.a. "sweet potatoes") has already placed her order.
Truth be told, Santha has been something of a Tupperware back-
slider in recent years. She hasn't bought any Tupperware in almost a decade. She has resorted to twisty ties and Ziploc bags and
Saran Wrap. She has let things spoil. She knows that at forty-two
dollars, the stack cooker is the most expensive item in the catalog.
But tonight she's got the Tupper Feeling. "Other things wear
away," Santha says. "But Tupperware goes on and on."

And Leia (a.k.a "lasagna"), who is a self-described Tupper-
holic, has ordered a new set of tumblers. "Not for me," she
quickly qualifies, "but for my relatives. My husband would pitch
a fit if I bought any more Tupperware for *our* house. I've got
cabinets that you open up and the Tupperware just spills out
onto the floor. My husband doesn't like the clutter. But see,
they keep coming out with new stuff. New colors. New lids. It's
always something."

IT'S THE LAST NIGHT OF JUBILEE, and a full moon is rising over
the cypress swamps at Tupperware headquarters. It's time for
the Wave-Off, the final farewell to the ladies as they depart for
home.

The Tupperware executives are standing on a platform in
front of Building A, dressed in *Wizard of Oz* costumes—Dorothy, the Tin Man, the Cowardly Lion, the Scarecrow, and Gaylin
Olson as the Wizard. Red floodlights illuminate the colonnade
behind them, and The Friendship Fountain constantly sprays
a fine mist over the scene. The giant rainbow made of sixty-
four thousand Tupperware lids arches across the sky.

A thousand vans are lined up bumper to bumper along the
Orange Blossom Trail, a mile-long procession of headlights
boring through the humid Florida night. Sheila Looney has
packed all her awards for the long trip back to Maryland. Now
she is waiting in her van with her husband Bob at the wheel, as
parking assistants direct the procession with fluorescent airport
beacons.

One by one the vans roll by the platform. The women throw open their side doors and furiously wave at the Oz characters. "Thank you!" they cry, some of them snapping off pictures. "We love you!"

"Bye Tupperfriends," the executives call back, squinting in the glare of the flashbulbs. "Come back!"

"We love you Gaylin!"

"Thanks for sharing!"

"Bye-bye!"

"You really socked it to us!"

The column of vans files out of the Tupperware driveway and turns north toward Orlando and the Gatorland Zoo, primed for another invasion of America.

"So long, Our World! See you next year!"

Gaylin heaves a momentary sigh of relief, but he knows this is no time to relax. Tomorrow morning another wave of two thousand salesladies will be arriving, and they will want to see Product.

Let Us Now Praise
Famous Fish

Richmond, Virginia

AT THE OSBORNE LANDING a few miles downstream from the
Virginia Capitol, forty-one fishermen are sitting in identical
nineteen-foot fiberglass boats, fiddling with their quivers of
graphite rods, rummaging through their giant plastic tack-
leboxes filled with plastic buzzbaits and crankbaits and worms,
plastic frogs and crawdads and minnows, and endless miles of
nylon monofilament line. Dawn is breaking. A tangerine sun is
just beginning to burn through the fog that has blanketed the
James River from the Chesapeake Bay to the falls above Richmond. The gray tidewater laps at the undersides of the boats,
and gives off a faint miasmal stench. The tournament officials
scurry over the docks with clipboards in their hands, checking
the last-minute details. The men will soon be roaring out to the
river channel in staggered heats, but now they sit idling in the
shallows, talking fish jive.

"You ready?"

"Yeah I'm ready!"

"You don't look ready to me!"

"Where you headin' today?"

"Appomattox Creek."

"Appomattox, huh? You going down there to rewrite that ole treaty, ain't ya bubba?"

"Nope, just doin a little fishin'. You?"

"Going *way* down. Down to my secret place."

"They say you got yourself a real honey hole down there, huh?"

"Sho-nuf."

"Ya lettin' anyone in on it?"

"Tell ya this: It's somewhere between here and the Chesapeake Bay."

"Why *thanks* for the big tip there, slim!"

Through all their macho banter, the fishermen can't conceal the nervous anticipation that burns in their faces, the hot flush of adrenaline. This is, after all, opening day of the Bassmasters Classic, the Super Bowl of fishing tournaments. The winner of the three-day competition will take home a cool fifty-thousand dollars and the world championship title. The windfall of corporate sponsorships that will rain down upon the victor will ultimately amount to more than a million dollars over his lifetime. Gathered this early August morning on the historic James River are the best bass fishermen in America. Each angler has earned his berth in the Classic by dint of ten months of qualifying competitions on the Bassmasters Trail, fishing in tournaments that ranged from the boulder-strewn St. Lawrence River in upstate New York, to the lime-green desert lakes of Utah and Nevada, to the murky old TVA impoundments in the very heart of the Bass Belt. A year of hard casting has come down to these three days. Now here they are, forty-one anglers thirsting for glory, sizing each other up, wondering who among them will be standing in the Richmond Coliseum three days from now with his day's catch flopping on the scales as twelve thousand fans howl in awe at the new King of Bassdom.

The Bassmasters. They are stolid men with thick, brown hides and crow's-feet around their eyes from constant squinting. They wear denim shirts crowded with the patches of their corporate sponsors: Zebco reels, Skeeter boats, Stren fishing line. They come from places like Arkadelphia, Arkansas; Broaddus, Texas, and Gravois Mills, Missouri. There is a musky smell about them, the brackish smell of the river. Their hook-scarred hands are redolent of outboard gasoline, Skoal tobacco, and gill slime.

The forty-one boats crouch in the water—broad and square in the sterns, sharp-nosed in the prows. Forty-one American flags fly over the transoms. The big Evinrudes splutter and cough, and blue fumes seethe from the frothy swirls of the propellers. The raspberry polyflake finish on the boats catches glints of the morning light. On board, the liquid-crystal instrument panels cast a dim green glow, as the gauges register the pH of the water, the temperature of the water, the light intensity of the water, the depth of the water, the structure of the bottom, and the presence or absence of fish. The swiveling captain's chairs rise from the carpeted casting decks, upholstered thrones surrounded by arrays of electronic footpedals and kill switches. The aerated livewells bubble with fresh oxygen. Boat by boat, the tournament officials peek into the livewells to ensure that none of the men has snuck any previously caught fish on board.

On the dock, a few extra-loyal wives, still half-asleep, wave their husbands off to battle. Also in the crowd is an eleven-year-old boy named Woody who rose at five this morning and rode his bicycle down to the boat landing to catch a glimpse of his favorite fishermen, the ones he'd seen on *The Bassmasters* cable television show countless times before. In a sweep of the eye, Woody can see the full pantheon, bassin' giants like Hank Parker, Tommy Martin, Larry Nixon, Guido Hibdon. There's Roland Martin, towheaded author and television star who has built a world-famous bassing resort on Florida's Lake Okeechobee. There's Gary Klein, the fair-haired Californian who claims he's never had a *real* job in his thirty-two years. There's Woo Daves, the local favorite, a little fireplug of a fellow out of Chester, Virginia. And in the far corner of the cove, keeping off to himself, is perhaps the greatest bassman of all time: Rick Clunn, the veteran from Montgomery, Texas.

There may be more consistent bassmen than Rick Clunn; there may be fishing personalities who are better known and better loved; there may even be a few in the bassing world who have earned more money over the years. But when it comes to high-stakes fishing tournaments like the Bassmasters Classic, Rick Clunn is the undisputed king. No one can outfish him in the clutch. He has won an unprecedented three BASS world fishing championships and the coveted Angler of the Year Award; he has also won major titles on rival bass fishing circuits, including two U.S. Opens and the Red Man All-American. All told, Clunn has earned more than a million dollars in tournament prize money, and twice that in endorsements and corporate sponsorships. When Clunn is having a good day—which is often—he is very nearly unstoppable. He fishes with a chilling, cyborg efficiency, which accounts for his nickname among sportswriters: "The Ice Man."

I have been selected to be the Ice Man's "observer" for the day. As part of tournament protocol, each of the pros is randomly paired each morning with a different writer, who serves as an official witness to discourage cheating. Many sportswriters have found these all-day outings to be ideal for conducting interviews with the pros, but this will not be the case for me. Rick Clunn is notorious for tuning out the world—his boatmate included. He can go a whole day without saying a word. He likes to shut out the extraneous dock-talk and contemplate the day's work in perfect silence. Even when the fishing is over and he's returned to the hotel, Clunn observes a strict regimen of mind purification. No TV. No newspapers. No heavy meals or unnecessary conversation. People often mistake his quirky introspection for rudeness. "I'm warning you," Clunn says as I climb into the boat. "I'm very antisocial when I get out on the water. I don't want you to think I'm being impolite. I'm just filtering out my externals. You're probably going to be bored out of your mind. All you're going to do is sit there for eight hours and stare at my butt!"

The details of Clunn's life story are well known to viewers of *The Bassmasters*: How he gave up his comfortable job as a computer programmer for Exxon. How his wife Gerri supported him and their two daughters through the lean years. How at the 1984 Bassmasters Classic in Arkansas, he caught a record seventy-five pounds of bass to take the tournament by storm, and then stood alongside Governor Bill Clinton and Vice President George Bush to tell the adoring crowds: "Only in America can a boy grow up to make a living chasing little green fish!"

Rick Clunn is something of a New Age mystic. A lot of the other fishermen think he's loopy, with all his strange talk of Zen Buddhism and *Jonathan Livingston Seagull*. He listens to cassette tapes of Shirley MacLaine. He says he experiences "visions." He has a black belt in hapkido, a Korean martial art that stresses mind control. He's been known to wear disguises out on the water so that, from a distance, the other fishermen can't recognize him. For reasons that no one can understand, he only buys hooks that are manufactured in Europe. Sometimes he camps by the lakeside the night before a tournament to get every cell of his body "in tune" with the energy fields of the water. "You have to achieve a spiritual connection to the environment," he explains. "You have to *be* the bass."

Whatever the other fishermen may think of Clunn's unorthodox methods, they can't argue with the results. Clunn is an intuitive genius at solving the great Rubik's Cube that is modern bass fishing. He can instantly break down the environment into its constituent parts—the current, the time of day, the season of the year, the wind, the clarity of the water, the approaching cold front or thunderstorm, the foliage, the submerged human garbage and the hundred other variables that factor into the vast and ever-changing calculus—and then superimpose that calculus over what he knows about the capricious behavior of the bass. "It's an enormous puzzle that you're constantly trying to put together," Clunn says. "If you want to catch a bass, you're going to have to understand his world down there. It's a tremendous challenge to your mental being."

Still, the Ice Man hasn't won a Bassmasters Classic in six years. This is the third year in a row that the tournament has been held on the dingy tidewaters of the James River, and so far Clunn has been jinxed. The first year, 1988, Clunn ended up in 18th place with a paltry 16 pounds. The second year he did a little better: 10th place, with a total weight of 22 pounds, 11 ounces. But this year, Clunn is confident that the trophy is his. How does he know? He had a vision. In fact, he looks like he's having a vision right now. He sits mute in his boat and stares vacantly over the iron-colored river, like a man in a voodoo trance.

An official tournament vessel noses through the throng of bass boats and circles in front of the dock. Inside the boat is a strapping man in a white cowboy hat who holds an electronic megaphone. "Uhhhh, gentlemuhn . . ." the man announces in a heavy Alabama drawl, with a note of solemnity in his voice. He clears his throat, removes his hat. The Bassmasters know the cue. They all bow their heads as Ray Scott, the man who more or less invented the sport of big league bass fishing, says the morning prayer.

"Heavuhnly Father ..." Scott begins, his megaphone slightly squeaking with feedback, "... bless each and evuhry one of these fishahmuhn here today. Lord, watch over'm as they make their way to their favuhrite holes this mornin'. Let them enjoy an All-American experience on the waddah, and return them safely to us. In Jesus' name, Aaaaaaaaaa*men*."

One by one, the fishermen blast off for distant points on the James. The fiberglass noses rise magnificently over the surface. Soon the sleek boats are hydroplaning at forty ... fifty ... sixty miles per hour. A few of the fishermen speed upstream toward the slumbering skyline of Richmond, but most turn downriver, gliding past the antebellum plantations and duck marshes of the Lower James, and on toward the salt line near Williamsburg.

Finally, Clunn's name is called, and we slip out of the cove for the river channel. The wives all turn from the dock and shamble back to their cars. But Woody, the eleven-year-old boy from down the road, doesn't budge. He wants Ray Scott's autograph. "Why sure, little fella," Scott says, bending down to sign the proffered sheet of paper.

Beaming, Woody hops on his bike and races home for breakfast, with the engines of the Bassmasters still roaring through the land.

> *I wanted to put that old muddy fisherman up on a marble pedestal. No longer would bass fishermen be looked upon as a bunch of good old red-neck country boys whose diets consisted of sardines and cracker barrel cheese, whose idea of dressing was fastening the top button on a pair of bib overalls, who could plow the south forty, run a trot line, and wear out two chaws of tobacco before the corn got hot in the moonshine still. Bass fishermen had always been thought of as refugees from hard work. No more.*
>
> Ray Scott, *Prospecting and Selling:*
> *From a Fishing Hole to a Pot of Gold*

RAY WILSON SCOTT IS THE FOUNDER AND PRESIDENT of the Bass Anglers Sportsman Society (BASS), a national federation of two thousand amateur fishing clubs that is headquartered in Montgomery, Alabama. Since its inception in 1967, BASS has been the organization chiefly responsible for turning the lazy pastime of the Deep South into a commercial juggernaut. The

BASS tournament circuit has created a new class of sports celebrities and helped fuel the technological transformation of angling in America. Today, Scott is recognized across the Bass Belt as a folk hero, the father of a new sporting universe for the rural man. To fishermen across the country, the jowly ex-insurance salesman in the trademark Stetson hat and lizard skin boots is known as "Mister Bass."

Drive down any interstate in America for five minutes and chances are good that you'll see one of Mister Bass's crested logos, with its leaping, gape-mouthed fish, pasted to the window of some mud-splattered Bronco or Suburban. There are an estimated 20 million bass anglers in the United States, and "bassing" represents the fastest-growing segment of the $28 billion sportfishing industry. More than 80 percent of all fishing tackle purchased in the U.S. is devoted to the capture of a single species of fish—*Micropterus centrarchidae*. Once the butt of jokes on *Saturday Night Live* (Dan Aykroyd got a lot of mileage out of a skit about the "Bass-O-Matic," a special blender that grinds up fish into tasty milkshakes), the bass has become the All-American sportfish. "The most sought-after critter in America," Scott calls it.

Scott's various angling ventures include a popular cable television show and *Bassmaster* magazine, a slick monthly journal with a readership of 2.5 million and an advertising rate of $20,000 per page. Scott's bass empire generates $30 million in revenues each year. "The whole thing has gone far beyond my wildest imagination," Scott says with an odd mixture of pride and embarrassment. "Now everybody's got the bug. These people are critically ill! I've met plenty of people who go from never having fished before in their lives to dropping twenty grand on bass equipment in a single week! Money is no object to them. It's that bass bug—it strikes them cold."

One of the afflicted is George Bush, who insists that *Bassmaster* was his "favorite magazine." In fact, Bush and Scott are personal friends and fishing buddies who have forged an unlikely political alliance. Scott is proud to tell you that he is "one of the few people in the world who has soaked in a hot tub with the President of the United States." Scott once served as Bush's presidential campaign chairman in Alabama and has openly endorsed him in his publications. For his part, Bush has lobbied behind the scenes for legislation favorable to bass fishermen and has even appeared at Bassmasters Classic weigh-in ceremonies, hurling the slimy fish onto the scales. The President and First Lady have fished with Scott on his private bass lake, just outside of Montgomery. When Mister Bass comes to Washington, he lunches with Bush at the White House, and on at least one occasion, Scott and his wife, Susan, have spent the night as guests in the Lincoln bedroom.

"You can argue that bass fishing is a huge waste of time and money," Scott admits. "But what a wholesome way to blow your paycheck! What a wholesome disease it is! The ancient Assyrians used to say that the gods do not subtract from a man's allotted lifespan the hours he spends fishing. The urge to fish is deeply embedded in the human soul. Theoretically, we came from the water. And the water still attracts us, pulls us like a magnet. Some of us want to swim in it. Some of us want to look at it. But there are others of us out there who have to *fish* it. It's a primeval motivation."

Ray Scott was enough of a student of human nature to realize that, "primeval" though it was, bass fishing needed high-profile personalities to bring it to the fore: heroes. He says the idea for a professional circuit came to him in a vision one night in 1967 after a squall had ruined a fishing trip to Mississippi's Ross Barnett Reservoir. "In a rainstorm, I had a brainstorm," he quips. He was an insurance salesman at the time (he'd gotten his start selling burial policies with the slogan 'A Nickel Cheaper, A Foot Deeper'), but his real passion was fishing. Living as he did in the Black Belt of Alabama, where the bass was rivaled only by native Hank Williams and the good Lord Himself as an object of devotion, Scott had an intuitive grasp for the potential magnitude of the bassing cosmos. Dollar signs swam in his head as he considered the possibilities: sponsors, stars, TV contracts. "I know this sounds like something Jim Bakker would say," Scott explains, "but it all rolled out for me, just like it was providential. I didn't ponder it for a second. I knew bass fishing was ready to emerge from the lily pads to the front page. I knew there was this subculture out there. I could feel the enthusiasm. All I had to do was roll away the rock and let that guy out!"

Ray Scott didn't *invent* the idea of the fishing tournament, of course; he just improved on it. Bass derbies and crappiethons were a time-honored tradition across the South. On Labor Day the local hardware store would announce a big fish-off, and all comers would pitch their money into a hat. But because most of these small-town affairs were poorly policed, cheating was rife. Wise guys would stuff buckshot down their fish's mouth when no one was looking, or sneak in lunkers they'd caught a year earlier and stored in their deep freeze.

Scott's first masterstroke was in designing the larceny-proof tournament. His solution worked on the principle of mutually assured detection: Every morning the fisherman would be randomly paired with another fisherman, and each would keep the other honest. It worked. Scott's first event—"The All-American Bass Tournament," held in June of 1967 on Beaver Lake in the Arkansas Ozarks—was scandal-free. The 106 anglers who showed up for that first tournament spread the word about Ray Scott's new organization. Fishermen signed up for his tournaments in droves. Within a year, Ray Scott had himself a bass fishing league.

But Scott knew that any self-respecting league had to have its Super Bowl, its Masters, its World Series. Thus the Bassmasters Classic was born.

First held in 1970 on Nevada's Lake Mead, the Classic is the crowning event of the tournament season, the grand invitational. In the early years, Scott kept the Classic's location a tight secret. On the appointed day, the anglers would board a chartered airplane like so many hostages, their destination unknown. Then, at thirty thousand feet, Scott would emerge from the cockpit, pull out an envelope, Academy Awards fashion, and announce the "mystery location." Nowadays, the Classics are too big for bush-league theatrics. Over the years the Classics have been held on such diverse waters as the Ohio River, Florida's Lake Tohopekaliga, and Lake Chickamauga, Tennessee. Other BASS tournaments can boast larger purses, but none has anything like the prestige or exposure of the Classic. There are no entrance fees: The pros must earn their spot. They have three days to prove their mettle. They are given brand-new, top-of-the-line Ranger bass boats with identical 150-horsepower outboard engines (all the equipment is publicly auctioned at the end of the tournament). Each morning at dawn the fishermen speed to their honey holes and sweet spots, sometimes traveling seventy miles or more before making the day's first cast.

Since bass fishing isn't exactly a spectator sport, the main attraction is the weigh-in ceremony, a kind of fishing pageant *cum* boatshow held each afternoon before crowds of ten thousand or more. While Scott works the audience in his rodeo announcer's brogue, the fishermen make their grand entrance. Seated in their boats towed by glistening Chevy trucks, they make a triumphal half-lap around the arena, like charioteers in the Circus Maximus. One by one, they hold up their fish for all to see. The bass are then placed in perforated plastic bags and weighed on an enormous set of digital scales.

Typically, the fishermen haul in more than seven hundred pounds of bass during a Classic, but it's not the massacre it seems. Few of the fish perish and none ends up in a frying pan. BASS practices a policy of mercy called "catch-and-release." All fish under twelve inches are immediately thrown back, and keepers are handled with extraordinary care. The contestants are penalized one ounce for every "deceased" fish they bring in. After the bass are weighed, BASS technicians place them in a metal holding tank filled with cold water and a bright green liquid called Jungle Tournament Formula, a "scientifically-designed" electrolyte potion that helps keep fish calm and infection-free until local wildlife authorities can return them to the river.

Though a special cash prize of $1,000 is awarded for the biggest fish caught each day, the tournament is ultimately decided on cumulative poundage: The Bassmaster with the largest weight tally at the end of three days wins the $50,000 check. Often the decision comes down to a matter of ounces.

More than a fishing tournament, the Bassmasters Classic is a carnival, a trade show, and a kind of family reunion. It is the annual mecca for the nation's bassheads, a theme park pavilion erected to the greater glory of a piscene god. Tens of thousands of fisherfolk come from all over the country to inspect the newest rods and reels, to finger the latest electronic paraphernalia, and to collect autographs from the pros. They plan their vacations around the Classic, dragging their poor wives and kids from booth to booth. They study the endless charts and diagrams purporting to explain the fish's breeding and feeding habits. They buy bass rings, bass belt buckles, bass tie clips, bass underwear. They buy hats that say things like "HAPPINESS IS THE THREE B's: BASS, BROADS, & BEER." They stare lustfully at the live bass swimming in bubbly green aquariums. There are banquets, cocktail parties, and seminars. Everyone in the fishing industry puts in an appearance: boat manufacturers, lure designers, outdoor writers, resort owners, fishing guides. For three days, they mill about the huge convention center, spinning fish stories, collecting freebie lures, and taking comfort in just being around so many others who are suffering from the same sickness.

Though Mister Bass is still the front man at the Classic, Scott has turned over the day-to-day management of BASS to Helen Sevier, a savvy former cookbook marketer. "Colonel Sanders didn't fry up a whole lot of chicken in his later years," he says of his diminished role. A sometime angler herself, Sevier is credited with devising the company's wildly successful marketing approach, which relies heavily on direct mail. Still, it's a little ironic that Scott chose a woman to rule BASS's overwhelmingly male kingdom. Women weren't even allowed to compete in the society's tournaments until 1991. In the late 1970s, a group of irate fisherwomen lodged a discrimination suit against BASS, and the case ended up in the New York Supreme Court. But the court sided with the male anglers, who contended that the presence of women would interfere with their right to urinate off the sides of their boats in privacy. Then fisherwomen developed their own angling circuit, Bass 'N Gal, and today the bassing universe remains largely self-segregated.

With Sevier at the company's helm, Scott has embarked on an unusual project that promises to do for deer hunters what BASS has done for fishermen. He's set up something he calls the White Tail Institute, a kind of hunter's think tank that conducts scientific studies on the foraging and breeding habits of the white-tailed deer, which he calls "the second most sought-after critter in America." Among its various projects, the institute is building a deer sperm bank for future eugenics studies. To that end, Scott has been collecting the testicles of trophy bucks. He's also marketing a high-protein variety of clover that he claims "the deer just can't resist." He advertises that all a landowner has to do is plant a plot of the new miracle seeds in the spring, and when deer season rolls around, it'll be a cinch to bag a trophy buck. Scott admits it all sounds a little strange, but says, "I think way out sometimes."

Scott attributes much of the success of his hunting and

fishing ventures to a phenomenon he calls "The Verticalization of America." The modern marketplace, he explains, is characterized not by broad cultures but by deep subcultures. With more time and money on their hands, Americans have become increasingly serious about the pursuit of leisure, and hundreds of specialized industries have sprung up to meet their demands for refined recreation. Today the serious bassman wants to practice his hobby with acumen and a sense of fashion. His sport has gone High Concept. It is now thoroughly Gore-Texed and bathed in liquid crystal. And because it has become a quite complicated and costly endeavor, bassing does not appeal to dabblers. The bassman can't just row out on the lake in a metal johnboat with a cane pole and a tin can full of hellgrammites. He's got to get himself over to Wal-Mart and buy a Humminbird depthfinder and a few of those new weedless spinnerbaits. He's got to subscribe to the bass magazines and join the local bass club with the cedar-shingled lodge on the lake at the edge of town.

Television has been at the heart of the sport's transformation. Dozens of weekly bass fishing shows are now airing on local and national channels—tips-and-tactics programs hosted by bassing celebrities like Jimmy Houstin, Bill Dance, and Roland Martin. *The Bassmasters* is most popular of all. The half-hour show is aired every Sunday over The Nashville Network (TNN), a cable channel that has proven enormously successful at mass-marketing the themes and values—real or imagined—of rural America. TNN offers its 48 million household subscribers a patriotic format of family-style cooking shows, stock car races, Winnebago tours, and country music videos. Spend an hour watching TNN's slick package of down-home "themecasting" and you begin to wonder whether there are any authentic country people left anywhere. TNN's viewers understand that bass fishing is no longer merely a pastime; it's part the rural "life-style." It's an expression of regional identity and class status—and, not incidentally, a pursuit that involves a good deal of keeping up with the Joneses. Today you can drive the poorest backroads of the South and Midwest and see ramshackle shanties with $25,000 Ranger boats proudly parked outside and gleaming satellite dishes that are no doubt reeling in *The Bassmasters* or *Bill Dance Outdoors*.

"There's a certain amount of peer pressure involved in

bass fishing—no question about it," Scott concedes. "People are parrots. They like to copy each other. They want to feel like they are part of some larger world. You can build a world around anything if you take the vertical approach. You've got to find that sleeping demand and amplify it, magnify it, exaggerate the need! In other words, don't try to do every species of fish. *Specialize!* Just pick one and do it better than anyone else. One of the great things about this crazy country of ours is that you can specialize in anything. Hell, you can specialize in salt and pepper shakers if you like. Or better yet, *just* the salt shakers. In my case I specialized in a fish, and built a whole world on it."

BUT IF YOU'RE GOING TO BUILD A UNIVERSE around a single species of fish, why the bass? What is it about *Micropterus* that's got the nation worked up into such a swivet?

It is not an easy question to answer. By most of the traditional yardsticks, the bass simply doesn't measure up as a sportfish. The muskie is a more aggressive fighter. The walleye tastes better. The trout is more elegant and makes a nicer trophy on the wall. The catfish yields a finer filet. A fisherman can fill up his stringer faster with perch or bream or crappie. And the bass is not especially large, usually weighing no more than five pounds.*

Even fanatics will acknowledge that the bass is not much to look at. Red Smith, the Pulitzer Prize–winning sportswriter, once described *Micropterus* this way: "Compared with the silver elegance of the Atlantic salmon or the radiance of the rainbow trout, the bass is no beauty. He is thick lipped and pot-bellied. Loop a watch chain across his bay window and he would look like a Thomas Nast caricature of vested interests." The bass is an extremely scaly fish with splotchy green flanks and a pale underbelly peppered with tiny black flecks that look like skin cancer. Its spiky dorsal fin gives it a vaguely prehistoric look. As if its exterior weren't ugly enough, the bass will graciously exhibit its insides, too: You can look down its yawning, cartilaginous mouth and plainly see its guts. Its gills open wide, exposing pulsing ringlets of blood-rich flesh.

---

*The world record largemouth bass weighed 22 pounds, 4 ounces, and was caught in 1932 in Montgomery Lake, Georgia.

Then too, the bass suffers from an identity crisis that is rooted deep in its history. From the day it was first scientifically described by the French naturalist Lacepede in 1800, the bass has been the redheaded stepchild of American angling. The specimen that Count Lacepede studied had been shipped to his Paris laboratory from America, and as it happened, it had a badly mangled dorsal fin which Lacepede erroneously assumed to be universal to the species. Lacepede thus gave the new fish the ill-deserved genus name *Micropterus*, or "small fin." For a century after Lacepede's flawed classification, and largely because of it, ichthyologists quibbled over the bass's physical attributes and failed to agree on a proper Linnaean nomenclature.

Local fishermen couldn't agree on what to call it either. Throughout the 1800s, the bass was variously known as the trout-perch, the green trout, the bronzeback, the blackback, and the oswego. And today, there are some twenty different varieties of fresh and saltwater fish that go by the name "bass," including the peacock bass, redeye bass, Suwannee bass, European bass, striped bass, and giant sea bass. The species that professional bass fishermen pursue is properly called the "black bass." But even this designation can create confusion, since the black bass, which is actually green, can either be large-mouthed or small-mouthed (the smallmouth is more commonly found in northern waters). And in tropical climes, where the black bass grows especially large, it is known as the "Florida bass," and considered by many to be a separate subspecies.

But the bass has something else going for it: a confounding personality. It is a moody, inscrutable phantom of a fish. "The reason we're all after the bass so much is that we can't figure him out," Ray Scott explains. "He's as unpredictable as Wall Street. The bass is a little like a cat. He's a solo operator. He doesn't pal around a lot. There's a certain mystique about him. You want to know what makes him tick. He'll drive you crazy!"

For all its feline fickleness, when the right bait floats by in the right way at the right time, and all the other environmental conditions are right, the bass can strike ravenously and without mercy. The bass undergoes a dramatic personality change, entering what is sometimes called "The Feeding Mode." It becomes, according to Red Smith, "the swaggering bully of lake and stream—truculent, greedy, overbearing." Says Rick Clunn: "He's a brute and a redneck and a predator. He'll hit just about any kind of bait, depending on his mood. He'll also strike for reasons unrelated to food. He'll snap at a lure just because he doesn't like the noise it's making. He would be scary if he could grow to fifty pounds. He'd literally eat children who were wading in the water—would just jump up there and take them off the bank."

Bassers like to compare their style of fishing to hunting, and often talk about their quarry as if it were not a fish at all, but some kind of menacing wild beast (a common term for a big bass is a "hawg"). It's hardly the "contemplative man's recreation" that Sir Isaak Walton rhapsodized in his 1653 paean to the English outdoorsman, *The Compleat Angler*. When old man Walton went "afishing," as he called his serene sport, his maxim was "Study to be quiet." But there is nothing quiet about modern bass fishing. It is a brawling, labor-intensive process, with bleeping electronic encumbrances and big engines grumbling at full throttle. "Bass fishing is like a chase," says Clunn. "You are *pursuing* something, not waiting for it to come to you. A lot of people like to go fishing as an escape from the demands of their life. They want a peaceful and uncomplicated situation. Well, bass fishing is not for them."

The contemplative man's fish, ever since Sir Isaak Walton's day, has traditionally been the trout. The modern bass fisherman differs from the trout angler of old not only in the brashness of his technology but also in the confrontational methods he uses to persuade the fish to bite. Trout fishing, at its essence, is a sport of deception: The trick is to tie the fly so expertly that it looks real, and to lay it down on the water with such artifice that the trout *believes* it's real. Bringing off this deception is made more difficult by the fact that the trout lives in clear, cold streams where visibility is good, and where the angler's movements are unobstructed by moss or algae. Once the trout catches a whiff of deception, the game is over.

But because the bass more often lives in murky waters, in dark, weedy lairs deep in the shadows of stumps and rotting tree limbs, it rarely gets a good look at its bait. But it doesn't need to. The bass is such an aggressive fish that it may strike at the slightest provocation: A strange movement in the water. A silver flash of light. An unfamiliar smell or color. It may strike out of curiosity, surprise, or pique. Thus the bass fisherman may try to taunt and rile his prey in the way that the matador

Champion Bassmaster Rick Clunn of Montgomery, Texas.

BASS founder Ray Scott and *Micropterus centrarchidae*.

Sunrise at the Bassmasters Classic.

C. BOYD PFEIFF

agitates his bull. Many of his lures are designed purely to grab the bass's attention. They shimmer and pop in the water. They are rigged with fluttery tassles and bright green skirts and spinner blades that swivel and whir through the weeds. They have names like the Bomber, the Hula Popper, the Devil's Toothpick, the Big, Bad LeRoy Brown. They are agile little annoyances that can invade all the bass's favorite hideouts. There are surface lures, deep-diving lures, and lures that bounce along the bottom. There are lures that are designed to travel through Sargasso Seas of hydrilla and milfoil weed without getting hung up. Some are amazingly lifelike replicas of real creatures—minnows, worms, crayfish—and some are bug-eyed mutations of warped Day-Glo plastic, melted monsters straight out of a Salvador Dali painting. Some are coated with the scent of pig fat to arouse the bass's sense of smell. Others have hollow cavities that are filled with tiny ball bearings which rattle loudly in the water. A trout wouldn't think of biting one of these garish torpedoes, but to the bass they hold a strange appeal, triggering some atavistic reflex to avenge violated turf.

The contrast to trout fishing raises a crucial point in attempting to understand bass fishing's ascendancy. For in many ways, the bass has risen in direct proportion to the fall of the trout, and sometimes at its expense. Modern bass fishing represents the American angler's declaration of independence from England. Before bass fishing came upon the scene in any organized way, outdoor literature in the United States was dominated by the trout/salmon aesthetic, an aesthetic that was overladen with Old World ideas about sport. For many Americans, "fishing" still conjured up Isaak Walton's pastoral image of the gentleman piscator, a "brother of the angle" wading his trout stream in solitude. His props consisted of a fly rod, a wicker creel, and a pair of Abercrombie & Fitch waders. Even when American writers like Hemingway celebrated trout fishing, they were building on a tradition handed down from Europe. "Fishing used to be for rich men in cute little knickers," Ray Scott says. "They wore neat little vests and yo-yo gadgets and made exotic yodeling sounds whenever they caught a fish."

James A. Henshall, a Cincinnati physician and naturalist author who was an early advocate of bass fishing, bemoaned the American overreliance on British angling styles as far back as 1881 in his treatise, *Book of the Black Bass*. "Most of our notions of gamefish are derived from British writers," Henshall lamented. "And as the salmon and the trout are the only fish in Great Britain worthy of being called game, they, of course, form the themes of British writers on gamefish. Americans, following the lead of our British cousins in this, have eulogized the salmon and brook trout as the gamefish *par excellence* in America, ignoring other fish equally worthy."

The "other" fish Henshall had in mind for America was, of course, *Micropterus.* "The black bass is eminently an American fish," Henshall argued. "He is wholly unknown in the Old World except where recently introduced, and exists, naturally, only in America." In Henshall's estimation, the scrappy, irascible bass behaved as an American sportfish ought to behave. It was the Everyman's fish. It was a survivor. It stood up for its rights. It was a creature of appetites. What it lacked in refinement and grace it made up for in sheer lust for living. While the effete trout might insist on the delicacy of a newly hatched fly, the bass would eat anything that was set before it. While the trout required a certain fragile balance of temperature and oxygen and current conditions, the bass could live practically anywhere, and could be caught any season of the year, any time of day, in any kind of weather. "He has the faculty of asserting himself," Henshall observed, "and of making himself completely at home wherever placed."

Henshall was remarkably prescient in this regard. For today, the bass is a truly national species. Broadly indigenous to the South and Midwest, it can now be found in every state of the union except Alaska, and has been successfully exported to scores of foreign countries. Like the kudzu vine, the stocked bass has flourished wherever it's been introduced, in some cases flourished *too* well. It can live in brackish tidewater rivers, sewage ditches, farm ponds, mountain lakes, municipal reservoirs—even the cooling ponds of nuclear power plants.

But nowhere has the bass thrived more prolifically than in the man-made lake. Indeed, it might well be said that bass fishing in the modern era owes its existence to a marvel of civil engineering: the multipurpose dam. Beginning in the 1930s, hydroelectric power projects such as those of the Tennessee Valley Authority have converted hundreds of the nation's streams and rivers into new lakes that have proven to be excellent habitats for bass. The U.S. Army Corps of Engineers has constructed more than four hundred multipurpose dams over the century, and hundreds more have been built by various private, state, and federal agencies. Today there are more than four million square miles of man-made reservoirs in the United States, which means four million square miles of Bass Country.

It also means thousands of square miles of former Trout Country that has been swallowed up. When a cold-water river is dammed, it becomes a warm-water lake. And while warm water is ideal for the bass, it can spell doom for the native trout (generally, the trout cannot survive in waters above 70 degrees Fahrenheit). Thus in many parts of the country, the construction of man-made lakes has effectively assured the dominance of the bass over the native trout as the local sportfish. James Henshall, always clairvoyant in fishing matters, foresaw this trend over one hundred years ago. "A prominent cause of the decline of the brook trout," he predicted in *Book of the Black Bass*, "is the erection of dams, which, though to be deplored, cannot be prevented. But in the black bass we have a fish able to defy many of the causes that will, in the end, effect the annihilation and extinction of the brook trout. . . . No doubt the bass is the appointed successor."

The coming of the dam has changed the nature of fishing all over the country, but its impact has been most profoundly felt in the South. The retreating glaciers left the northern states pocked and gouged with tens of thousands of lakes—including the Great Lakes—but in the South, natural reservoirs are fairly rare. Before TVA, the southern angler usually had to content himself with a muddy, mosquito-infested river whose unpredictable waters might run dry in the summer and flood in the spring. But when the Great Lakes of the South were created, the Dixie fisherman suddenly had a controlled environment with a steady water supply and a virtually unlimited number of holes to fish at a greater variety of depths than he'd ever known. Now he found himself in a boat exploring the sparkling coves and nether reaches of the lake. Fishing had become a three-dimensional experience.

The lure of the man-made "impoundment" had the effect of dragging a dimly understood and vaguely disreputable folk-sport into the full glare of the twentieth century. Before World War II, bass fishing was a largely uncharted phenomenon pursued in feral swamps and bayous by sharecroppers and coal miners on their day off, the proud crackers that James Agee had written about in *Let Us Now Praise Famous Men*. Bass angling tips were passed down from father to son, and in some households the trove of fishing wisdom was considered as precious as the oldest family heirlooms. Each region boasted its own styles and preferences. And since there was scant national literature on the habits of the bass and techniques for its capture, an aura of secrecy surrounded the fish.

The dam shattered that secrecy. The new "fake lakes" acted as magnets, drawing the bass fishermen out of their hollows and creeks and putting them out on the open water where everyone could watch and learn. And to their pleasant surprise, the anglers found that their old friend the black bass had taken well to its new artificial environment, had taken to it, in fact, the way RC Cola took to the Moon Pie. They found that the bass loved to hide in the ground structure that had been inundated during the creation of the lakes and left behind to rot on the muddy bottom—the abandoned homes, the submerged forests, the long-forgotten barns and churches and fencerows. Working these underwater graveyards, a new generation of sportsmen began to study the behavior of the bass in a more disciplined way. The crackerbarrel "afishianado" stepped aside for a bold new breed of specialist angler. In the afternoons, the bassmen would gather on the docks to share tips and refine their techniques. Gradually, a loose-knit society began to form.

And then one day in 1967 a fast-talking insurance salesman from Alabama called the society to order.

BBBRRRRRRRRRRRRrrrrrrrrrrrrrrRRRRRRRRRRRRRrrrrrrrrr!!!!

The James River valley slides by at sixty miles an hour. Foam spews over the bow. I am sitting deep in my bucket seat, cinched in tight, my lifevest buckled. Rick Clunn is at the wheel, his head tucked behind the windshield. Watching him negotiate the river channel, I realize that in addition to being an expert fisherman, a Bassmaster must also be something of a speed demon, a Nascar racer of river and lake.

Twenty miles downstream, Clunn kills the engine and glides to his first hole. He opens the bright red locker and selects one of his five rods. And then, without saying a word, he climbs to the casting deck and goes to work.

Rick Clunn is a lean, tautly built man with ginger-brown

hair. He speaks softly in a Texas Gulf twang that is as sharp as turpentine. He is forty-four years old, but has an ageless face that could belong to a boy of fifteen or a man of sixty. He has frosty, slate-colored eyes that seem simultaneously spacey and intense. There is a jittery restlessness to his movements in the boat, but his face is calmly absorbed in concentration, his mental energies neatly husbanded. He works his mouth into strange contortions. His tongue curls and slides around with his casts, as if *it* is doing the casting. He has the surefootedness you'd expect from someone who spends 130 days a year in a bass boat. His tiny feet look like suction pods on the casting deck. Sometimes he stands on one leg and drapes the other over the bow, keeping it cocked at the knee, so that from a distance he looks like a stork. He works the foot-powered trolling motor like a wah-wah pedal, inching the boat toward his chosen targets in quiet spurts of humming energy.

Today he is wearing polarized sunglasses, fuschia shorts, and a denim shirt discreetly sprinkled with a few company logos—companies, he says, that he actually believes in: Daiwa. Tracker Boats. Poe's Plugs. A sticker on Clunn's tacklebox says, "DON'T MESS WITH TEXAS."

Watching Rick Clunn fish is an exhausting experience. He is what is known as a "Run 'n Gun" fisherman, which means that he moves around a lot, bouncing from hole to hole in a frenetic effort to "eliminate unproductive water." It is not uncommon for him to cover 150 miles in a day. Sometimes he will stop at a hole, make a single cast, and then head downriver ten miles before stopping again. Once he finds a "productive" stretch of water, he works at breakneck speed. It is said that Clunn is the fastest caster in the sport, averaging around five thousand tosses per tournament. He can't seem to keep still. Now he's kneeling, now he's sitting down, now he's standing up again. He is constantly changing rods, tying on new lures, checking the depthsounder. His movements are carried out with an urgency bordering on desperation. He works as if each cast may be his last. He skips lunch. If he sees one of his colleagues downriver, he does his best to avoid him. His eyes methodically scan the water, searching for promising holes. He always seems to be thinking three or four casts ahead, like a rock climber strategically plotting his course. The barrages of casts keep coming so fast that the component sounds begin to blur together: the wheeze of the line overhead, the splash of the fat lure in the water, the rapid grinding of the reel's gears.

Clunn catches his first bass on a bogus worm in a pile of submerged riprap. The initial strike is fierce, but the battle is over in five seconds. Clunn lands the bass without fanfare, removes the purple worm from its gristly maw, and tosses the fish into the livewell. "Two pounds," Clunn says, his tone expressionless. He hurls his lure back into the James as if nothing has happened. The captured fish thumps against the side of its tank. At regular intervals, the timers in the livewells pop on, and fresh oxygen pumps into the swishing chambers.

Five minutes later Clunn is working a surface lure along the edge of a rotten dock, threading it in and out of the creosote pilings. Suddenly he spots a suspicious-looking ripple thirty yards off. He glances over at the Humminbird depthsounder and sure enough, scads of fish (little red blurbs) dart across the high-definition screen. *WheeeeeeeeezeSplooosh*. He hits the spot on a dime, taking care to avoid the mossy ledge to the left, the clump of cattails to the right, and the livewire overhead. But nothing bites. *WheeeeeeeezeSplooosh*. Another perfect cast. This time—*Bam!* A strike. The rod buckles under the weight. Clunn hauls in his second fish of the day, but he is unimpressed. "Pound," he mutters, placing it in the livewell. "Maybe pound'n a quarter."

Clunn may catch as many as twenty bass during a day's fishing, but he is allowed to bring only five to the weigh-in ceremony. Thus he must constantly cull his livewell, replacing the smaller specimens with ever larger ones to ensure that the final collection represents, in effect, the day's "greatest hits."

Sportswriters often compare bass fishing to golf. They note how the bassman moves from hole to hole, sizing up his terrain, selecting his rod and lure with the same discrimination that a linksman uses in choosing his iron. But as I watch Clunn fishing, the comparison that keeps coming to my mind is not golf but *dentistry*: He methodically works the river, flossing the banks, brushing the weeds, scraping the stumps clean, constantly changing his tools for greater precision, taking little X-ray pictures of the unseen cracks and cavities—laboring, all the while, in a confined world of swiveling chairs, pneumatic booms, bubbling chemicals—until, suddenly, the fish answers the command

and bites down hard, so that Rick Clunn, River Dentist, may finally pull the offending specimen up by the roots.

RICKEY HOLMES CLUNN grew up in Hurricane Country, in the little town of La Porte, Texas, on the blustery shores of Galveston Bay. He caught his first bass when he was four. One of his earliest childhood memories is of wading a river in his underwear. At an age when other kids were playing football and riding bikes, he was running around the local farm ponds, stocking them with bass. When he was a teenager, he used to wake up at dawn and hike over to a rice reservoir near his house, where he'd fish until he heard his mother honking the car horn. Then he'd jump into the car, usually with a stringer full of smelly fish, and change clothes on the way to school.

Clunn spent three restless years at the University of Texas in Austin, switching majors four times before dropping out in disgust and bewilderment. "I didn't know what I was searching for," he recalls. "Nothing felt right. All I knew was that I liked to fish. But the University of Texas didn't exactly have an angling curriculum."

Clunn moved to Houston and landed a job in the computing department of Exxon. For seven years he worked as a programmer and systems analyst. "I started to accumulate the things I perceived to be 'Happiness': the house, the two-car garage, the executive position with the retirement plan. The whole package. It was the ideal life I had been raised to believe in. But I was miserable. I would look down from that tenth-floor office and see the people scurrying around like ants. I realized that I had become one of them. I had become an ant."

Clunn had never lost his love for fishing, though, and in 1969 he joined the Pasadena Bass Club east of town. By the late sixties, organized bassing had become a popular phenomenon all over East Texas. There were some 170,000 square miles of man-made reservoirs within a day's drive of Houston, including two of the premier bass fishing hotspots in the United States: Sam Rayburn and Toledo Bend. Clunn traveled around to these lakes and won enough local tournaments to realize that he was an ace at competitive fishing. Meanwhile, he heard about an organization out of Alabama that was now putting on big-money tournaments across the South. As he understood it, people were

actually making a living at this new gig. Professional sportfish-
ermen? It all sounded too good to be true. "My whole life I'd
been mediocre at everything I'd tried. But here was one thing—
the only thing—that I was really, really good at. I knew in my
heart that I could be as good as anyone else in the world."

So one day in February of 1974, Rick Clunn, aged twenty-
eight, walked into the Exxon building in Houston and put in
his two weeks' notice. He would languish in a sterile office no
longer: He was going to be a Bassmaster. His friends thought
he was crazy. His wife, Gerri, figured he was going through "a
phase." His father told him he was going to starve to death.

Clunn and his wife sold their house in Houston and moved
fifty miles north to Lake Conroe, where he started a fishing
guide service. "I was going to treat bass fishing just like any
other business venture," Clunn says. "I'd give it three years to
succeed or fail. But I just got deeper and deeper into it. Bass
fishing became another woman for me. After six months, I
knew I'd never go back."

Clunn's rise was meteoric. He qualified for the Bassmasters
Classic that first year, and finished respectably, in sixteenth
place. At the next year's Classic in North Carolina, he jumped
to eighth place. And in 1976, he ran away with the trophy. A
year later, when he won the Classic a second time, his father
stopped telling him he was going to starve.

Suddenly Clunn was in demand. Lure designers beat a path
to his home. Boat manufacturers burned up his phone line with
offers. Endorsements and sponsorships came out of the blue.
There was talk of a Rick Clunn TV show, a Rick Clunn book,
even a Rick Clunn board game. "I had to try hard not to be
consumed by own success," Clunn says. "I had to keep re-
minding myself: I didn't get into this sport to be a businessman
or an actor on TV. I got in it to be a fisherman."

And something else happened that Clunn had never
counted on: He became a celebrity. Kids wanted his autograph.
People treated him with a strange new deference at the lure
seminars he gave at Kmarts and hardware stores. The mailman
delivered letters that were addressed, simply: "Bassmaster,
Montgomery, Texas." Clunn had mixed feelings about stardom.
"It's a fascinating and strange and sometimes worrisome thing,"
he says. "Of course, I enjoy being respected for my ability in
my chosen profession. The energy of the crowds is intoxicating.

It can literally lift you out of the boat. You can feel it rushing through you. It kind of makes you understand why rock stars love to perform. But I don't like the idolizing. I don't think it's healthy. At the Classics, I've had grown men coming up to me crying their eyes out. It was kind of hard to relate to. I have to tell those people: Get yourself a life!"

Clunn began delving into what he calls "the mental stuff" early in his professional career—in the mid-1970s. He found that by visualizing the next day's fishing, he could predict the outcome of his tournaments in sometimes uncanny ways. He could predict how many fish he'd catch. He could even predict where the bass would be, and how large. Sometimes he would experience magical days on the water, days in which everything played out just exactly the way he'd visualized it. Sometimes the fishing would be so precisely executed, so beautifully choreographed—so nearly perfect—that he felt he had broken through a mental barrier and entered a higher realm of pure intuition. In those moments, he felt a clarity of perception that was almost frightening to him. He called it being "In the Flow."

"It was kind of like skipping through a door into a new dimension," Clunn explains. "It usually would come at a point of pure exhaustion in which I was ready to give up. My intellect would shut down and suddenly something else would take over."

Athletes in other sports had described similar states of euphoria. Tennis players called it "The Zone." Runners sometimes spoke of "going through the wall." The problem, for Clunn, was that these moments of inspiration did not occur with any consistency, and they did not last long, sometimes only a few precious minutes. They could backfire, too: A moment of pure "intuition" could prove to be nothing more than a dumb hunch that led him on a wild-goose chase. "It was a mystery to me. How could I access this thing? How could I control it? What part of my being was it coming from? I knew there was something else going on here that I had to understand."

So Clunn hit the books. He read Whitman and Thoreau. He read the Koran. He studied Hindu and Buddhist philosophy. He read a smattering of Plato and New Age literature. He devoured biographies of great historical figures, men like Mozart, Einstein, and Pasteur, to find out how they experienced their breakthroughs. Over time, Clunn began to develop an angling "philosophy." He felt that the only way he was going to improve his fishing was to step *outside* of it. His regimen was simple: Pare down your life. Follow your instincts. And integrate yourself with the total fishing environment.

You might be fishing in a cove one afternoon when a bird flies over your head. That bird is not inconsequential. It may provide clues to the whereabouts of bass. It may be that the bird is pursuing shad or crayfish. It may be that it is eyeing a particular insect in the water. "Everything is made of one hidden stuff," Clunn says, quoting Emerson. "It is a giant play out there, and we are all actors in it—the birds, the fish, the water, the wind. And humans, too. We sometimes think we are superior to the natural world, apart from it. We keep forgetting that we are nothing but little molecules and electrons, an energy field."

For Clunn, tapping into the Hidden Stuff is a matter of consciously turning on the unconscious. This is a tricky task which Clunn compares to "exercising an atrophied muscle." It is a matter of meshing yourself so completely with the environment that you "become" the water, become the fish, become the lure threading through the weeds—like the Zen warriors who imagined they were arrows. Clunn says, "Fishing, to me, is just a small scenario in all the scenarios of life. It's a pure vehicle for learning about the inner mind. As soon as I stop learning, I reckon I'll quit and do something else."

IT'S LATE IN THE AFTERNOON, and the day's fishing is almost through. Clunn is working beside a collapsed duckblind at the mouth of a small creek when a fine drizzle starts pecking at the water surface. He climbs into his neoprene rainsuit "system" and remains dry. Across the creek, obscured behind a stand of cypress trees, is an antebellum mansion with a greensward sweeping down to a boathouse. Clunn spots the cypress trees, and starts working along their roots, bombarding the unseen folds and pockets. *WheeeeeeezeSplooosh.*

He glances at his watch. He grimaces. A half-hour until check-in. The impending deadline reanimates him, and he executes his casts even faster.

Suddenly I notice that another boat has pulled beside us. In the boat are three men with binoculars. They are not fishermen; they are *spectators*. Evidently they've spent the day tailing the Bassmasters in the hope of gleaning hot bassin' tips. "Oh

my God!" one of them gasps. "It's Rick Clunn! Right there!
LOOK! Right *there*! Rick Clunn!! Shhhhh! What's he usin'?"

But the Ice Man is oblivious to their presence. He has
stopped fishing for a moment, and seems to be daydreaming.
He turns his face up into the rain, and stares at a flock of birds.

"A-a-a-a-a-ND NOW, LADIES AND GENTLEMEN . . . it's . . . MISTER
BASS!"

Ray Scott stands beside the digital scales and grins mischie-
vously at the roaring crowds packed into the Richmond Coliseum. *Also Sprach Zarathustra*, the theme from *2001: A Space
Odyssey*, booms over the loudspeakers, and spotlights swirl
through the arena. Scott wears an electric blue coat, a necker-
chief, and his usual Stetson hat. He holds a wireless microphone
in his hand. A giant laser image of a bass is dancing in the air
over his head, its flickering outlines etched in lime green.

"Richmuhn, Viginiah!" Scott shouts to the crowd. "Let's
make lotsa racket today! Let's blow the soft stuff off the roof!"

Today is the final weigh-in of the 1990 Classic. The pit of
the coliseum is carpeted in AstroTurf and landscaped with plastic green shrubs. Hanging from the rafters are bunting adver-
tisements from the Classic sponsors: MotorGuide trolling
motors, Delco Voyager batteries, Wrangler jeans. Behind a blue
curtain, BASS statisticians diligently plug numbers into their
computers. Cameramen from *The Bassmasters* roam the arena
taking footage.

One by one, the forty-one fishermen emerge from the main
portal and display their fish. As it happens, Rick Clunn is the
last man to come out of the chute. The crowd gives him a warm
and boisterous welcome, but no one expects much from the Ice
Man this year. He's had a mediocre tournament, and is far back
in the standings: tenth place. To win today, he'll have to bring
in 11 pounds, 9 ounces of bass, which would be an astounding
feat. "He's gotta have a lot of weight," Scott informs the crowd.
"It's going to be very difficult. But Rick Clunn is no ordinary
fishermuhn. It always pays to lay a little of yo' money on Rick
Clunn."

Clunn digs into his livewell, and pulls out a plump bass.

"Lip him!" Scott shouts. "Hold him up nice 'n high! He's
proud to be here!"

Clunn raises the fish above his head, its gills flaring, its tail flopping wildly in the air. The ten thousand humans let out a bloodcurdling scream, a scream that sounds a million years old. A dot-matrix sign on the scoreboard displays a running commentary:

N*I*C*E C*A*T*C*H, R*I*C*K!!!!

While Clunn reaches for another fish, Ray Scott keeps the patter going—"Whoa! Look at him! He's about to give himself a hernia on that one!"

Clunn drops a second big fish into the plastic bag. Another primal scream erupts from the humans.

"Look out!" Scott's voice booms. "Two bass! Look at that! Another James River beauty!"

W*H*A*T A L*U*N*K*E*R!

Clunn pulls out another one, even bigger than the first two.

"He gonna win this thing!" Scott says, his voice now tinged with genuine surprise. "I believe he's gonna win it! He got any more?"

Clunn digs out still another one.

"Bingo! We *definitely* got us a winner!"

N*I*C*E G*O*I*N*G, R*I*C*K!

Clunn places a fifth fish in the plastic bag and saunters up to the grandstand, where Scott and the BASS technicians are waiting. The digital screen shows that Clunn's catch weighs 18 pounds, 7 ounces—the largest single stringer caught in the three James River Classics. Scott drapes his arm around Clunn's shoulder and for the first time today is speechless.

R*I*C*K C*L*U*N*N, C*H*A*M*P*I*O*N B*A*S*S
M*A*S*T*E*R

Clunn is smiling from ear to ear. In the glare of the cameras, he holds up $50,000 worth of black bass.